D1212144

POLICE
AND THE SOCIAL ORDER IN
GERMAN
CITIES

LIBRARY
I.U.P.
Indiana, PA

363.230943
Sp33p

POLICE
AND THE SOCIAL ORDER IN
GERMAN
CITIES

THE
DÜSSELDORF
DISTRICT,
1848–1914

Elaine Glovka Spencer

NORTHERN ILLINOIS UNIVERSITY PRESS
DeKalb   1992

∞

© 1992 by Northern Illinois University Press
Published by the Northern Illinois University Press,
DeKalb, Illinois 60115
Manufactured in the United States using acid-free paper
Design by Julia Fauci

Library of Congress Cataloging-in-Publication Data

Spencer, Elaine Glovka, 1939–
Police and the Social order in German cities:
the Düsseldorf District, 1848–1914 / Elaine Glovka Spencer.
p.   cm.
Includes bibliographical references and index.
ISBN 0-87580-170-6 (acid-free)
1. Law enforcement—Germany—Düsseldorf (Regierungsbezirk)—
History.   2. Police—Germany—Düsseldorf (Regierungsbezirk)—
History.   3. Düsseldorf (Regierungsbezirk)—Social conditions.
4. Düsseldorf (Regierungsbezirk)—Politics and government.
5. Germany—History—1848–1870.   6. Germany—History—1870–1918.
I. Title.
HV8209.D87S64   1992
363.2'3'094355—dc20   92–1279
CIP

A000005419791

For my daughter, Laura

CONTENTS

List of Tables x

Preface xi

ONE   Prussians and Rhinelanders to 1848   3

TWO   Revolution and Reaction, 1848–1858   24

THREE   Police for Industrializing Cities, 1850–1878   44

FOUR   · Policing Urban Life, 1850–1878   61

FIVE   · The Empire and Its Internal Enemies, 1871–1890   76

SIX   Big-City Police, 1890–1914   89

SEVEN   Police and Daily Life, 1890–1914   109

EIGHT   Police and Organized Workers, 1890–1914   126

NINE   On the Eve of War and Beyond   140

Conclusion   155

Appendix   165

Notes   175

Bibliography   225

Index   239

TABLES

1. Police Personnel, 1848 and 1858   35

2. Police Personnel, 1863–1888   50

3. Essen Police, 1860–1874   52

4. Police Personnel, 1890–1913   90

5. Most Commonly Recorded Ordinance Violations in Duisburg   118

A-1. Krefeld Police, 1853–1913   166

A-2. Departures from Düsseldorf Police, 1877–1911   168

A-3. Penalties for Ordinance Violations in Duisburg, 1864–1909   170

A-4. Reported Crimes in Duisburg, 1864–1913   172

PREFACE

Nineteenth-century industrial cities, with their expanding populations, altered occupational structures and social relationships, clashes of divergent life-styles, uneven economic growth, juxtaposition of wealth and power with poverty and disenfranchisement, and proliferation of oppositional ideologies, spawned increased concern among both national and local elites about provisions for the protection of property and the maintenance of order. Fears of collective violence, especially in the middle decades of the century, heightened such concern and crystallized demands for more rigorous and uniform enforcement of existing laws or for creating new restrictions. Responsible for the preservation of ever-larger concentrations of wealth and productive capacity, the representatives of increasingly powerful and centralized bureaucratic states and the champions of the new industrial order placed ever-greater emphasis on guaranteeing predictably compliant lower-class behavior. Growing awareness of the provocative and inflexible nature of military responses to problems of maintaining domestic order, along with the increasing reluctance of armies to devote substantial manpower to such a divisive and distracting task, led to mounting demand for reliable civilian alternatives. At the same time, commercial and industrial expansion generated resources that made augmented public expenditure on law enforcement feasible, and the establishment of representative institutions helped to legitimate such allocations. As a consequence of these developments, urban policing took on unprecedented significance with uniformed patrolmen becoming, before the century ended, the most visible and ubiquitous representatives of governmental authority.[1]

Such changes transcended national frontiers. But of course the police also bore the strong imprint of the particular society they served, a linkage emphasized, for example, in Wilbur Miller's *Cops and Bobbies* (1977), a comparative study of the development of the New York and London forces between 1830 and 1870.[2] Even greater than the differences between the emerging New York and London police were the differences between Anglo-American experience and that of continental European societies. To date, however, historians have investigated the development of policing in continental countries less intensively than they have the history of law enforcement in Great Britain and the United States.

Historians of German central Europe, in particular, have until recently given relatively little attention to the police, certainly compared to that lavished on the more glamorous military and on the administrative bureaucracy. To be sure, there has been some interest in the police of the Weimar Republic, the republican era being one of large-scale civil disturbances. Hsi-huey Liang's 1970 study recounts frustrating police struggles in Berlin for control of the city's often turbulent streets between the end of the First World War and the Nazi seizure of power. Peter Leßmann's 1989 history of the Prussian *Schutzpolizei* covers the same years.[3]

For an examination of the first half of the nineteenth century, we now have Alf Lüdtke's studies of Prussian coercive forces. In his 1982 book (recently translated into English), Lüdtke stresses the still negligible development of urban police institutions before the revolutionary upheavals of midcentury and the state's continued reliance until that time on the army for the routine maintenance of domestic order.[4]

Studies of the German police between 1848 and 1914—the crucial years that witnessed the formation of the first large, bureaucratic police forces in central European cities—remain limited. East German historian Dieter Fricke's narrowly focused 1962 book on the Berlin political police from 1878 to 1890 was for years the only frequently cited work. More recently, other historians, especially Wolfram Siemann, have added to our knowledge about the development of the political police in Germany.[5] Such works neglect, however, the great bulk of what most policemen did and how they interacted with the various components of society.

In spite of recent historical interest in popular protest, crime, and deviance, the forces employed by German states to respond to such challenges still have not received the attention they deserve, especially with respect to how they functioned in daily contact with ordinary citizens. This remains true even after the 1986 publication of Albrecht Funk's informative work on the Prussian police from 1848 to 1918. Funk chose to focus primarily on legal and administrative decision making in Berlin, not on rank-and-file policemen and day-to-day law enforcement in the provinces.[6]

Papers presented at a conference organized by Herbert Reinke, Düsseldorf, 22–23 June 1990, and at a session organized by Alf Lüdtke for the Deutscher Historikertag, Bochum, 29 September 1990, suggest a currently broadening German interest in the history of policing. Reinke kindly provided copies of the programs of both meetings, along with information about his work-in-progress on the police in Rhenish cities. Ralph Jessen's *Polizei im Industrierevier: Modernisierung und Herrschafts-praxis im westfälischen Ruhrgebiet 1848–1914* (1991) unfortunately arrived too late for detailed consideration in this book. An insightful study of policing in an industrial region contiguous to the district examined in my work, Jessen's volume offers many points of comparison, especially for the years from the 1890s to the First World War, the period covered most fully in his study.[7]

My interest in the policing of nineteenth-century German cities grew out of my earlier investigation of the history of labor relations in Ruhr heavy industry before the First World War. I began my study of the police at a time when I was completing a book on Ruhr employers.[8] Common to both topics is the question of how the exercise and legitimation of authority were altered as a consequence of industrializa-tion, urbanization, and the expansion of the central state. In the present study, I am especially interested in what the emergence of the police in German central Europe as a prime symbol and instrument of state power in daily life reveals about changing values and social relationships and about the nature of the interaction between bureaucracy and society in Germany before World War I.

Because sources for the study of the German police between the revolutions of 1848 and the beginning of the Great War are both voluminous and widely dispersed and because comparatively little schol-arly work on the subject has been done, especially on the local and regional level, I decided to combine a brief survey of national develop-ments based primarily on printed materials with a case study of a single administrative district (*Regierungsbezirk*) based on archival research. In selecting a district for closer investigation, I looked for one that had a diverse and rapidly growing urban and industrial population prior to 1914. I chose the Düsseldorf district, the northernmost subdivision of the Prussian Rhine province. The Düsseldorf district was the most populous of five districts comprising that province, the others being those administered from Aachen, Cologne, Trier, and Koblenz.

Prior to Bismarck's wars, Prussia had twenty-three administrative districts, subsequently increased to thirty-two. During the second half of the nineteenth century, no other Prussian district—Berlin being a special case—became as densely populated or as highly urbanized as the Düsseldorf Regierungsbezirk. By 1871, 82 percent of the district's population lived in towns and cities of two thousand or more, compared to only 36 percent in Germany as a whole.[9] By 1910, one out of every nineteen Germans lived in the Düsseldorf district (population 3,418,388), and it boasted eight municipalities—out of forty-eight in all of Germany—with over one hundred thousand inhabitants.[10]

The district's cities were notable for their variety. Of the eight whose populations had passed one hundred thousand by 1910, three (Elberfeld, Barmen, and Krefeld) were long-established centers of textile production. Düsseldorf, the district's administrative center, specialized—after midcentury—in the metal-finishing industries, becoming Europe's leading producer of piping. To the north, in the heavy-industrial Ruhr, whose western portion lay within the district, were the coal-, iron-, and steel-producing cities of Essen, Duisburg, Mülheim an der Ruhr, and Hamborn, municipalities whose greatest expansion was concentrated in the last prewar decades.

To Prussian authorities, the cities of the Düsseldorf district gave periodic cause for concern both because of their escalating proletarian populations and because one or more of them at some time before 1914 exhibited virtually every political, social, or demographic characteristic viewed from Berlin as potentially disruptive. The district's population included, as the nineteenth century progressed, increasing numbers of migrants coming from ever more distant places who were disproportionately young and working class—and in the case of the heavy-industrial Ruhr, disproportionately male.[11] In addition, the district's population was religiously, and in some areas even ethnically, divided. Further, massive strikes, most notably those in the coal-mining industry in 1889, 1905, and 1912, riveted national attention on Prussia's industrial heartland. Increasingly wealthy and influential urban and industrial elites, confronted with unsettling change (including much they themselves initiated), demanded that government do more to guard them against the criminal, the disorderly, the disreputable, and the disrespectful—always, they insisted, at minimal cost and inconvenience to well-to-do taxpayers. Only partially mitigating official apprehensions about developments in the district's cities were their geographic isolation from the capital, their comparative prosperity through much of the late nineteenth and early twentieth centuries, and the presence of some of Germany's largest and most authoritarian industrial corporations.

In presenting my account of developments in the cities of the Düsseldorf administrative district between 1848 and 1914, I have focused particularly on periods that witnessed major changes in either the amount of resources allocated to policing or in the organization, composition, and functions of law enforcement agencies. Especially important are the early and mid-1850s (years of political reaction and economic transformation), the late 1860s and the 1870s (years of nation building, the emerging challenge of organized labor, and dramatic economic volatility), and the 1890s and beginning of the twentieth century (years when mass politics and mass strikes appeared increasingly threatening to defenders of the urban status quo). In explaining the timing of important changes in the police and their role in the life of the district's cities, I have paid special attention to both the conflicts and cooperation between local and national elites.

Sources consulted for this study include the records of the Rhine province in the state archive in Koblenz, the documents of the Düsseldorf district in the state archive in Düsseldorf, and police records in the city archives of Düsseldorf, Essen, Duisburg, Krefeld, and Wuppertal (the city of Wuppertal being the product of the 1929 union of Elberfeld and Barmen). I also made some use of materials—originally collected for my book on Ruhr employers—from the historical archive of the Gutehoffnungshütte and the Bergbau Archiv.

I was received with great kindness and helpfulness at all these institutions. The documents made available yielded abundant information about the recruitment, training, discipline, and daily lives of the police, at least for the late nineteenth and early twentieth centuries. For the early and midnineteenth century, when the Düsseldorf district's urban policemen were still few in number, sources proved less adequate. As a consequence, the early chapters of this book do not give as complete an account of the lives of rank-and-file policemen as I would have liked.

The archives provided valuable information about the means the police used in their efforts to control individual and collective behavior, the determination of priorities in law enforcement, the timing of increases in funding and allocation of manpower, the response of elite and nonelite groups to innovations in policing, and the changing nature of the interaction between the state and urban society. The advantages of studying the development of policing in a cluster of cities rather than in just one were that gaps in the record for a single municipality could often be made good elsewhere and local developmental peculiarities could be put into perspective on the basis of comparisons with experiences in neighboring urban centers.

Besides police documents, the city archives also provided published annual municipal reports—most complete for the last prewar decades and in the cases of Düsseldorf, Duisburg, and Krefeld—containing valuable quantitative data on local police forces and law enforcement. In addition to information on the size, composition, and cost of urban police departments, these reports also give—although with varying completeness and following no consistent format either from city to city or over time—an accounting of felonies, misdemeanors, and contraventions of local ordinances identified and responded to by the police as well as of a variety of services provided to the public, municipal authorities, and the state.

Eric Monkkonen in his very suggestive studies of the American police in the nineteenth century has discussed at some length how the detailed quantitative information contained in such reports can be used to measure changes over time in the role of the police.[12] Useful as police reports are, however, the police could exercise great discretion as to what they recorded. The police accounts need to be carefully compared with and supplemented by information, usually qualitative, supplied by their administrative superiors, local supporters, and—often most revealing—their critics.

My research in Germany was made possible, in part, by grants from the American Philosophical Society, the National Endowment for the Humanities, and the Graduate School of Northern Illinois University. Portions of this work have appeared previously as parts of articles published in *Journal of Social History* (1985), *Central European History* (1986), and *Journal of Urban History* (1990). I benefited from the helpful comments of the editors and the anonymous referees of those journals. Further useful suggestions for improvements were provided by the editors and referees of Northern Illinois University Press.

For friendly hospitality and unfailing good cheer during my research trips to Germany, I would like to record my gratitude to the Dehnen family of Cologne. As always, my husband, George W. Spencer, deserves warmest thanks for providing all possible help and encouragement. In particular, he ran our household during my absences and volunteered his editorial expertise at every stage in the writing of this book. Finally, I acknowledge my debt to Hans Rosenberg, who provided me with inspiration and good advice for almost three decades. I regret that he did not live to see this work completed.

POLICE
AND THE SOCIAL ORDER IN
GERMAN
CITIES

CHAPTER ONE

Prussians and Rhinelanders to 1848

THE LEGACY OF PRUSSIAN ABSOLUTISM

As the nineteenth century began, amidst the upheavals of the Napoleonic wars that would leave Prussians standing watch on the Rhine, Prussia was an absolutist state with extensive police powers but few policemen, a situation common in Europe at the time.[1] Already noted for its army and administrative bureaucracy, the realm of the Hohenzollerns showed few signs of becoming a leader in the provision of innovative and effective civilian policing. Indeed, the prior entrenchment of strong, prestigious administrative and military institutions, combined with the absence of serious challenge to central authority in eighteenth-century Prussia, had discouraged extensive experimentation in law enforcement.[2] In Prussia, as in neighboring states, the decades before the coming of Napoleon had witnessed only the merest beginnings of policing as a separate and prominent function of government, distinct from both general civil administration and adjudication, and implemented by a body of specially designated, full-time personnel. But an increasingly pervasive police presence in the nineteenth century came to represent a crucial extension of state power. Before the century's end, Prussia—like its neighbors—added to its long-established ability to tax, conscript, and judge its subjects the capacity to maintain routine surveillance over many of their daily activities.[3]

In their earliest efforts to establish the police as a specialized agency to deal with public safety and law enforcement, Prussia's rulers drew, although at a remove of several decades, on the experience of French absolutism. Paris became the model for Berlin, as Berlin subsequently became the model for other Prussian cities. The model stressed state control over municipal initiative in policing. As long as the Prussian monarchy survived, impetus for changes in the police continued to originate more often in the capital than on the local level. In this respect, Prussia resembled other continental states, in contrast to the more decentralized Anglo-American experience.

In France, the seventeenth century witnessed increased efforts by the Bourbon monarchy, in the aftermath of the midcentury civil wars of the Fronde, to fashion police institutions designed to serve the security needs of the state. In 1667, King Louis XIV appointed a lieutenant general of police for Paris, France's first specialized state official for policing. The new royal appointee presided over a force consisting of 48 *commissaires*, 20 inspectors, 120 sergeants, and 130 court bailiffs. He and his men were responsible for overseeing the maintenance of public order in the French capital as well as for such essential urban services as the regulation of traffic and the cleaning and lighting of streets. These responsibilities reflected an emerging definition of policing that was narrower than its usual continental European, early modern equivalence with civil administration, although still broad by twentieth-century standards. The appointment confirmed the monarchy's intent to bring the vital function of enforcing state-approved order more directly under the control of the central government.[4]

In Prussia, state agents specifically designated as police personnel made their initial appearance in the eighteenth century.[5] In 1742 the Berlin police (Berlin's population was about 68,000 in 1740) were reorganized with a royal appointee as director. The new police director was the city's former mayor with a new title. Initially, six part-time police magistrates were assigned for districts in the central city and twelve for outlying areas. These men were available to the public to take complaints and depositions. Their use of the French title *commissaire de quartier* (later rendered into German as *Polizeikommissar*) reflected the immediacy of the Parisian precedent. The commissaires had at their disposal nine rank-and-file policemen (*Polizeidiener*), supervised by two officers. More numerous than either the commissaires or the Polizeidiener were the approximately forty part-time night watchmen employed by the municipality.[6]

In 1747 the city specified the responsibilities of the local police to include overseeing the provisioning of Berlin and the operation of its markets, keeping track of all travelers and other individuals—such as beggars, vagabonds, peddlers, and Jews—deemed inherently suspicious, inspecting all establishments serving alcohol or offering popular entertainments, making certain the streets were quiet and clean and that traffic moved smoothly, overseeing relations between masters and servants, and supervising the night watch.[7] This list of duties reflected contemporary notions of the most likely sources of unrest, disruption, and inconvenience in urban life.

In the eighteenth century, being a rank-and-file policeman was a lowly, even a tainted, occupation that entailed direct contact with social outcasts and participation in punitive actions.[8] Such commonly assigned tasks as running errands for administrative and judicial officials, enforcing street cleaning ordinances, keeping watch over taverns, and hushing noisy children at play were judged to require little aptitude, training, or even strength and vigor. The state designated invalided soldiers as the group from whose ranks Polizeidiener were to be recruited, an economical way of making provision for the support of at least some former army men.[9] Although significant adjustments in qualifications were later made, the enforced reliance of the police upon the army as the preferred source of recruits survived as long as the Prussian monarchy itself, with the manpower needs of the military routinely given precedence over those of the younger and less-esteemed civilian force.

With only a minimal police presence even in the capital, the Prussian monarchy continued throughout the eighteenth century to rely upon inherited methods of maintaining order. In the countryside, landed estate owners were primarily responsible for the exercise of police powers. In urban centers, town magistrates were expected to ensure that reasonable tranquillity and security prevailed. In carrying out this task they utilized not only whatever bailiffs and watchmen—often part-time, elderly, and sometimes otherwise unemployable—they had at their disposal, but also enlisted the cooperation of various corporate bodies, especially the guilds, as well as heads of households for monitoring those in their charge. In addition the military played a major role, on a day-to-day basis in garrison cities and on an emergency basis elsewhere. Private citizens, too, could be mobilized to keep watch and to respond to disturbances, especially where the army was not close at hand.[10]

The incursions of the French at the beginning of the nineteenth century raised serious questions about the security of the Prussian state, internally as well as externally. Bureaucratic reformers, their influence temporarily strengthened by the crisis, addressed the issue of the future of policing in the context of their proposed reordering of Prussian administration. Two of their decisions had lasting significance.

First, in Baron von Stein's 1808 city ordinance, policing—deemed an essential aspect of sovereignty—was explicitly reserved as a prerogative of the central state. Even where, as was to be the case in most municipalities, the police were administered by communal authorities, such men were to carry out this function as representatives of the Crown, not of the town council.[11] This bureaucratic determination to shield policing from local control survived into the twentieth century. Not for Prussia, or for other continental European states for that matter, was the American alternative of legitimating the police by making them answerable to locally elected officials. In the United States, the police would become symbols of both local corruption and local independence. In Prussia, they would become neither.[12]

Second, the Prussian reformers, in direct imitation of the French, sought to extend the power of the central state through creation in 1812 of a gendarmerie, a military constabulary staffed by men recruited from the army, led by former military officers, and distributed in small units throughout the countryside. The new gendarmes were subject to military discipline but were at the disposal of civilian authorities for maintaining order. They were frequently dispatched to deal with riotous behavior.

Unlike communal policemen, gendarmes were typically mounted and provided with firearms. Although meant primarily for rural policing and for keeping vital lines of communication open across the state, gendarmes were also assigned, given the dearth of reliable alternatives, to cities. Berlin received an initial complement of fifty gendarmes and until 1848 had approximately as many gendarmes as communal policemen.[13]

Originally intended to be a substantial force of nine thousand men, greatly enhancing the presence of the central government throughout the state, the gendarmerie was cut in 1820 to 96 sergeants (*Wachtmeister*) and 1,240 privates (*Gemeine*), leaving Prussia much less well supplied with gendarmes on a per capita basis than were its smaller neighbors. Whereas Prussia had only one gendarme for every 6,000 to 8,000 inhabitants, Hanover had one for every 4,300, Braunschweig one for every 2,000, and Oldenburg one for every 1,700.[14]

In Prussia, landed estate owners in particular had objected to the challenge to their police powers represented by a sizable gendarmerie. In addition, the always influential military resisted the allocation of a substantial share of scarce resources to the new force. Given the formidable obstacles to the expansion of the gendarmerie, its numbers remained essentially frozen between 1820 and 1848, in spite of a 46 percent increase in Prussia's population. According to Karl-Joseph Hummel, by 1848 Prussia had only one gendarme for every 11,800 inhabitants, whereas Bavaria had one for every 1,131.[15]

Lacking both a large gendarmerie and sizable, reliable communal police forces, leaders of the Prussian state before midcentury continued to assign a central role in maintaining order to the military, thereby contributing to increased popular resentment of the army. In emergency situations, contingently mobilized civic guards also continued to protect property and hold the disorderly at bay. Over time, however, the central government became increasingly reluctant to permit recourse to such volunteer guards, uncertain of its ability to control them in every instance and also worried that reliance upon volunteers undermined the credibility of public agencies. Government officials also feared that politically aware citizens might attempt to transform the duty of self-defense into a right.[16] At the same time, in those Prussian towns and cities where class society was beginning to displace the corporate order, growing consciousness of social divisions within the civic guards themselves caused the more well-to-do members, in spite of their dominance of leadership roles, to become uneasy about the reliability of such forces.[17]

Uneasiness about volunteers did not, however, transform the economically fortunate into advocates of the expansion of paid policing. Whatever concerns they harbored about crime and disorder during the often economically difficult years of the early nineteenth century, urban elites resisted allocating increased sums for police personnel. In part, as Albrecht Funk has suggested, town councils had little incentive to replace the traditional watchmen and bailiffs under their control with more expensive specialized urban policemen who would be paid from municipal funds but would be subject to increased state oversight.[18] In addition, during the years of post-Napoleonic reaction, the close association of policing with intrusive political surveillance (especially of newly emergent bourgeois associations) also dampened local enthusiasm.

During the early nineteenth century, bourgeois liberals kept a wary eye on the state's use of both the army and the police. Although they valued order highly, liberals wished society to be as self-regulating as possible. They objected to any innovations they regarded as leading toward the creation of an oppressive *Polizeistaat*. In their thinking, a Polizeistaat was a government that made itself offensive both because of its arbitrary political repressiveness—especially its utilization of police spies—and because of its needlessly capricious and paternalistic intervention in the daily lives of citizens.

Prussian liberals identified such practices primarily with French influence. In 1829 they were presented with a more attractive model by the formation of the London Metropolitan Police. A large uniformed but unarmed force of over three thousand men, the Metropolitan Police dwarfed at its creation all other police institutions in the world in total numbers and (with a single exception) in the ratio of police to population. The exception was the Dublin police. According to Stanley

Palmer, the Irish capital in 1808 had one policeman for every 238 inhabitants, compared to one for every 4,170 in London at that time. Designed to help preserve minority rule in turbulent Ireland, the forbidding Dublin police would, however, serve primarily as a model for later colonial forces, not for would-be European police reformers.[19]

By 1830 London had one policeman for every 416 inhabitants. In a major departure from past practice, the new force was designed to provide coordinated around-the-clock preventive patrol of the British capital. Emphasis shifted from police reaction to deeds reported to efforts to prevent criminal and disorderly acts through continuous and conspicuous police presence.[20] Although the Metropolitan Police was much more ambitious and expensive than anything anyone at the time contemplated for Prussia, the very existence of a major capital (the world's largest city, in fact, with a population close to one-and-a-half million) that was willing and able, unlike Berlin or Paris, to rely upon an unarmed civilian police force rather than upon its military garrison as the first line of its security was appealing to liberals.[21] The police commissioners in London were successful, at least as far as bourgeois observers abroad were concerned, in projecting the image of an impartial agency subordinated to law and exercising its powers with restraint.[22] The example would not be forgotten in Prussia in the revolutionary upheaval of 1848.

THE CHALLENGE OF NEW LANDS

In their efforts to enforce a prescribed order in daily life, Prussia's nineteenth-century leaders confronted the challenge of incorporating new territories, first in the aftermath of the Napoleonic wars, then following the wars of unification. Of these lands, none was of greater importance than the Rhine province. This crucial border area, composed of territories granted to Prussia in 1815 by the Congress of Vienna and organized as a single province in 1822, presented its new Protestant overlords with the daunting prospect of governing an additional population of nearly two million that was four-fifths Catholic and that had just experienced up to two decades of French rule.[23] During succeeding decades, large-scale urbanization, industrialization, and political mobilization would dramatically transform large segments of this westernmost Prussian possession.

The acquisition of new Rhenish lands added substantially to the social and economic diversity of the Prussian state. The Rhineland had in many ways more in common with neighboring lands to the west than with Hohenzollern territories to the east. More densely populated than other Prussian provinces and more open to foreign influences, the Rhineland was to become the home of some of Germany's most notable early commercial and industrial entrepreneurs as well as an early center of liberal sentiment. Neither Prussian officials nor influential Rhinelanders considered immediate and complete integration of the new province into the institutional structure of the Hohenzollern monarchy feasible. As a consequence, the Rhineland continued until midcentury to use Napoleonic legal codes and institutions of local administration rather than their Prussian counterparts.[24]

The imposition of Prussian rule brought large numbers of Prussian soldiers but only a handful of Prussian police officials to the Rhine, few being available in any case. Little was done initially to change day-to-day policing. Indeed, the gendarmerie in the Rhineland was much more thinly spread under the Hohenzollerns than it had been in the days of the French.[25] In 1839 the chief administrative official (*Oberpräsident*) of the Rhine province noted that large border counties (*Kreise*) with populations of thirty to forty thousand were served by only two to four gendarmes. These gendarmes, the Oberpräsident reported, were so occupied with keeping track of strangers passing through their jurisdictions that they had time for little else.[26]

Communal policemen remained few in number and poorly regarded. For the 1,136 communities of the Rhine province's Trier administrative district, for example, Polizeidiener in 1839 numbered only fifty-five, with most police duties still devolving upon watchmen, foresters, field guards, and town magistrates.[27] During the crisis of March 1848, the *Regierungspräsident* (chief district administrator) in Trier would point in helpless frustration to the "total insignificance" of the local police, a situation he regarded as the result of years of inaction by higher authorities.[28]

The state did make special provision for the province's two largest municipalities, Cologne and Aachen, with populations in 1816 of 50,187 and 32,070 respectively, as well as for the province's administrative center and chief fortress, Koblenz, population 13,042. These three cities were chosen to join twenty-two others elsewhere in Prussia that had royal police administrators. The mayor of Cologne reported that local inhabitants were horrified at the prospect of such an ominous intrusion, fearing in particular that the Prussian practice of authorizing the police to use corporal punishment would be introduced along with the new royally appointed police president.[29] When in 1830 the number of royal police administrators for Prussian cities was reduced to ten, the three

for the Rhine province remained in place, an indication of the importance Berlin attached to maintaining surveillance over its newly acquired
borderlands.[30]

Even in the largest Rhenish cities, however, resources available for
law enforcement did not expand dramatically during the first decades of
Prussian rule.[31] In Aachen in the early 1830s, for example, when the
city's population was almost forty thousand, the police department had
nine rank-and-file policemen and three officers.[32] In 1839 Prussia's
minister of the interior authorized six additional Polizeidiener and two
more officers for Aachen, with increases also planned for Cologne and
Koblenz. He cautioned, however, in what amounted to an indirect
comment on Rhenish attitudes toward the Prussian police, that such
substantial additions should be introduced gradually to avoid rousing a
negative response from the local population.[33]

For Prussian officials in the Rhine province, given their limited resources
for the routine maintenance of public order and their suspicions of a
population so recently subject to French rule, crowd-generating activities
of any kind were cause for concern. Certainly an event of the magnitude of
the Trier pilgrimage of 1844, which brought an estimated half-million
people to a town of approximately twenty-five thousand over a period of
fifty days, could not help but arouse bureaucratic anxieties.[34] But even much
smaller, long-established popular festivities were suspect. Authorities
viewed with disdain celebrations whose primary activities were eating,
drinking, dancing, and noisemaking and condemned them as morally and
physically debilitating, as a drain on the economy, and as a potential source
of disorder.

Local urban elites, whose own celebrations increasingly took place at
home or in private clubs, often shared this view and encouraged officials to
rein in periodic popular exuberance. Provincial authorities usually hesitated,
however, to recommend outright prohibition of customary festivals, aware
of the widespread resentment this would produce.[35] The resentful were
certain to include not only would-be celebrants but also tavern keepers and
others with economic interests at stake. Government officials therefore
advocated recourse to prohibition only when the political situation appeared
particularly threatening. Otherwise they opted for limiting duration, imposing curfews, and discouraging innovations.

Rhenish carnival, with its masks and disguises, its traditions of popular
license, and its institutionalized disorder, was cause for special concern. To
facilitate surveillance, Prussian officials maintained throughout the nineteenth century a regulation—originally introduced by the French during
their years of occupation—requiring those who wished to wear masks in
public during carnival to purchase identifying cards daily and to display

those cards on their persons.[36] In a move designed to rob carnival of much of its customary intent, police were held responsible for ensuring that costumes did not offend religious, moral, or social sensibilities or cause embarrassment to prominent individuals. Officials were joined in their efforts to tame carnival by urban elites who strove to reorganize local celebrations into a series of staged events that assigned most of the urban populace the role of passive spectators. The elaborately planned Cologne carnival of 1823 provided the much-imitated model. In the 1830s and 1840s, however, the proliferation of more democratically oriented carnival associations and the increased injection of political satire produced a resurgence of official displeasure.[37]

Carnival was not the only festivity that caused concern. Prussian authorities also took a dim view of local parish festivals (*Kirmessen*), which were more notable for their merrymaking than for their piety. The government reported numerous complaints, presumably from business interests, about the disruption of work caused by such celebrations. However, concern for popular and clerical reaction precluded outright prohibition. Although the Catholic clergy favored limiting the more disreputable worldly trappings of the festivals, they did not wish the observances themselves banned. Authorities adopted the policy of limiting the duration of annual Kirmessen to no more than the customary two or three days and of forbidding entirely the reportedly growing practice of scheduling festivities on the Sundays before and after the actual event. Ordinances to this effect were issued in 1820 and 1834.[38]

Beyond limiting the duration of festivals, local authorities despaired, given the frequently lamented inadequacies of communal police forces, of making much headway in altering the nature of boisterous public celebrations. Where authorities attempted to use police for this purpose, the results were often the opposite of those intended. In Cologne in the late 1830s and early 1840s, for example, official concern about the St. Martin's Kirmes prompted increased police surveillance. Policemen so assigned, however, were regarded as provocative by the celebrants and became the target of teasing and rock throwing. In August 1846, such incidents culminated in a bloody confrontation, recourse to the military, and creation of a temporary volunteer citizen force to patrol the streets.[39]

In the Rhineland, Berlin's civil and military representatives were nervous not only about crowd-generating events and the disorder that might arise from them but also about the possible infiltration of the border province by democratic agitators from France, Belgium, and the states of southwest Germany.[40] Government officials sought to identify and root out all sources of political dissent, this being regarded as a vital undertaking at a time when disorder had become increasingly perceived as linked with politically motivated opposition. Although, to quiet criticism, political policing with its Napoleonic associations had been officially abolished by 1816, reputedly on the grounds that it had existed only as a wartime expedient, well-founded rumors of the continued operation of secret agents roused Rhenish liberals to complain about police repression.[41]

One important spokesman of Rhenish liberalism was David Hansemann, wool merchant in Aachen and future 1848 cabinet minister. In memoranda composed in 1830 and 1840, he spelled out his critique of Prussian policing. In the Rhineland, Hansemann believed, given its special historic development and economic head start, "modern, forward-looking principles" demanded recognition. He saw the province's residents, especially its bourgeois inhabitants, as unwilling to accept the heavy-handed rule customary in Prussia's eastern lands.[42] Political policing, Hansemann argued, discredited the monarchy in the eyes of its Rhenish subjects.[43] And, he added, the repeated use of a proud military for routine maintenance of domestic order led to unnecessary brutality and precipitous recourse to arms.[44]

Yet Hansemann, like other liberals, was far from denying the need for strong and vigilant policing. Liberals paired their opposition to reaction from above with a horror of the potential of those below for unrestrained and disruptive behavior. Hansemann saw a serious threat to order in the growth of democratic forces fostered, he believed, by the advent of industrialization, increasing geographic mobility, the extension of education and military service, and what Hansemann described as moral and religious decline among the lower classes. He believed urban entrepreneurs had a special vested interest in cooperating with the Crown in police matters. He argued that merchants and manufacturers stood to suffer more from disorder than did landed estate owners. The latter, Hansemann suggested, might even benefit from increases in food prices following periods of political and social upheaval. Urban businessmen could only lose.[45]

The concerns Hansemann articulated found resonance throughout the urban areas of the Rhine province, including the cities of the Düsseldorf administrative district. Although these municipalities initially were not highly regarded as meriting special attention in matters of public safety and criminal justice, some of them soon would be as the district took its place in the forefront of German industrialization.

THE DÜSSELDORF DISTRICT AND ITS POLICE

Bounded to the north and west by the Netherlands, to the south and southwest by the Rhenish districts administered from Cologne and

Aachen, and to the east by the Prussian province of Westphalia, the Düsseldorf Regierungsbezirk was bisected from south to north by the Rhine River, which added to its comparative openness to the outside world. In 1816 the district had 591,098 inhabitants, increasing to 908,777 by 1849.[46]

Even before midcentury, manufacturing was beginning to transform portions of the district. Along the Dutch frontier, most of the population continued to depend upon agriculture for its livelihood, but on the left bank of the Rhine, cottage industry had long supplemented agriculture, especially around the textile centers of Krefeld and Mönchengladbach. More vigorous was the urban and industrial development on the right bank, especially that related to textile manufacturing in the valley of the Wupper and iron working in the surrounding Bergisches Land.[47] By 1843, when 60 percent of the Prussian population was still dependent for its livelihood upon agriculture, the comparable figure was only 24 percent in the Bergisches Land.[48] Meanwhile, in the 1830s and 1840s, the first deep mine shafts were being sunk north of the Ruhr River around Mülheim and Essen and the Ruhr coalfield's first successful coke-fired blast furnaces were just coming into operation at midcentury, harbingers of massive industrial development to come.

In 1816 the district's largest city was its administrative center, Düsseldorf, with 23,391 inhabitants. Düsseldorf's population stagnated, however, in the first half of the nineteenth century and was soon surpassed by the district's most important textile manufacturing centers—Elberfeld, Barmen, and Krefeld, bustling cities whose populations approximately doubled in the three decades from 1816 to 1846.[49]

Especially noteworthy were Elberfeld and Barmen. By 1840 more than sixty thousand people lived in these adjoining early industrial cities on the Wupper, which jointly constituted the second-largest urban concentration in the Rhine province, after Cologne, and the sixth largest in Prussia. Approximately half of the population of the two cities worked in textile manufacturing or related industries.[50] By those above them in the social hierarchy, the workers of Elberfeld and Barmen were regarded as an unstable and demoralized proletarian mass. Contemporary observers, including Barmen's most famous native son, Friedrich Engels, especially noted the copious consumption of alcohol among local workers. Elberfeld had in 1829 the exceptionally high ratio of one public drinking establishment for every 115 inhabitants.[51] St. Monday was reportedly vigorously observed, in spite of bourgeois efforts to entice young workers into more wholesome activities and more regular work habits.[52]

The slightest sign of agitation among workers in the two cities—even so much as the posting of an announcement for a weavers' meeting—caused immediate consternation in Prussian officialdom. And each year the first of May, a day for paying rent and moving households for much of the population, aroused nervous concern among authorities.[53] Defenders of the existing order, however, took some comfort from the 1841 construction of the Düsseldorf-Elberfeld railroad, which made possible the rapid transportation of soldiers from Düsseldorf's approximately twenty-five-hundred-man garrison to the cities on the Wupper at the slightest hint of trouble. However, even though the military was readily available to restore order, officials and property owners increasingly worried about the damage that could be done to vulnerable workplaces before the army was able to take charge of the situation.[54]

In the Düsseldorf district until midcentury, even where, as in Elberfeld and Barmen, social and economic change was marked, police forces expanded slowly at best and their composition altered little. Surviving reports on urban policing of the period are fragmentary but give a picture of resistance to major transformation, especially if increased expenditure would result. State officials and local property owners, while sharing a common concern about crime and disorder, had not yet come to view urban policemen as a major part of the answer. They continued to turn to the military, the gendarmerie, and bourgeois self-defense, in combination with appeals to parents, teachers, churchmen, and employers to make use of their authority in the defense of the status quo.

In 1828, for instance, unrest among hand-loom silk weavers in Krefeld, precipitated by a proposed lowering of wages by an average of 15 percent to enable local manufacturers to meet Swiss competition, focused official attention on the meager peacekeeping forces available in that city. With a population of 17,976, Krefeld maintained one Polizeikommissar and five Polizeidiener, or one full-time communal policeman for every 2,996 inhabitants. The local *Landrat*, the chief county administrator and the man responsible for oversight of policing throughout his jurisdiction, described one of the patrolmen as useful but three others as weaklings and noted that the fifth had been suspended for fraud. The Landrat added that for special occasions such as fairs and church festivals, the gendarmerie reinforced the city police. He described one of the three gendarmes stationed in his county as reliable, one as preferring peace and quiet, and the third as physically weak. Krefeld's night watch personnel he characterized as largely worthless.[55]

In 1839 the Krefeld Landrat was still expressing his concern about inadequate police personnel for the growing manufacturing city, which now had about 25,000 residents, largely textile workers whom he viewed, in terms often used by officials of the time, as "readily inclined to excesses of every sort."[56] By 1853, when Krefeld had a population of 42,286, its police department had grown to include ten rank-and-file policemen (now called *Polizeisergeanten* rather than Polizeidiener) and three officers, but the ratio of full-time communal police to population had failed to improve since 1828, now being one for every 3,253 inhabitants.[57]

In fast-growing Elberfeld (population 26,770 in 1837 and 34,956 in 1843), the number of Polizeidiener increased from six to eight in 1838 and from eight to ten in 1844. In explaining the need for the 1844 increase, the mayor pointed not only to the growth in population but also to the increasing range of services the city police were expected to provide. As the centralizing state made ever greater administrative demands upon the city, the city, lacking substantial alternative personnel, loaded implementation onto the police. Thus, policemen were required to spend more and more of their time on such matters as enforcing school attendance and smallpox vaccination, gathering census data, and distributing tax forms.[58]

Offsetting the 1844 decision to hire additional police personnel in Elberfeld was the simultaneous choice not to pension and replace three of the eight Polizeidiener already employed, men who because of age (the oldest was sixty-one), physical disability, or limited intelligence were regarded by their superiors as incapable of providing full service. Rather than shoulder the cost of pensions for the three, the city council decided to continue to use them to run errands and take care of similar undemanding tasks.[59]

In recruiting policemen, towns and cities in the Düsseldorf district, as elsewhere in the Prussian monarchy, had from the 1830s onward more flexibility than they had previously enjoyed. No longer confined to hiring military invalids, they could now also draw from the ranks of able-bodied former noncommissioned officers, provided they had at least nine, later twelve, years of army service. Local appointments to the police required the approval of the district administration and necessitated proof that the appointee had the requisite military background. Final appointment was to follow successful completion of a six-month probationary period. District officials complained, however, and would continue to do so for decades to come, that cities did not always clear appointments properly or draw recruits from state-approved sources.[60]

For Prussian authorities, the advantages of using former noncommissioned army officers as policemen included the oft-repeated observation that such men were experienced in both accepting and enforcing discipline. They were also, incidentally, experienced in writing at least brief reports. Another perceived advantage was the prospect that most of them would not be native to their places of employment. Men born locally were regarded as generally less desirable as police recruits than were outsiders because of the ties of kinship and friendship likely to link local applicants to segments of the town's less prosperous population.[61] A lack of local attachments was even more important for communal policemen than for gendarmes. Gendarmes were subject to periodic relocation. Local police personnel were not.

Once appointed, policemen were admonished to keep their distance from the citizenry. Uniformed at all times, as a constant reminder to themselves and others of their special state function, they were forbidden to accept gifts of any kind, even a free drink. Authorities further attempted to avoid police entanglements with local society by prohibiting policemen or their wives from engaging in private economic ventures.[62] Such prohibitions proved, however, difficult to enforce. Exceptions were granted, and many infractions were tolerated. In particular, the acceptance of gratuities remained common practice, widely regarded as a necessary supplement to limited incomes.

Before midcentury, the salaries of rank-and-file policemen were frequently described by Polizeidiener and their superiors as being pitifully low. And so they were, at least as measured against the incomes of higher police officers or against the amount deemed necessary to maintain a family with even modest pretensions to respectability. Salaries for Polizeidiener appear, however, in a more favorable light when compared with the incomes of the majority of their fellow urban residents.

In Krefeld, rank-and-file policemen earned 140 talers a year in 1828 and 150 talers in 1829, plus a clothing allowance of 13 talers. Krefeld's sole Polizeikommissar had an annual income of 600 talers.[63] The district's gendarmes, more highly regarded than communal policemen, received a starting salary of 250 talers a year in 1829.[64]

In Düsseldorf in 1832, Polizeidiener earned 128 talers a year, while the Polizeikommissare earned 400 talers, and the *Polizeiinspektor* (a royal appointee in that city since 1824) drew a 1,000-taler annual salary from the state.[65] By comparison, Hugo Weidenhaupt, reporting on Düsseldorf in 1825, lists the Regierungspräsident as the city's highest-paid resident, with an annual salary of 3,500 talers. Privy councillors and judges earned from 800 to 1,600 talers a year, and the mayor 1,200 talers. Workers in the building trades had an estimated annual income of at most 150 talers, usually less.[66]

By 1848 the salaries of Düsseldorf's rank-and-file policemen ranged from 180 to 204 talers a year, plus allowances for uniforms and housing.[67] For that same year, Friedrich Lenger estimates that fewer than half of Düsseldorf's master artisans earned more than 100 talers annually and that fewer than one-eighth earned over 200 talers.[68] At the end of the 1840s, Ruhr miners earned on average approximately 100 talers a year.[69] Textile workers in Barmen and Elberfeld in the 1840s earned between 2 and 4 talers a week when work was available, which was not always the case.[70] Polizeidiener had, at the very least, the advantage of a steady income.

For rank-and-file policemen, prospects of improving their financial fortunes through promotion were extremely limited. At most, they could aspire to become Wachtmeister. Communal police officers (Polizeikommissare and Polizeiinspektoren) were recruited separately, not promoted from the ranks. Like their subordinates, police officers were normally expected to have long years of military service but differed in needing a secondary education, not just the elementary schooling characteristic of Polizeidiener.

Understandably, the reliability and incorruptibility of police officers were regarded as even more crucial than was the case with lowly Polizeidiener. The state expected communal police officers to act as its eyes and ears in local affairs. Much less was expected of Polizeidiener in this capacity because of the low opinion their superiors held of their intellectual abilities and social origins. The surveillance role of police officers was considered crucial at a time when even the elites of urban society, given their often liberal leanings, were not to be completely trusted. Under such circumstances, police officers might well find themselves caught between the expectations of the cities that paid them and the state they ultimately represented.

Such, for example, was the experience of Krefeld Polizeiinspektor Leonard Walther. In July 1847, the Krefeld city council organized a reception honoring the return of its noted liberal representative to the United Landtag, an assembly that had earned the king's displeasure by refusing to grant requested loans to the state. After Deputy Hermann von Beckerath, member of a locally prominent silk manufacturing family, had been greeted by spokesmen for the city council, the chamber of commerce, and various bourgeois associations, Walther spoke a few words of welcome in the name of the city's police. District officials were outraged and Walther was sternly censured, despite his presumably accurate claim that he only did what Krefeld's city council and most notable citizens would have condemned him for not doing.[71]

Whether officers or rank-and-file personnel, full-time communal policemen conducted most of their business during daylight and evening hours. At night, after shops and taverns had finally closed and most honest citizens were assumed to be safely in their beds, patrolling the streets was left to part-time night watchmen, with at least one representative of the day force on duty to process arrests and to handle other police business beyond the authority of watchmen. Most larger towns and cities paid their night watch, although some continued to rely at least in part on citizen participation, despite growing resistance to unpaid duty. In Essen (population 6,391 in 1840), for example, citizens were used to supplement the regular four-man night watch during the extended hours of winter darkness. This citizen watch apparently functioned to the satisfaction of authorities, and Essen's mayor reported that no thefts had occurred in the town during the institution's existence. To deal with those individuals who refused to participate, the Essen town council in 1841 proposed a fine to cover the cost of hiring replacements.[72]

Numerous challenges to the imposition of watch duty led the district administration in 1847 to evaluate the legal basis of such demands for service. District officials concluded that neither Prussian nor French law (Napoleonic law remained in effect in the Rhine province until 1851) required regular watch duty from townsmen. At most, citizens could be called upon in emergency situations such as riots, floods, or shipwreck.[73] Otherwise, state authorities concluded, towns would have to pay for nighttime patrol.

Although paid night watches were becoming the norm, they were not paid much. In 1847, for example, privates in the Elberfeld night watch received an annual salary of 28 talers for service every third night.[74] Obviously, only the poorer members of a community would be interested in such pay for nighttime duty. In Mülheim an der Ruhr, for instance, when a new watch was created in 1828, thirteen out of thirty members were identified as day laborers, five as porters, one as a miner, and the remaining eleven as representing a variety of trades ranging from carpentry to shipbuilding. Although without the long military service required of daytime policemen, all had served in the army, a qualification regarded as important even at this lowly level.[75]

The newly recruited night watchmen in Mülheim ranged in age from 25 to 46, with the average being 34.3 years. Mülheim's was, however, a new force, and elsewhere night watchmen often continued to serve to a debilitated old age. Thus, when in 1844 the mayor of Barmen proposed a reorganized and expanded watch, he stipulated, as a departure from the established practice of employing the aged and disabled in what amounted to a form of poor relief, that no one over 50 should be permitted to serve. His proposal to create a larger and more vigorous night watch met the resistance of the city council. The council, representing property-owning interests, argued that because of the increased taxes that would be required, the plan was opposed by "virtually the entire population." Since the state, however, had the final word in matters relating to policing, and Barmen with its expanding proletarian population was regarded as requiring special attention, the council was forced to give way.[76]

In Elberfeld in 1847, the primary stated purpose of the city's night watchmen was to ensure the security of persons and property and to maintain peace and order in the city. In particular, they were to watch for suspicious individuals, especially those carrying bundles. If such persons could not properly identify themselves and explain why they were out at night, they were to be taken to be questioned and, in some instances, searched, by the Polizeisergeant on duty. Watchmen were also expected to keep an eye out for prostitutes plying their trade, make certain that street lanterns remained lighted, and report all fires and other mishaps, while holding themselves in readiness to render assistance as needed. They were further required, without extra pay, to reinforce the daytime police whenever crowd-generating festivities took place.[77]

For the day forces, primary responsibility consisted of keeping track of the whereabouts of individuals, especially newcomers and persons without families or a demonstrably steady, legitimate source of income. Such monitoring of people on the move was initially not too difficult as long as towns were reasonably small and strangers readily recognizable. Inns and boardinghouses called for special attention.

Since local authorities and property owners widely regarded serious disorder and crime as being caused by outsiders, great importance was attached to the surveillance of strangers. The Napoleonic era had ushered in the age of the documented citizen. Newly arrived individuals were required to register with the police. Innkeepers, landlords, and employers were expected to aid the police by reporting the comings and goings of an increasingly mobile population.[78] Characteristically, when in 1834 a reported upsurge in thefts and assaults in the Düsseldorf district roused official concern, the government assumed that the best way to tackle the problem was for the police to tighten their procedures for granting licenses for itinerant trades so that only individuals judged reliable would be authorized to travel through the district in pursuit of their livelihood.[79]

When crimes were reported, investigation was the responsibility of the Polizeikommissare. The Kommissare interrogated suspects, decided the initial disposition of persons arrested, made certain that court orders were implemented, and presided over house searches, seizures of evidence, and the execution of arrest warrants. Barring crimes in progress or the imminent flight of a suspect, the lowly Polizeidiener were supposed to undertake arrests and intrusions into the homes of citizens, especially at night, only under the direction of a Kommissar.[80]

On the rank-and-file policemen devolved not only the law enforcement duties assigned them by the Kommissare but also myriad miscellaneous tasks relating to taxation, school attendance, immunization, and other administrative errands. In addition, they were responsible for day-to-day surveillance of public places. According to the 1847 instructions for Elberfeld Polizeisergeanten, their regular duties included reporting such common violations as newcomers failing to register their residences, the sale of pictures that might be deemed religiously or morally offensive, the smoking of uncovered pipes in the streets (a fire hazard), individuals practicing usury, and the presence of prostitutes. Characteristically, many of the violations monitored by Polizeisergeanten did not produce readily identifiable victims, making the policemen's activities appear especially intrusive to those unfortunate enough to be cited for infractions of any of a multiplicity of petty ordinances.[81]

The police's response to prostitution occasioned particular debate. In 1844, officials from the district's department of the interior argued that the central government had made a mistake in ordering the closing of police-regulated brothels. The one exception still allowed was the fortress town of Wesel with its three authorized establishments, their clienteles segregated by class.[82]

Many local authorities believed that the prohibitions of regulated brothels had caused an increase in sexual improprieties and illegitimate births in the general population. Special concern focused on the possible consequences for the concentrations of young women working in such expanding textile towns as Krefeld, Elberfeld, and Barmen. The warnings of doctors and Landräte about the ill effects for public health and morals resulting from the closing of regulated brothels notwithstanding, the counterargument, that the government could not permit itself to be perceived as sanctioning immorality, prevailed for the time being—at least officially.[83]

An 1839 report on the communal police in the Düsseldorf administrative district by Regierungspräsident Freiherr von Spiegel gives a summary evaluation of their effectiveness as viewed by the man charged with oversight of their activities. Von Spiegel described the communal police as adequate for carrying out their normal duties—from monitoring fairs and religious processions to responding to fires and tavern brawls. He failed to detect any strong sentiment for the expansion of local forces, especially as parsimonious town councils (state-appointed in the Rhine province until 1845 and elected on the basis of a plutocratic three-class system of voting thereafter) were reluctant to pay more for that purpose.

But the Regierungspräsident was far from being completely satisfied. The primary cause of his concern was inadequate provision for dealing with outbreaks of collective violence, especially if they should occur in more than one place at a time. He also worried about the problems of countering the dissemination of political propaganda and of monitoring the movement of individuals along the border. For such activities, he regarded the communal police as worthless—no matter how their numbers might be increased—and called instead for a strengthening of the gendarmerie. Von Spiegel characterized that body, in contrast to municipal police forces, as a flexible and dependable instrument of state policy with the added advantage of being respected, even under the most agitated circumstances, by the district's lower classes.[84]

The significant strengthening of the district's gendarmerie desired by the Regierungspräsident failed, however, to take place before midcentury. From two foot and forty-three mounted gendarmes in 1823, the district's force increased to thirty-nine foot and thirty-five mounted gendarmes by 1849. But since the district's population grew during that period from 623,063 to 907,151, the number of inhabitants per gendarme changed little, declining slightly from 13,846 to 12,259.[85]

With the communal police regarded as of limited utility in confronting any but the most routine local disturbances, the gendarmerie remaining only a nominal presence in much of the district, and the military being concentrated in garrison towns and reluctant to disperse its forces in response to civil disturbances, property owners in urban centers before 1848 continued occasionally to resort to self-help. Indeed, the government reluctantly found itself forced to call on them to do so.

During riotous demonstrations by Krefeld silk weavers in 1828, for example, the perceived inadequacy of local police and gendarmes, even backed by twenty to thirty citizens who came to their aid, led to the sending of a detachment of fifty hussars from Düsseldorf. However, once order was restored, military authorities were anxious to have their men return as quickly as possible and argued that much of Krefeld's population also wished them to leave in order to free the city of the continued costs of quartering troops. Faced with the prospect of the early withdrawal of military forces, local silk manufacturers proposed the creation of an armed voluntary security force to aid the police in case of need. Their proposal drew upon the precedent of a citizen militia that had existed during the wars of liberation.[86]

The district administration voiced reservations about the reliability of a volunteer force that anyone could join and then serve or not serve at will. Instead, the government insisted that the force—initially approved for a period of three months—be organized on terms to be determined by state officials. One hundred men would be carefully selected by local authorities and would be subject to fines if they failed to respond to demands for service in emergency situations. Reflecting the purpose of the security force to respond to worker protest and to protect property, the majority of the men chosen to participate were owners and managers of textile firms, and most of the rest were merchants and professional men. The individuals selected were not permitted to excuse themselves on grounds of pressing business. The local Landrat pointed out that they had been chosen precisely because they had extensive business interests and as a consequence stood to lose more than others in case of renewed tumult.[87]

A flurry of activity involving civic guards followed in 1830 as the district experienced reverberations from revolutionary activity in France, Belgium, and scattered German cities. In that year, guards were mobilized to reinforce police and gendarmes for patrol duty in Elberfeld, Barmen, and Düsseldorf. In the case of Barmen, the guard consisted of 880 men, of whom 30 were mounted. The district administration, while appreciative of the service, expressed its determination to direct the course of events.[88] A royal order retroactively legitimated the guards, while stipulating that students and day laborers—reputedly for their own good—must be excluded from membership.[89]

With the restoration of approved order, civic guards were demobilized, but the idea remained alive, to be revived in times of stress. Essen, for example, a city with a 60 percent Catholic majority (a percentage comparable to that for the district as a whole), was shaken in 1845 by a Protestant-Catholic clash accompanying the annual Corpus Christi procession. Divisions within the peacekeeping forces themselves emerged, with a gendarme bringing charges that one of the city's two Polizeidiener, a tax collector, and a local court official had, as Catholics, participated in the procession and then had refused to join the gendarmes in their efforts to control the demonstrators.[90]

In the wake of attacks on law enforcement agents and on the Essen town hall, local authorities approved the formation of a civic guard armed with weapons from the armory.[91] In a subsequent letter to the district administration, forty of Essen's bourgeois residents strongly argued the need for such a guard, to consist of all the city's "reliable and right-thinking" citizens come together to protect life and property against the "rage of a fanaticized proletariat." The authors of the letter pointed both to the weakness of the local police and to Essen's distance from the closest garrison, precluding timely military intervention.[92] The issue was not whether the military could be relied upon to quell riots but rather how much damage might take place before their arrival, a particular concern at a time when protesters frequently targeted the residences and workplaces of unpopular employers and officials for demolition.

Into the 1840s, citizen involvement continued to be solicited from time to time not only to counter collective violence but also to deal with criminal acts by individuals. In 1846, for example, following reports of a series of robberies around Krefeld, the Regierungspräsident called upon district residents to join communal policemen and gendarmes in patrol. Court and police officials used the occasion to argue their need for additional personnel, which would make reliance on volunteers unnecessary, but they continued to count themselves fortunate if additions kept pace with population growth.[93] Under these circumstances, the district's communal police continued to form a relatively small part of the peacekeeping force, foreshadowing the comparatively minor, if controversial, role they would play in the tumultuous events of 1848–49.

CHAPTER TWO

Revolution and Reaction, 1848–1858

POLICING A REVOLUTION

As indicated in chapter 1, urban police forces in the Düsseldorf district prior to 1848 were of little help in cases of serious challenge to the existing order, nor were they really expected to be. The revolution at midcentury underscored their limitations. Not only were municipal policemen too few in number and too little respected to make much difference in the face of large-scale collective protest, but often their very presence inflamed already tense situations. Uniformed policemen were conspicuous symbols of state authority and provocative reminders of past and present grievances about the exercise of power in the realm of the Hohenzollerns. Police agents and the buildings housing their operations were prime targets for citizens wishing to give dramatic expression to their discontent. Especially subject to attack were local jails, whose typical inmates in the 1840s were individuals accused of such poverty-related offenses as poaching or theft of food or fuel. During especially turbulent episodes in 1848 and 1849, local policemen often felt compelled to adopt a passive role or even to leave town entirely. Flight, for example, was the choice of all but one of Elberfeld's policemen during that city's May 1849 uprising.[1]

The general tendency of the local police to maintain a prudently low profile during the months of greatest upheaval was reinforced by frequent shifts in the identity of their superiors and in the character of instructions emanating from Berlin. Prussia had five ministers of the interior during 1848, an indication of the volatility of domestic affairs. Düsseldorf, like Berlin, had three police chiefs in that year.[2] Equally uncertain was the legal situation. Policemen were often left unsure which laws they were expected to enforce and with what degree of strictness.

Especially unclear to local agents were changing instructions regarding public meetings and political publications. Guidelines for action altered rapidly in accordance with the ebb and flow of revolutionary and counterrevolutionary activity.[3]

Not all local policemen tried to remain as inconspicuous as possible. Some sacrificed their careers by aligning themselves with the losing side of the political struggle. Disagreements about where legitimate authority lay complicated the situation for police officials. A notable case involved Polizeiinspektor Zeller of Düsseldorf. Appointed as head of that city's police in August 1848 to provide the kind of vigorous leadership his sixty-four-year-old predecessor had reportedly long since ceased to demonstrate,[4] Zeller opted in November of that year to back local forces, including the city council, in calling for a tax strike. The strike was to protest the Crown's collection of monies not authorized by the beleaguered Prussian National Assembly. Zeller publicly announced that he would not permit the participation of Düsseldorf's police in the collection of such funds. The royal government responded to the tax strike with the imposition of a state of siege that ended not only Düsseldorf's resistance but also Zeller's brief tenure as the city's police chief.[5]

Of course, what the urban police did or failed to do in 1848 and 1849 was of secondary importance compared to the role of the military. The army, not the police, was the ultimate guarantor of the Prussian monarchy. As befitted the strategic importance of the Rhineland, nearly one-third of the Prussian army was stationed in that province.[6] The potential effectiveness of this concentration of military force as an instrument for maintaining domestic order was enhanced by the Rhineland's well-developed rail transport.

The use of soldiers in 1848 was, however, recognized as being even more provocative than reliance on the police. Royal authorities initially hesitated to use the army, at least until support for the revolution had begun to wane. Such restraint reflected not only fear that use of the military would provoke bloody encounters that might lead to a general uprising in the Rhine province but also concern about the reliability of rank-and-file soldiers.[7] Even more questionable was the dependability of the Landwehr, and indeed the call-up of those militia units of citizen-soldiers for use as counterrevolutionary forces in southwestern Germany was to provide the immediate spark for the uprising in Elberfeld and elsewhere in May 1849.[8]

Having at their disposal only limited police forces of dubious quality and being initially reluctant to make extensive use of the military, officials in the Düsseldorf district in 1848 acquiesced, as they had during past crises, in the hasty recruitment of civic guards (*Bürgerwehren*).⁹ On these volunteer forces was to devolve much of the responsibility for preserving communal order and protecting property during the early months of the revolution. City councils and the urban elites they represented hastened to sponsor such organizations not only because of immediate concern about possible damage to property and disruption of business but also because the law held cities financially liable for losses caused by local uprisings. After the revolution, for example, the courts compelled the city of Barmen to compensate the mayor of Elberfeld because Barmen residents had not been prevented from crossing into Elberfeld to help in the demolition of the mayor's house.¹⁰

The composition and goals of Bürgerwehren varied from place to place and questions about their reliability clouded their brief existence. In Elberfeld and Krefeld, proletarian demonstrations in March 1848 resulted in damage to manufacturers' property. In Burg, near Solingen, center of the Bergisch cutlery trade, craft workers demolished a recently established iron foundry. The foundry was mass-producing cheap goods that threatened the economic survival of craftsmen using traditional techniques.¹¹ In the centers of early industry in the Düsseldorf district, preventing recurrences of such outbursts (relatively rare though these actually remained in manufacturing areas) was the primary preoccupation of the bourgeois leaders of hastily formed civic guards.

Shooting and gymnastic societies mobilized their members to aid the Bürgerwehren in their tasks. Bourgeois citizens collected contributions to help with the purchase of uniforms and firearms and called on the government to supply weapons from its armories.¹² Although the army initially resisted such demands, during the revolution the government distributed 9,933 firearms to volunteers in the Düsseldorf district or slightly more than one weapon for every one hundred inhabitants. Sabers were also supplied.¹³

If cautious merchants and manufacturers were likely to see the Bürgerwehren first and foremost as emergency defenders of property, other, more democratically inclined participants conceived of them as representing an important step away from capricious and intrusive military and police intervention in daily life and toward the greater self-reliance and empowerment of the citizenry. The Bürgerwehr embodied the right of citizens to bear arms, as opposed to the state's claim to monopolize the legitimate use of force.

In Düsseldorf, a city still lacking the sharp class divisions to be found in the district's manufacturing centers, the city council initiated the formation of a Bürgerwehr that ultimately had close to 2,500 members, including workers. The members had the right to elect their own officers. As chief they chose Lorenz Cantador, a merchant and colonel of the local shooting society and also a leading democrat. For Cantador, the city's Bürgerwehr, equipped with 1,038 firearms and 200 sabers, was the "armed guard of freedom." At the time of the November 1848 tax strike in Düsseldorf, the Bürgerwehr declared itself in permanent session, pledged its support to the Prussian National Assembly, and joined in searching the city's post office to make certain that tax money was not being forwarded to Berlin. After imposing a state of siege, the royal government called for the disarming and disbanding of Düsseldorf's civic guard and for the arrest of its chief.[14]

Troubling for government officials was not only the political unreliability of some Bürgerwehr units but also their questionable effectiveness. The initial enthusiasm of many volunteers waned after the first days or weeks. Not only disagreements within the Bürgerwehren about political issues but also competing claims on the time of members, especially those with substantial business interests, led to reduced participation.[15] In addition, when really serious disorder threatened, volunteers might well prove reluctant to risk challenging armed protesters.[16]

By the time the last of the Bürgerwehren were disbanded in 1849, the government and local men of property regarded their recent experiences as ample proof of the inadequacies of amateur policing. State officials were strengthened in their suspicions of local initiatives. But if the Bürgerwehren had no future, the trauma of revolution did stimulate an innovation of lasting significance in the development of Prussian policing, the *Schutzmannschaft*. Originally created to patrol the politically sensitive capital, this new royal police force ultimately became the model for urban police departments throughout Prussia.

Although designed for Berlin, the Schutzmannschaft at its creation incorporated proposed changes being debated throughout German central Europe during the months of revolutionary upheaval. The bitterness aroused by military intervention in domestic affairs had highlighted the need for a reliable civilian alternative. Official distaste for amateur policing and local initiatives suggested that the state itself would have to allocate substantial new resources for routine surveillance of daily life. The demonstrated unpopularity and lack of credibility of existing urban police institutions pointed up the need for extensive reorganization.

Authorized by the monarchy in June 1848 (during the liberal Camphausen ministry), the Berlin Schutzmannschaft went far beyond all previous efforts to provide urban police forces in Prussia. On the eve of revolution the capital, with slightly more than 400,000 inhabitants, had only a motley collection of 112 communal policemen and 121 gendarmes. By July 1848, over 1,200 of a projected 2,000 men had been selected for the new Schutzmannschaft, this greatly expanded force to be paid from state funds.[17] To make them more acceptable to their fellow citizens, the Berlin Schutzmänner recruited in 1848 and 1849 were typically local out-of-work artisans with an average of only three years of military experience, not the superannuated noncommissioned army officers characteristic of other Prussian police forces. And to emphasize their civilian character, the new recruits were given uniforms cut in a civilian mode, including top hats adorned with numbers identifying the individuals wearing them. London's Metropolitan Police constituted the obvious model.[18]

Conceived in the midst of revolution, the Berlin Schutzmannschaft was highly controversial during its early years. Conservatives were initially suspicious of the new institution, representing as it did part of the legacy of 1848. Speaking before the newly created Prussian Landtag in 1849, Düsseldorf's deputy, Graf Villers, argued that the Schutzmannschaft represented an unnecessary extravagance. He believed that the previous system of maintaining small numbers of policemen for routine duties and calling in the army to handle significant disturbances had been both economical and effective.[19]

Although the Schutzmannschaft survived the attacks of its critics and the entrenchment of political reaction, it did so in significantly altered form. In particular, its civilian trappings were soon jettisoned. By 1850, spiked helmets had replaced top hats on the heads of Berlin Schutzmänner. Gone, too, were the identifying numbers. And most significant, the military became, as for other Prussian police forces, the primary source of recruits. By 1852, nine years of military service had become the prerequisite for entrance into the Schutzmannschaft.[20] Twelve or more years with the armed forces continued to be preferred for communal police recruits. Requiring a somewhat shorter term of military service as preparation for the Schutzmannschaft reflected not a desire for a less militarized police in the capital (the opposite actually being the case) but rather for a force younger and more vigorous than those serving in provincial cities.

POSTREVOLUTIONARY REORGANIZATION

Internationally, the 1850s witnessed major initiatives in the reorganization and extension of urban policing. In the United States, the largest East Coast cities—drawing on the experience of the London Metropolitan Police—took the controversial step of putting their policemen into uniform.[21] In France in 1854, Emperor Napoleon III, himself a one-time London special constable, approved a threefold increase in the Paris municipal police, from approximately one thousand to approximately three thousand men. Intended to reassure the Parisian bourgeoisie in the wake of the coup that had attended the creation of the French Second Empire, the new patrolmen, like their London counterparts and the Berlin Schutzmänner in their first years, bore identifying numbers.[22]

In England, the wide gap between the provision of police for the capital and for the rest of the country was partly closed after the passage in 1856 of the County and Borough Police Act, stimulated by fears of the domestic consequences of the Crimean War and of the end of the overseas transportation of convicts. For early 1856, Stanley Palmer lists eight middle-sized English towns (20,000–100,000 population) as having 1,241 to 2,259 residents per policeman. The new act set a target of one policeman for every 400 to 800 inhabitants in large cities and one for every 1,000 to 2,000 in nonurban areas. By 1861, according to V.A.C. Gatrell, the average number of inhabitants per policeman in England and Wales ranged from 504 for the metropolitan police, to 792 for borough police forces, and 1,489 for county forces.[23]

For policing in the Prussian provinces, changes in the 1850s were less dramatic. Of the changes introduced in 1848, the most lasting would be the state's commitment to providing more substantial resources and more rigorous supervision. Even with the allocation of more money, however, the costliness of the Berlin Schutzmannschaft precluded its immediate duplication in other, less politically sensitive Prussian municipalities. Thus in 1849 the Landtag, fearful of renewed disorder, approved 756,432 talers for urban policing, compared with the state's allocation in the previous year of only 337,301 talers. But nearly four-fifths of the larger amount was intended for the capital.[24]

Although during the 1850s Berlin's Schutzmannschaft was frequently criticized in Landtag debates as needlessly expensive and as a consequence experienced more cuts than increases, the capital continued to be incomparably more closely policed than any other Prussian city. By 1859, for instance, Berlin had 1,150 Schutzmänner or 1 for every 397 inhabitants. In that same year, no other Prussian city had fewer than 1,396 inhabitants for every full-time policeman.[25]

Outside Berlin the government provided modest increases for provincial cities with royal police administrators. In 1849 there were eight of these (Königsberg, Danzig, Posen, Potsdam, Breslau, Magdeburg, Koblenz, Cologne, and Aachen) with a combined population of 575,814. These cities had a total of 149 Polizeisergeanten, or 1 for every 3,864 residents. By 1859, the population of these eight cities had increased to 666,211 and the number of Polizeisergeanten to 233, or 1 for every 2,859 inhabitants. In 1859 the highest state expenditure for policing in any of these eight cities was .37 talers per capita for Königsberg compared to 1.03 talers per capita for Berlin.[26]

As a general rule, aside from Berlin, Prussia's postrevolutionary government avoided expensive innovations in policing and concentrated instead, as a first step, on purging local forces of individual policemen who had proven either especially incompetent or politically unreliable in the recent turbulent past. Those believed guilty of collaboration with the revolutionaries were quickly removed. In the aftermath of the Elberfeld uprising of May 1849, for instance, Minister of the Interior Otto von Manteuffel (minister president, 1850–58) ordered that punishment should be meted out not only to rioters but also to any state or local officials who had failed to do all they could to counter disorder.[27]

High on the list of the accused was Polizeisergeant Samuel Scheffler, who had placed himself at the disposal of the committee of public safety formed in Elberfeld in May in defiance of royal authority. Scheffler argued that he had only cooperated with the democrats in an effort to put himself in a position to protect his neighbors from bands of radicals, but his superiors refused to accept his plea. Not only was Scheffler dismissed, but he was also ordered to pay the costs of his hearing and of the substitute who had been employed during his suspension.[28]

Weeding out individuals deemed incompetent or insufficiently committed to the royal cause continued through the early 1850s. Among those retired during that period was Krefeld's police chief, Polizeiinspektor Leonard Walther. As noted in chapter 1, Walther had already attracted unfavorable attention from his superiors as a result of his 1847 welcoming speech for United Landtag Deputy Hermann von Beckerath. In 1851, following numerous complaints about the aging Walther's inadequate performance, royal authorities were further annoyed when they received reports that policemen under his command had failed to expel from a theater audience a patron wearing a red jacket in honor of the anniversary of the revolutionary events of 18 March 1848. Walther attempted to justify the inaction of his subordinates by arguing that expelling the offending democrat would only have resulted in increased disruption, but his superiors were not prepared to listen.[29]

Retirement from communal police service, whether forced or voluntary, brought with it no guaranteed pension. In Walther's case, although he had served Krefeld for twenty-three years, the city denied any legal obligation to provide him with continued support. However, while rejecting the principle of entitlement, the city did agree, on "grounds of fairness," to continue to pay Walther 400 talers a year (half his previous salary), subject to annual review of the municipal budget.[30] Krefeld intended to meet the costs of Walther's revokable pension by cutting in half the salary appropriated for a new third Polizeikommissar.

With still very restricted resources available for urban policing in the provinces, state officials believed that the best investment of their funds was in vigorous leadership. In searching for replacements for those police officers who had been dismissed or retired, royal officials sought individuals they believed capable of becoming forceful administrators, committed without qualification to the counterrevolutionary tasks of the 1850s and capable of imposing rigorous discipline on those under their command. Such, for example, was the approach adopted in seeking a replacement for Walther in Krefeld. The royal government informed the city that to make possible the offer of a salary high enough to attract someone of proven ability, capable of rectifying what were described as long-standing deficiencies in the city's police, the state would pay half. Krefeld provided 400 talers a year, and the state matched that amount.[31] The individual selected was Eduard Viedebantt. Viedebantt, a man with extensive police experience in a number of Prussian cities, had worked most recently for the political police in Cologne, investigating the likes of Karl Marx and Ferdinand Lassalle.[32]

In its postrevolutionary efforts to guarantee the maintenance of approved order, the state increased its direct supervision of policing important provincial cities. As noted in chapter 1, the Prussian government insisted throughout the nineteenth century that policing was exclusively its prerogative, strictly excluded from the otherwise substantial domain of municipal self-administration. Liberal efforts during the revolution of 1848 to secure for elected representatives a meaningful role in controlling municipal police and thereby to establish the principle of local accountability failed to survive the triumph of monarchical counterrevolution. After the revolution, as before, mayors who functioned as police administrators did so in the name of the king, taking their directives in these matters from royal officials, not from city councils. Such councils, elected on the basis of a plutocratic three-class franchise and open ballots, provided no meaningful representation for the urban lower classes. Nevertheless, Prussia's leaders refused to regard the property owners represented in city councils as acceptable partners for setting police priorities. The role of urban elites was largely limited to the provision of funds, and even on such questions they could be overruled.

But after the experience of 1848, royal officials found even these guarantees of their monopoly of police powers inadequate. During the years of postrevolutionary reaction, they lacked confidence in urban administrators. They viewed mayors as too liberal and too dependent upon local elites, even though that dependence was limited by the right of the royal government to confirm the election of municipal administrators and to monitor their activities. When state authorities had special doubts about individual mayors, they made use of the new Prussian police law of 11 March 1850 to deny such men even delegated authority over the police.[33] That law gave the interior minister the right to place administration of police forces in cities of his choosing in the hands of state-appointed directors. In the Düsseldorf administrative district, he exercised this option for Düsseldorf, Krefeld, Elberfeld, and Barmen, the latter two neighboring cities to share the same royal police director.[34]

The new police directors in Düsseldorf and Elberfeld-Barmen were not only state appointees but were also among seventeen Prussian police officials required to make weekly reports of local political developments directly to Berlin's ambitious reaction-era police president, Carl Ludwig von Hinckeldey. From 1854 until his death in 1856, Hinckeldey was not only head of the Berlin police but also held the newly created post of general director of police in the ministry of the interior, a controversial position that lapsed when he died.[35] Reports to Hinckeldey circumvented the normal transmission of information through the district and provincial hierarchies and were symptomatic of efforts in the early and mid-1850s to create a more centralized and independent police. The ambitions of the Berlin police president were, however, realized only in part. The administrative bureaucracy did not care to be circumvented. With the return of more settled conditions, direct reports from provincial police directors to the Berlin police became less frequent and ceased altogether by the end of the decade.[36]

Throughout the 1850s, urban spokesmen repeatedly protested the appointment of state officials to administer municipal police forces. The potential was high for friction between state-appointed police chiefs and local elites. Haughty representatives of centralized authority, often with little knowledge of or sensitivity to local priorities, royal appointees acted as state watchdogs against any manifestations of renewed political opposition, including liberal associations drawing support from local business and professional leaders. Particularly contentious, for instance, was the relationship between Düsseldorf's elites and that city's royal police director, Franz von Falderen, appointed in November 1848.

Falderen, a former cavalry lieutenant and most recently the appointed mayor of a small town near Solingen, was selected by royal authorities for his new position because he was regarded as "an energetic man of loyal disposition."[37] In Düsseldorf he saw his primary task as combating any resurgence of the "subversive party."[38] Falderen's reports stressed continuing local unrest and the resulting need for vigorous, uncompromising measures.

Falderen complained that his efforts were hampered by the agitators' sympathizers on the city council and in the mayor's office. Arguing initially that the communal and police administration of Düsseldorf should be united in the hands of the same person, presumably himself, he later settled for stressing the complete independence of the police from the city administration. He emphasized that Düsseldorf's policemen should be free from any threat of dismissal by local officials.[39] Falderen's liberal critics, echoing charges being leveled during the 1850s against the Berlin Schutzmannschaft, accused him of sanctioning illegal arrests and tolerating physical abuse of prisoners.[40]

In the immediate postrevolutionary years, provincial authorities backed Falderen. Thus, the district administration sharply reprimanded the mayor of Düsseldorf for permitting the city council to discuss policing. The mayor was also forced to apologize for ordering a display of flags in the city without first securing the approval of the police.[41] By the mid-1850s, however, administrative officials had come to see the abrasive and controversial Falderen as a serious liability. Accused of financial improprieties, he was, by 1855, on the verge of indictment. He was saved from that fate by timely hospitalization for mental and physical disabilities.[42]

More often than not, however, the primary issue raised during the 1850s by civic leaders was not so much who should administer the police as who should pay for them. Finances mattered more to many urban property owners than did local accountability. Some even envied Berlin its royal police force because the state bore most of the cost. Provincial taxpayers complained that they were being called upon to subsidize the policing of the capital while also being required to pay for local forces.

The cities of Düsseldorf, Krefeld, Elberfeld, and Barmen, with state-directed municipal police, seemed to be in the worst possible situation. The state directly controlled their forces through appointment of the police chief, but the city covered all costs except the director's salary.[43] And the royal directors themselves, though drawing their salaries from the state, cost the cities substantial sums to meet what seemed to frugal town councils extravagant demands for housing, carriages, office space, and additional personnel.[44] The councils found state appointees typically unwilling to accept the facilities that had been provided for their city-employed predecessors. Elberfeld's royal police director, for example, cost the city 400 talers a year for rent and 300 talers a year for horses and carriage in the mid-1850s, a time when the annual salary for one of the city's Polizeidiener was 220 talers.[45]

The campaign against the state-appointed police directors started to bear fruit at the end of the decade, as the years of arbitrary counterrevolutionary repression gave way to the short-lived "New Era." In 1858 the new regent, the future William I, replaced the reactionary cabinet of Otto von Manteuffel and Count Westphalen with one composed of more moderate individuals, even some who were mildly liberal. For the Düsseldorf district, the New Era brought the return of the police forces of Düsseldorf and Krefeld to municipal administration in 1860. A similar transfer for Elberfeld and Barmen was completed in 1863.[46]

The state's change of heart on this matter had to do only in part with continued liberal protestations in the Landtag. Also important was the prospect of escalating costs. Throughout the 1850s, state and city officials had differed on interpreting the financial provisions of the 1850 police law. The state claimed that if it chose to appoint its own director for a municipal force, it incurred no cost other than his salary. The cities claimed that in such cases the state was obliged to pay the salaries of all the full-time men on the force. Municipalities did not hesitate to take the state to court on this issue. Finally, in 1861, a judicial ruling settled the dispute in their favor.

The state offered the cities the opportunity to continue the previous arrangement voluntarily, but they refused. Faced with the prospect of supporting substantial additional personnel, the financially hard-pressed Prussian state dismantled the royal police directorates formed during the 1850s, retaining royal police forces in only eleven provincial cities. None of these was located in the Düsseldorf district, although three (Cologne, Aachen, and Koblenz) survived elsewhere in the Rhine province.[47] Where royal police directorates were dismantled, the state reluctantly agreed to reimburse the cities for police salaries they had paid during the 1850s. In Krefeld, the reimbursement amounted to the substantial sum of 35,441 talers.[48]

THE POLICEMAN'S LOT IN THE 1850S

Beyond the experiments with royal police directors, provincial police forces remained little altered during the 1850s in either size or composition. A government report summarized in table 1 compares the provision of police personnel in four urban police districts (cities and surrounding villages) in the Düsseldorf Regierungsbezirk in 1858 with the situation a decade earlier. The numbers indicate no significant quantitative improvement. Barmen and Düsseldorf registered only

slight drops in the ratio of inhabitants to full-time communal policemen, from 4,341:1 to 4,062:1 and from 2,485:1 to 2,460:1, respectively.
The Bergisch metalworking town of Remscheid registered a striking
decline in the number of inhabitants per policeman, from 6,233:1 to
4,953:1, but the actual increase in personnel in that case was only one
Polizeikommissar.[49]

Of the four police districts listed in the report, Düsseldorf, as
administrative center, continued to be much better supplied with policemen than were its neighbors, even though Düsseldorf also had the added
protection of a large garrison. In the three manufacturing centers

TABLE 1

Police Personnel, 1848 and 1858

Police District	Population	Full-time Policemen	Inhabitants per Policeman	Gendarmes
Barmen				
1848	34,730	8	4,341	2
1858	44,681	11	4,062	See Elberfeld
Düsseldorf				
1848	42,241[a]	17	2,485	11[c]
1858	49,200[b]	20	2,460	6[d]
Elberfeld				
1848	43,131	16	2,696	4
1858	53,420	13	4,109	5[e]
Remscheid				
1848	12,467	2	6,233	—
1858	14,858	3	4,953	—

Source: Nachweisung über die Zahl der executiven Polizeibeamten in den Städten
Düsseldorf, Barmen, Elberfeld, und Remscheid gegen Ende der 1840er Jahren und
zu Ende des Jahres 1858, Staatsarchiv Koblenz 403/6595.

Note: In this and all subsequent tables, the number of full-time policemen given
refers only to the executive police, i.e., those whose duties included enforcing the
law and maintaining order or supervising those who did. Excluded are those who
had purely administrative or clerical functions.

[a]This number includes 2,500 military personnel.

[b]This number includes 2,351 military personnel.

[c]This number represents the entire county.

[d]This number represents gendarmes under the police director for Düsseldorf.

[e]This number represents gendarmes under the police director for Elberfeld–Barmen.

(Elberfeld, Barmen, and Remscheid), armed representatives of the state were less plentiful. Elberfeld actually lost three policemen. When its police department was reorganized under a royal director, the three had been retired as unsuitable for active service. In their place, five gendarmes were put at the disposal of the police director for Elberfeld-Barmen. Gendarmes were deemed more effective than city policemen for the control of collective actions although less satisfactory for routine urban patrol.

In 1859 Elberfeld's royal police director stressed that the force at his command was totally inadequate for patrolling a major industrial city. Nevertheless, he advised against pressing the city council to pay for additional personnel because he regarded the municipal budget as already overburdened.[50] In that same year, Elberfeld officials noted with relief that despite the decade's inflationary pressures, allocations for policing had remained essentially unchanged for several years.[51]

Stagnant municipal police budgets militated not only against significantly increasing the size of urban forces but also against making service in them more attractive. In particular, policemen lamented the decline in purchasing power of their salaries. The stability of their incomes, an advantage in deflationary years, worked against them in the inflationary mid-1850s. Wholesale food prices in Germany rose sharply from an index figure of 56 in 1850 (1913 = 100) to 127 in 1855. Wholesale prices for industrial raw materials and semifinished goods climbed from 84 in 1850 (1913 = 100) to 118 in 1857.[52] In Ruhr mining, the average price of a ton of coal rose from 5.20 marks in 1850 to 9.00 marks in 1856.[53] Wages in that industry also climbed, Ruhr miners earning an average of 111 talers in 1850 and 186 talers in 1857.[54]

Policemen, at least in the larger cities, continued to be better paid than most workers, even skilled workers, but they feared the gap was narrowing. As noted in chapter 1, in Düsseldorf in 1848 Polizeisergeanten earned from 180 to 204 talers a year, plus allowances for uniforms and rent. In spite of the inflation of the mid-1850s, their pay was not increased until 1858, when their salaries ranged from 230 to 280 talers a year.[55] In Krefeld in 1849, Polizeisergeanten earned 200 talers a year, without additional provision for uniforms or rent. Their salaries were raised modestly to 220 talers in 1852 and then to 240 talers in 1859. By comparison, the mayor of Krefeld earned a salary of 2,000 talers in 1856, his assistants (*Beigeordnete*) received 1,000 talers each, the police chief 800 talers, and the Polizeikommissare 500 to 600 talers each.[56] In Düsseldorf in 1854, workers averaged an estimated 90 to 150 talers a year.[57]

Hard pressed in inflationary times to maintain their accustomed standard of living, rank-and-file municipal policemen submitted frequent petitions for relief. Well informed about pay rates in neighboring cities, they mentioned any discrepancies they believed would strengthen their case. They invariably described themselves as married men with large families consisting of as many as seven or eight children. They noted that a substantial portion of their income—almost half was the perhaps exaggerated claim of a petition signed by seven Krefeld Polizeisergeanten—had to be expended on job-related costs. Prominent among such costs was the payment of informers.[58]

Another major expense, except where—as in Düsseldorf—the city covered the cost, was the purchase and care of uniforms; Düsseldorf budgeted 33 talers per man per year for this purpose.[59] Royal officials frequently complained of the shabby appearance of many communal patrolmen. For their part, policemen, though attaching importance to dressing appropriately for their role as representatives of the state, found the price of new uniforms prohibitive. Men employed by smaller towns where pay was substantially lower than in the larger cities (150 talers a year in Langenberg—between Elberfeld and Essen—in 1858, for instance) considered this expense especially burdensome.[60]

Reluctant to grant raises that would become part of the base pay of policemen but cognizant of the ravages inflation was inflicting on fixed incomes, cities opted more often than not for annual gratuities. This practice placed policemen in the position of being perpetual supplicants for special favors from their superiors.[61] An additional means of supplementing the income of rank-and-file policemen in inflationary times was to divide among them the money allocated for positions that fell vacant, with the understanding that recipients of the extra pay would have to perform the extra work.[62]

Not only rank-and-file policemen but also their officers submitted frequent petitions for financial relief. Petitions from Polizeiinspektoren and Polizeikommissare stressed not only the loyal and energetic service they claimed to have rendered, especially in 1848 and 1849, but also the expense of maintaining a suitable standard of living, including the costs of carriages, maids, and education for numerous sons.[63] Even Polizeiinspektor Falderen, with an annual state-paid salary of 1,400 talers in 1854, joined in requesting a yearly supplement. Among his expenditures he listed trips to Belgium, France, and England, necessary, he insisted, to offset the strain of his position.[64] He did not mention, however, that his rank itself brought with it certain opportunities for relaxation. In Düsseldorf and in all other cities with royal police administrators, a choice box at the theater had to be permanently reserved for the use of the police chief, his family, and visiting police dignitaries, a claim based on a very broad reading of the police obligation to censor all theatrical productions.[65]

To be worthy of their pay and gratuities, policemen were expected to be continuously available. They were required, if at all possible, to dwell in the neighborhood they patrolled and were not to leave without permission. Their superiors wished to know where they were at all times. In addition to being available for all contingencies, policemen were called upon to work long hours. In Düsseldorf in 1860, for instance, the regular shift for Polizeisergeanten began between six and eight o'clock in the morning, depending on the time of year, and extended (with breaks) to eleven o'clock at night.[66]

In Krefeld Polizeisergeanten, after their regular duties, were expected to gather every evening at 10:45 to oversee the closing of the taverns. They were to continue patrolling the streets in pairs until all was quiet, only then turning over surveillance to the night watch. The Krefeld police chief, while recognizing that the hours demanded were exhausting, claimed that he was unable to offer any relief as long as the number of men at his disposal remained inadequate.[67] To save on pensions, cities did continue, however, the practice of assigning lighter duties to men who because of age or disability were not equal to the full rigors of the job.[68]

Not only were policemen required to work long hours, but they were also expected to submit without question to rigorous discipline of a military character. Following liberal efforts in 1848 to make the police more civilian, Prussian officials in the reactionary 1850s, as already noted in the case of the Berlin Schutzmannschaft, reemphasized the army as the appropriate model for police appearance, bearing, and relationship to their superiors and the public.[69] Government officials sought to strengthen the link between the army and the police by stressing the requirement that communal policemen should be recruited from the ranks of former noncommissioned officers who had qualified for civil employment by completing long years of military service. Elaborate procedures were devised to ensure that exceptions to this rule were granted only when an exhaustive search had found no qualified *Militäranwärter* (former noncommissioned officers with the requisite service records) available to fill a vacancy.[70]

REPRESSIVE STRATEGIES

The purging or retirement of the most incompetent and politically unreliable urban policemen, the preferment of vigorous and unyielding police chiefs, the increase in state coordination and supervision, and the renewed insistence on making the police as militarized as possible constituted Berlin's program for preparing provincial police forces in the 1850s to serve as effective instruments of centralized authority, even without appreciably expanded resources. In the postrevolutionary era, the state intended the police to play a highly visible role in forestalling or monitoring all activities that could conceivably lead to renewed political opposition or disorder of any kind. The police were instructed to give the broadest possible definition to what might constitute a threat to the status quo and were granted great latitude in their choice of methods for combating any such threat. Although still too few to be deemed capable of countering significant collective protest, the provincial police were expected to help substantially by preventing protest from manifesting itself in the first place. The primary role of the police, as viewed by their superiors, was to deal with early symptoms of unrest and political mobilization before discontent had a chance to become a serious threat.[71]

For the Prussian state in the 1850s, a crucial function of the police was surveillance of politically active individuals. The central government, more than ever, regarded the police as its indispensable eyes and ears. Vital for this purpose was the Prussian association law of 11 March 1850, issued on the same date as the new police law. The law regulating associations sharply curtailed in practice the right of free association guaranteed in principle by the Prussian constitution of 1850. The police were empowered by the association law to disband political organizations if they infringed prohibitions against the presence of women, students, or apprentices or if they gave evidence of attempting to coordinate their activities with those of like-minded organizations in other cities. The association law required all political organizations to keep the police informed of their statutes, membership, and meeting plans, and to admit uniformed policemen to their gatherings so that they could record the proceedings and squelch any provocative statements or actions.[72]

The Prussian police made the fullest possible use of the association law. Under its terms, political associations were broadly defined as those—no matter what their stated purpose might be—that in any way attempted to influence public affairs. Gymnastic societies, for example, given their association with ideas of national unity and freedom, could be defined under the 1850 law as political associations and suffered a significant loss of membership in the 1850s due to the resulting police pressure. In Düsseldorf the police had disbanded the local gymnastic society in 1849. A new one was not established until a decade later.[73]

The conspicuous presence of one or more uniformed police officers at political assemblies served as a constant reminder to Prussian citizens of the state's watchfulness for ideological deviance and confirmed the lasting popular equation of the police and political repression. Police responsibility for press supervision, reconfirmed in the Prussian press law of 12 May 1851, strengthened this identification. Editors of newspapers and any other publications of under twenty pages were required to make certain that police authorities received a copy of every issue they produced. Police officers scrutinized all local publications for offensive or subversive material. In addition, they controlled the issuing of permits for distribution of handbills and pamphlets and monitored the book trade.[74]

The state also expected policemen to continue monitoring closely the movement of individuals, issuing travel passes for local inhabitants, and checking the credentials of visitors.[75] They were required to register all residents and to report to Berlin the presence of political suspects. The revised and expanded registration order of 1857 stipulated that all new residents had to report their addresses within fourteen days. Landlords and employers were expected to make certain that their tenants and employees complied with these regulations. Innkeepers had to supply the police daily with lists of overnight guests. Householders also had to report to the police any nonresidents who spent the night in their homes. Regulations regarding registration were enforced with particular strictness in the case of the poor.[76]

Special attention focused on keeping track of individuals without fixed addresses. Suspicious travelers without proper identification could be compelled to return to their places of official residence.[77] Wandering journeymen, especially those who had spent time abroad in cities regarded as sources of dangerous political ideas and associations, such as London or Zurich, were subject to particular scrutiny.[78] In 1852, in an order that remained in effect until 1861, the minister of the interior informed the district administration that Prussian journeymen were to be forbidden to visit Switzerland, that non-Prussian journeymen who had been resident in that country should be denied entry into Prussia, and that any returning Prussian journeymen should be subjected to special surveillance.[79]

The careful attention to those who traveled extended even to those individuals, such as railway men, whose occupation brought them into frequent contact with travelers. The government feared that politically unreliable railway employees might use their positions to aid in the transport of suspicious individuals or publications.[80] The police were expected to watch railroad stations with special care, since railroads symbolized the vastly augmented potential for mass movement that, in combination with the demands of an expanding economy, would soon make impractical efforts to oversee all travelers.[81]

The burden of numbers never led, however, to abandonment of the registration of residents. Registration, though cumbersome and frequently circumvented, served a multitude of purposes. It provided information not only for political and criminal investigations but also for tax collectors, for school, health, church, and military authorities, and even for businessmen interested in debt collection. Prussian policemen were amazed that their British counterparts could function without comparable means of keeping track of residents.

In their efforts to forestall the mobilization of political opposition, state authorities called on the police to respond immediately and vigorously to any attempt to instigate demonstrations within their jurisdictions.[82] Linked to this in the postrevolutionary era was concern for more rigorous maintenance of public order in general. During the early and mid-1850s, Prussian authorities demanded of the police careful surveillance, and sometimes outright prohibition, of all crowd-generating gatherings, however innocuous their stated purpose. One consequence was that Catholic clergymen found officials more willing than they had been before 1848 to comply with clerical wishes regarding stricter limitation of drinking and dancing on Sundays and religious holidays.[83] Where public festivities were permitted during the 1850s, authorities sternly instructed organizers about their responsibilities. Thus, before the master silk weavers in Krefeld could stage their annual celebration in 1851, their representatives had to meet with the police and provide detailed plans and assurances of lawful behavior, especially guaranteeing to eliminate "any political or socialist tendencies."[84]

Among places where people gathered, taverns were especially suspect as possible sites of political discussion and organization, as well as of disorder, idleness, and immorality. In the 1850s the police made increased use of their licensing powers in an attempt to limit the number of drinking establishments; they targeted those that catered to the lower classes or were suspect because of political associations. The police focused particular attention on those tavern operators who attempted to increase business through the holding of dances. Officials strove to keep the number of such events, especially those relating to Kirmes celebrations, to a minimum.[85]

In 1858 the advent of the New Era brought a reevaluation in the capital of policies relating to popular entertainments. Eduard Heinrich von Flottwell, the new minister of the interior, chided the administration of the Rhine province for excessive zeal in its campaign against public dances and Kirmes celebrations and accused it of doing more harm than good. Flottwell perceptively argued that while ordinary people were willing to put up with a great deal in regard to restrictions and limitations perceived as customary, they greatly resented even the most modest of new regulations designed to change their daily lives.[86]

As the 1850s drew to a close, not only the regulation of amusements but also the whole reaction-era approach to policing was subject to reconsideration. As memories of revolutionary upheaval lost some of their immediacy, Prussian liberals stepped up their criticism in press and Landtag of the state's toleration of high-handed and capricious police behavior. Revelations of serious financial irregularities and disregard for legal procedures, especially on the part of the expensive and conspicuous Berlin Schutzmannschaft, helped strengthen the argument of those who charged that the police should be held more strictly to account. Among those advancing such arguments were representatives of the justice ministry, who resented police uncooperativeness and especially the practice of arresting and holding individuals for extended periods without court sanction.[87]

Excessively capricious and intrusive behavior by uniformed personnel damaged the credibility of the police in particular and the legitimacy of state authority in general. In an effort to dampen liberal criticism by making police behavior more predictable and more respectful of existing legal norms, the New Era government not only purged those police officials most closely associated with the abuses of the immediate postrevolutionary years but also required far more careful reporting of police activities and closer cooperation with the courts.[88] At the same time, police forces were advised to reduce the number of penalties imposed for minor violations and to focus more narrowly on individuals who deliberately and maliciously disregarded ordinances. Those whose transgressions were deemed to be the product of ignorance or misinformation were to be merely instructed or warned, not fined or jailed.[89]

The onerous system of police surveillance of released convicts was also greatly reduced. In the 1850s and early 1860s, this assignment had been a major commitment. In 1862, for example, when Krefeld had only sixteen full-time policemen, they were responsible for supervising 302 former prisoners.[90] The rigor of police surveillance was such that some convicts reportedly regarded it as worse than imprisonment.[91] According to the Essen Landrat in 1863, many prisoners requested permission to emigrate after their release rather than face obtrusive police oversight that made "obtaining housing and honest employment impossible."[92] During the 1860s, the scope of this practice was drastically curtailed. By 1869–70, the Krefeld force was responsible for only 87 former convicts, by 1879–80 for a mere 24.[93]

As the Prussian government proceeded with the dismantling of some of the most repressive and capricious policing practices of the postrevolutionary years, it did so with growing confidence in its ability to maintain order. Even if the police were to be more limited by the law than in the past, the existing legal system, which encompassed such legislation as the Prussian law of association and the laws regulating the registration of residents, combined with the continuing lack of local police accountability, still guaranteed great latitude for police action.

CHAPTER THREE

Police for Industrializing Cities, 1850–1878

STATE AND LOCAL EXPECTATIONS

From the perspective of urban elites in the Düsseldorf district during the years of postrevolutionary reaction, the state's demand on community-supported police forces often seemed intrusive and irrelevant to local concerns. Resentment was particularly strong when bourgeois associations and activities were subjected to police surveillance and intervention. While state officials pressed their demands on police officers in the provinces to keep them well informed about local developments and to act vigorously to preempt renewed political mobilization, civic leaders had their own notions about the uses of police personnel.

In the 1850s urban administrators and town councillors continued to regard the policemen they employed as convenient personnel for carrying out a wide variety of routine tasks. Police chiefs complained that their subordinates were required to spend much of their time serving as "communal errand boys" instead of properly fulfilling their peacekeeping and surveillance functions.[1] The chief of the Elberfeld police sought to drive home this point in a letter to the mayor by listing assignments given to the city's thirteen Polizeisergeanten during January 1850. In addition to routine patrol of the city and surveillance of such public events as markets and theater performances, duties assigned to Elberfeld's Polizeisergeanten in that month included delivery of 251 summonses, identification of 441 young men liable to military service, including actual call-up of 44, processing 439 cases of truancy, and compiling a list of 1,582 individuals subject to the tax on dog owners.[2]

As late as 1877, Krefeld's Polizeiinspektor was complaining that his

Polizeisergeanten were spending most of their time as messengers for tax collectors, the military, school inspectors, and poor relief administrators, among others. Replying to parsimonious taxpayers who believed that patrolmen should make themselves useful by tending to miscellaneous tasks as they made their rounds, the Polizeiinspektor enumerated his objections. In particular, he noted the difficulty of keeping close track of his men because they so frequently departed from their assigned routes to tend to other matters. In the process of running errands, Polizeisergeanten also were frequently placed in situations leading to the offer of gratuities by members of the public, a practice officially frowned upon but difficult to curb. Finally, Krefeld's Polizeiinspektor believed that the use of policemen as menials seriously undermined their prestige and credibility.[3]

Police chiefs complained not only that their patrolmen were overburdened with errands but also that they could not be properly supervised because their officers were inundated by masses of paperwork. The dispersed nature of police patrol makes it inherently difficult to supervise, but the problem was made worse because officers were kept largely desk bound by the multiplicity of local and state regulations entailing police certification and recordkeeping. The police were expected to make certain that urban inhabitants were registered, immunized, schooled, taxed, counted, and monitored in a variety of other ways. Visits to police headquarters by residents and visitors alike were routinely required. In the 1850s just issuing and validating all the papers citizens needed for various purposes was a major task for small police departments. In Barmen in 1857, for instance, the police issued 1,448 travel passes and other forms of identification and validated 3,404 passes for visitors. In addition, they issued 5,138 permits for temporary and permanent residence.[4]

Also making substantial claims on the time of police officers were the state prosecutors (*Staatsanwalten*), who were established throughout Prussia in 1849. Into the 1860s tension remained high between the police and the Staatsanwalten.[5] Prosecutors were empowered to call upon the Polizeikommissare to aid them in collecting evidence for use in court and in carrying out other court-determined assignments. The power of court officials to requisition the services of police officers for their own purposes led to many disagreements. Düsseldorf's Polizeiinspektor Falderen, doubtless putting the worst possible light on the situation, complained that the demands of the courts on his Kommissare were so great that they had almost no time left for police duties.[6]

One response to the problem was to divide the Kommissare between those who specialized in functioning as auxiliaries of the court and those who tended to tasks assigned them by the police hierarchy. In Düssel-dorf in 1860, for example, one of the city's three Polizeikommissare was designated to handle criminal investigations and related court business at the behest of the state prosecutor, the remaining two to concentrate on other police responsibilities.[7] A difficulty inherent in such an arrange-ment was that when the Polizeikommissar assigned to help with court cases left the city's police force, he would take with him much of the department's accumulated knowledge about and experience in criminal investigation.[8]

For police chiefs concerned about the multiple and conflicting de-mands made upon their subordinates, one solution was to shift some routine recordkeeping and service functions from the police to nonpo-lice personnel. The Krefeld police chief in 1852, pointing to Düsseldorf as a precedent, suggested that responsibility for making certain all children were vaccinated against smallpox be transferred from the police to another communal agency, with the understanding that the police would cooperate as needed to force recalcitrant parents to comply.[9]

The Prussian state, however, joined urban administrators in resisting significant reduction in the array of police functions. Such opposition arose from more than just the lack of ready alternatives. For the state, a primary advantage of a police responsible for overseeing a wide variety of areas (such as street lighting and cleaning, fire fighting, school attendance, weights and measures, insurance contracts, and master-servant relations) was that such broad responsibilities helped justify the appointment of more policemen than local elites would otherwise have deemed necessary. Into the 1870s the answer given to critics who wondered why policemen should be employed to run errands or sit behind desks tending to routine clerical tasks was, as argued by Minister of the Interior Friedrich Graf zu Eulenberg, that such men were thereby kept available for deployment in the streets in case of an emergency. They represented a reserve force, to be kept busy with various bureau-cratic tasks until needed to respond to civil disorder.[10]

Eulenberg also spoke against greater specialization of the police on the grounds that manpower could be more fully utilized if individuals in a single agency could be switched from function to function as the need arose. If separate staffs were maintained for each communal function, some men might be left underemployed on occasion.[11] In addition, performing a wide range of tasks permitted the police to penetrate many aspects of daily life and also to save on pensions by providing continued employment at lighter duties for older or partially disabled men.

Although, during the remaining decades of the nineteenth century,

Prussian police did shed some of their tasks, new ones were added as governmental responsibilities expanded. Thus, in 1878 Düsseldorf Polizeiinspektor Hellwig pointed to an overall increase rather than decrease in the tasks confronting his Kommissare. In particular, Hellwig claimed, they were required to spend more time than before overseeing the inspection of such commodities as milk, butter, bread, and meat, regulating the sale of drugs, supplying retirees with the affidavits they needed to collect their pensions, inspecting factories, providing workbooks for workers under age twenty-one, and supervising delivery of an ever-expanding number of writs.[12] Prussia's police continued into the twentieth century to exercise functions broad enough to elicit amazement from British and American observers.

The desire to have as many men as possible available for emergency use may have served not only to retard police specialization but also to delay the transition from part-time to full-time night patrolmen. Night watchmen, who typically served only every second or third night, were more numerous than personnel for daytime patrol. They therefore represented a substantial reserve that could be called upon for service whenever a threatening situation occurred. In Düsseldorf in 1858, for example, the city had one Polizeiinspektor, five Polizeikommissare, and fourteen Polizeisergeanten, but forty-six night watchmen.

The city of Düsseldorf in the 1850s specified that preference in hiring men for night duty be given to those age twenty-four to fifty who had served in the army or who had been trained in crafts that required strength (such as masonry, carpentry, and blacksmithing).[13] Although not regarded as the equal of the daytime police in intelligence and discipline, night watchmen were increasingly expected to be at least reasonably physically fit. For major public celebrations or any situation deemed potentially disruptive, the city's night watchmen could be mobilized along with the day force to create a sizable contingent for guaranteeing public order.

Although civic leaders in the district's biggest cities could muster a peacekeeping force of several dozen men when the need arose, they continued to regard the police in their employ as suitable for dealing only with the most routine aspects of maintaining order. In cases of serious disturbance, local property owners continued to advocate reliance upon state-supported soldiers and gendarmes, who were considered both more effective and less of a financial burden for cities than enlarged police forces. Administrators and councilmen in Elberfeld and Barmen, in particular, would argue until the end of the century that as important centers of German industry, the neighboring cities needed not more police but rather a military garrison.[14] The state, however, repeatedly rejected such requests, in part because the stationing of troops in industrial surroundings was deemed ruinous to military discipline.

The relative stagnation in the number of policemen employed by the cities of the Düsseldorf district into the 1860s, despite a major surge of urban and industrial expansion since midcentury, reflected the continuing disinclination of city councils to give policing a high priority. Even the presence of more numerous and much enlarged industrial establishments failed at first to alter the situation substantially. Insofar as major employers were seriously concerned about guaranteeing their property and safeguarding the conditions necessary for uninterrupted operation of their works, their initial impulse was to invest in fences and safes and to hire gatekeepers and watchmen, not to press for larger and more effective communal police forces.

In Krefeld in 1861, for instance, in line with this self-help orientation, manufacturers responded to the problem of traffic in stolen silk by forming the Association against Silk Theft. Initially this organization concentrated on the offer of rewards. Then, in 1864, the silk manufacturers proposed to contribute two hundred talers annually to the city to cover one-third of the salary for a Polizeikommissar to be assigned to work with them on investigating the disappearance of their goods.[15] In making their proposal, the employers reminded Krefeld's mayor of the city's dependence on silk manufacturing.

Elsewhere individual employers entered on their own into agreements with city administrations to pay the salaries of patrolmen to be stationed near their concerns. They thereby incurred an obligation relating directly to their own interests as an alternative to supporting more intensive policing for the city as a whole. Of Essen's seven rank-and-file policemen in 1864, for example, one was assigned to and paid for by the Krupp steelworks (6,600 employees) and a second was assigned to and paid for by the Stinnes family's Victoria Mathias mine (1,297 employees). Alfred Krupp also supplied Essen with eight watchmen for patrol between the city gate and his factory on Sunday and holiday evenings.[16]

Such arrangements were by no means peculiar to Prussia. In England, for instance, the Police Act of 1840 authorized the appointment of additional constables at the expense of private individuals. In the 1860s and 1870s, according to Carolyn Steedman, such privately subsidized constables represented up to 25 percent of northern county and borough forces.[17]

ADDING RESOURCES

By the mid-1860s Prussian officials, preoccupied first by the constitutional conflict and then by Bismarck's wars and the incorporation of new territories, were becoming less tolerant of the reluctance of frugal town councils to make more substantial provision for policing their communities. For the next decade and beyond, cities and the state vigorously debated the issue of the appropriate size for urban police forces and the amount of communal resources to be allocated for their support.

An early step toward making cities in the Düsseldorf district more responsible for their own security was the reassignment in the mid-1860s of gendarmes serving in urban areas. The appropriateness of gendarmes for urban police work had been a matter of discussion for years. Town councils generally favored the use of as many such men as possible, both because they were paid by the state and because they were reportedly more likely than communal policemen to command respect from urban workers. Also, in garrison cities like Düsseldorf, gendarmes had much more latitude than did communal policemen in taking action against delinquent soldiers.[18]

Gendarmes did, however, have serious limitations in an urban context. According to Düsseldorf's Polizeiinspektor Falderen, gendarmes were effective when a show of force was required but were otherwise largely useless for regular police service.[19] A recurring problem relating to the use of gendarmes was the potential for conflict between the military authorities who commanded the gendarmerie and the civilian officials who made use of their services.[20]

In 1865 the state, against the wishes of city and district administrations, declared its intent to withdraw gendarmes from a number of cities with communal police on the principle that the cities had both the responsibility and the resources to provide their own patrols.[21] This decision was quickly implemented as gendarmes were reassigned to work with the army during the wars with Austria and France and to help in the policing of recently acquired lands. The reassigned gendarmes had to be replaced by newly hired Polizeisergeanten (three were hired in Elberfeld, two in Krefeld).[22] When in 1865 the minister of the interior accepted Alfred Krupp's offer to pay the salaries of two gendarmes, he did so with the understanding that the new men would patrol outside the city limits of Essen. Town councils continued into the 1870s to renew their requests for gendarmes, but they were reminded that the obligation to pay for urban policing was theirs.[23]

While state officials were forcing the district's cities to find replacements for withdrawn gendarmes, they also were pressing for the appointment of more communal policemen in general. They focused particular attention on those cities that were experiencing rapid urban and industrial growth, which was viewed as inherently disruptive. Authorities continued, as in the 1830s and 1840s, to regard newly arrived workers as "restless" and "given to excesses of all kinds." Complaints from influential citizens, discomfited by signs of rapid social change and encounters with newcomers who exhibited what seemed strange and threatening ways, reinforced these concerns. As industrializing cities received more attention, the administrative center of Düsseldorf lost its accustomed preeminence in the allocation of police personnel (see table 2).

In this context, references to urban crime became more common in official correspondence, even though a compilation of reported felonies and misdemeanors (*Verbrechen* and *Vergehen*) in the Düsseldorf district from 1858 to 1866 revealed that by far the most common of all violations remained the essentially rural phenomenon of wood theft. In the late 1850s, reports of wood thefts exceeded all other entries taken together and constituted more than 40 percent of the total through the early and

TABLE 2
Police Personnel, 1863–1888

Police District	Population	Policemen (Day Force Only)	Inhabitants per Policeman
Barmen			
1863	58,104	12	4,842
1874	82,000	34	2,412
1878	90,000	52	1,731
1887–88	106,000	65	1,631
Düsseldorf			
1864	54,690	19	2,878
1874	76,500	36	2,125
1878	86,000	43	2,000
1887–88	123,000	64	1,922
Elberfeld			
1864	62,008	19	3,263
1874	80,000	38	2,105
1878	89,000	48	1,854
1887–88	110,000	64	1,719

Sources: Reports from Oberbürgermeister, May 1874, Staatsarchiv Düsseldorf, Regierung Düsseldorf 30218; Vergleichende Übersicht des Polizeiexecutivpersonals, 18 November 1878, Stadtarchiv Düsseldorf III 4350; Übersicht über das Personal und Kosten der Gemeindepolizeiverwaltungen 1887–88, Stadtarchiv Krefeld 4/938.

mid-1860s. As a result, the rural county of Kleve, not one of the district's urban centers, had the highest reported crime rate in the Düsseldorf Regierungsbezirk.[24]

If, however, wood theft is excluded, those who read the statistics did have reason for concern about conditions in the district's largest industrial cities. Take for example Elberfeld and Barmen, jointly representing the most significant manufacturing center in the district. In 1861, when Elberfeld and Barmen had 9.5 percent of the district's population, they reported 23.7 percent of all cases of theft and 19.9 percent of all cases of assault.[25] The numbers, of course, do not reveal whether this disparity was due to actual higher incidence of such violations in the two cities or only to more complete reporting.

Among the district's industrial cities in the 1860s, fast-growing Essen attracted particular official attention. Between 1861 and 1864 the population increased by 50 percent, from 20,751 to 31,224, with most of the newcomers being laborers. Officials noted a marked increase in thefts to 111, plus two burglaries, reported in 1864 compared with 52 thefts and no burglaries in 1861. But they claimed to be far more concerned about assaults upon individuals, with fifty-one, resulting in two deaths, reported in 1864 compared with fifteen assaults in 1861 (see table 3).[26] The police described Essen streets as quiet on workdays, when long hours of industrial employment served to discipline the proletariat, but as unsafe or at least unpleasant for bourgeois citizens, especially ladies, on Sundays and holidays.[27]

Local property owners and communal administrators in the district's industrializing cities felt ambivalent toward the state's demands for more policemen. Certainly they shared official concerns about the behavior, especially the leisure behavior, of an emergent industrial working class, and about the safety of life and property in a changing social milieu, but they remained reluctant to allocate the needed monies and uncertain that more policemen represented the best response.

Consider again the case of Essen. In 1864 the city council, at the urging of the state and in a move intended to help improve decorum in public spaces, agreed to the appointment of three additional rank-and-file policemen beginning in the following year. These additions brought the number of Polizeisergeanten to ten, with two officers. Within four years the city's population had grown by another ten thousand and reports of property crime, especially burglaries (forty-five in 1868 compared with two in 1864), had increased dramatically.[28] At this point, the state demanded further additions to the police force. The mayor, however, replied that the existing force was adequate for the city's needs and the council voted down the requested increase.[29] The Essen Landrat

TABLE 3
Essen Police, 1860–1874

Year	Population	Full-time Policemen	Inhabitants per Policeman	Property Crimes (per 10,000 inhabitants)[a]	Violent Crimes (per 10,000 inhabitants)[b]
1860	18,435	5	3,687	29.3	12.5
1861	20,751	5	4,150	27.9	7.2
1862	21,368	6	3,561	37.0	17.8
1863	23,925	6	3,987	44.3	12.9
1864	31,224	7	4,460	41.3	17.0
1865	33,666	8	4,208	69.5	21.7
1866	35,099	12	2,925	52.1	13.2
1867	40,695	12	3,391	57.0	10.3
1868	41,753	12	3,479	49.8	11.7
1869	42,813	12	3,568	—	—
1870	43,598	12	3,633	—	—
1971	47,212	13	3,632	—	—
1872	52,000	17	3,059	—	—
1873	56,356	25	2,254	—	—
1874	60,000	28	2,143	—	—

Sources: Oberbürgermeister, Essen, to Regierung Düsseldorf, Abteilung des Innern, 22 May 1874, Staatsarchiv Düsseldorf, Regierung Düsseldorf 30218; Polizeianzeige, 1859–68, Stadtarchiv Essen XIII/1.
[a]Property crimes include theft, burglary, arson, fraud, and counterfeiting.
[b]Violent crimes include homicide, assault, and robbery.

wondered how the council could regard its provision for policing as sufficient when the mayor himself admitted that he carried a loaded revolver with him on New Year's Eve, an always boisterous occasion celebrated in the streets by the discharge of firearms and firecrackers.[30] State authorities, convinced that the situation was unacceptable, ordered the city to appropriate money for three additional recruits. In 1871 they called for two more. The city, however, delayed taking action on either demand until 1872.[31]

Elsewhere, reports of additions made to the district's urban police forces in the 1860s parallel the pattern suggested by Essen. Despite growing concern about urban crime and the unsettling presence of increasing numbers of newcomers, additional policemen were appointed only sporadically, often in response to outside pressure. And the additions that were made did little more than keep pace with the rapid growth of urban population.

The 1870s, by contrast, brought a significantly more willing and generous allocation of resources for policing. By the end of the decade, due to a combination of intensified state insistence and the increasing preoccupation of local elites with maintaining order and protecting the social and political status quo, the ratio of urban policemen to population in the district's major cities improved substantially. In Krefeld, for example, the number of inhabitants per policemen in 1870 was virtually identical to what it had been in 1854 or 1864. But by 1874 the number of residents per policeman had been cut by nearly a thousand. (See Appendix, table A–1. Compare tables 2 and 3.)

In the 1870s the state's growing concern with urban policing found clear expression in the significant increase of resources it was prepared to allocate for the Berlin Schutzmannschaft. In 1851, that force had been reorganized with a complement of 1,213 officers and men. During the next decade, that number remained essentially unchanged, despite an almost one-third increase in Berlin's population. Then in the early and mid–1860s, with the Schutzmannschaft subject to repeated liberal attacks for its overbearing manner and hard pressed to defend itself against serious charges of corruption and abuses of power, the number of Schutzmänner actually decreased to 1,066 in 1866, despite the city's accelerated population growth. Whereas in 1852 Berlin had one Schutzmann for every 344 inhabitants, by 1868 the ratio was one for every 615. Large increases in manpower in the 1870s, however, brought the ratio close to its earlier level, with one Schutzmann for every 350 residents in 1880. In that year, the Berlin Schutzmannschaft numbered 3,204 officers and men.[32]

In Landtag debates in 1872, 1874, and 1878, which preceded increases in the size of the Berlin force by 49.4 percent, 12.6 percent, and 41.3 percent, respectively, the government and its supporters presented their arguments for more policemen. The reasons centered less on reported crime and the overall growth of urban population than on the feared consequences of proletarianization and the advent of organized labor. The Paris Commune of 1871 served as a dire portent. In 1878 Minister of the Interior Graf zu Eulenburg made very clear the link between the new antisocialist law and that year's successful quest for one thousand additional Berlin Schutzmänner.[33]

Government officials and like-minded deputies repeatedly referred to the potentially unsettling consequences of major pieces of liberal legislation that had accompanied national unification and guaranteed freedom of internal migration (1867), abolished anticombination laws (1869), and granted greater occupational and entrepreneurial freedom (1869). Increased freedom, the argument went, made more policemen necessary.[34] What could no longer be prohibited had to be carefully monitored.

While providing significantly expanded resources for policing the capital, the state stiffened its demands for complementary additions to communal forces, especially in rapidly industrializing regions such as the Düsseldorf district. At the same time, urban elites proved less resistant than they had earlier. In part, their greater willingness reflected a more positive view of the state and the police as its servants. Having moved beyond the postrevolutionary reaction of the 1850s and the constitutional conflict of the 1860s, the Prussian state now offered liberals the satisfactions of nation building, combined with accelerated economic development, and appeared more as protector than repressor of bourgeois society. Many local property owners shared Berlin's concerns about a rapidly changing society and the advent of organized labor. As in the capital, fears of crime, though important, played a lesser role as a justification for expanding police forces.

Germany's first major strike wave, from 1869 to 1874, strongly reinforced growing bourgeois concerns about the security of life, property, and the existing order. Both the prosperity of the early 1870s and the depression years that followed added to the uneasiness of the propertied classes. In the first years of the decade, defenders of the status quo feared that higher wages and greater choice of employment would result in less deferential workers, more prone both to crime and to protest. At the same time, rapid inflation sparked major popular protests in the new empire, such as those over rents in Berlin in July 1872 and over beer prices in Frankfurt in April 1873 (leaving eighteen dead in the latter case).[35] Such actions heightened concerns recently unleashed by the Paris Commune. With the economic downturn after 1873, urban elites worried that increased unemployment would remove workers from industrial discipline and might make them desperate enough to resort to individual criminal activity or—worse yet—to violent collective protest. Simultaneously, early socialist electoral successes (40 percent or more of the vote, for example, in the Elberfeld-Barmen electoral district in 1874, 1877, and 1878)[36] conjured up visions of a growing threat not only to private property and existing political institutions but also to religion, morality, and the family. In the cities of the Düsseldorf district, as in Berlin, expanding police forces were part of the immediate prehistory of the antisocialist law.

Essen is an example of a city that had been previously slow to comply with the state's wishes for the hiring of more police personnel, but then began in the early 1870s to make significant improvements in the ratio of policemen to population (see table 3). This initiative came in the immediate aftermath of the turbulent summer of 1872, which saw not only Essen's first mass coal strike but also popular disturbances that accompanied the Kulturkampf-inspired expulsion of the city's Jesuits. Essen's mayor cited attacks on policemen and night watchmen by a disgruntled population as a major reason for increasing the size of the force. With more manpower available, he hoped, policemen would be safer and more effective because more of them could be assigned to patrol in pairs rather than singly.[37]

Elsewhere in the Düsseldorf district in the 1870s, additions to urban police forces were less directly prompted by specific local incidents of popular challenge to elite dictates. Indeed, manpower increases in that decade became routinely linked to population growth and to the size of police forces in comparable cities. Proposals for such procedures had often been made in the past but they had been only partially and inconsistently implemented. Now both local and state authorities agreed on a concerted effort to establish consistent guidelines. In Barmen in 1875, for example, the city council approved the hiring of fourteen additional Polizeisergeanten (up 46 percent) as well as six additional night watchmen (up 15 percent). The stated purpose of the increase was to bring the ratio of police to population in Barmen in line with that of Aachen.[38] In 1878 Düsseldorf's administration argued for making future increases in police personnel proportional to those in neighboring cities.[39] By 1882 Elberfeld had made it a rule to add two Polizeisergeanten for every five thousand additional inhabitants.[40] The big advantage for both state and civic leaders of making the size of police forces dependent on population and on comparisons with other cities was to lift the issue from the realm of periodic controversy to something approaching an automatic procedure. The intent was to present policing as an essential and noncontroversial public service, beyond politics. At least as far as the urban elites of the Düsseldorf district are concerned, by the 1870s the concept of the need for sizable and expanding urban police forces had entrenched itself, and earlier disagreements with state authorities about the police and their role in city life had eased.

THE POLICEMAN'S LOT IN THE 1870S

Confronted with increasingly heterogeneous urban societies and the emergence of organized labor, advocates of more effective police forces for Prussian cities emphasized that additional attention needed to be paid to quality as well as quantity of personnel. Urban administrators complained, however, that hiring both more and better policemen was proving difficult.[41] During the early 1870s, unprecedented economic growth meant increased competition from other potential employers. And even when alternative employment opportunities declined later in the decade, appropriate candidates remained hard to find.

The position of Polizeisergeant in a growing industrial city had a number of unattractive features that discouraged applicants. Among these was the presence of hostility and disdain from at least part of the urban population. Policemen attempting to make arrests complained that they were subject to frequent verbal and sometimes physical abuse, a problem that would ease somewhat in the next decade, in part due to the introduction of closed wagons for the transport of prisoners.[42] In Duisburg, for example, reported challenges to representatives of state authority were particularly frequent in the final troubled years of the 1870s. Reports of individuals resisting, slandering, or attacking public officials, including policemen, or attempting to free prisoners, soared from an average 22.6 per year from 1870 to 1874 to 40.4 per year from 1875 to 1879, dropping back to 20.4 per year from 1880 to 1884. The peak number of reports came in 1876 with 60 incidents recorded.[43]

In Krefeld in 1873, ten longtime Polizeisergeanten complained that the dearth of applicants had become so serious that unqualified and poorly motivated individuals were being hired, men with whom they had no wish to be associated.[44] "Unqualified" meant to the older Polizeisergeanten individuals without the normally required twelve years of military service. The Krefeld Polizeisergeanten made their complaint in a petition for salary increases, an issue all interested parties recognized as crucial to the problem of recruitment of suitable personnel. Attention also focused on the issue of salary because of the strong inflationary pressures of the early 1870s. As in the 1850s, police personnel frequently appealed for more money to help them support their families in a manner appropriate for representatives (however modest) of the state.[45]

According to Gerhard Bry, the cost of living in Germany rose from an index figure of 64 in 1870 (1913 = 100) to 80 in 1873.[46] During those same years the price of a ton of Ruhr coal soared from 5.72 to 11.00 marks.[47] Cities in the Düsseldorf district were compelled to provide their police personnel with some financial relief. In Düsseldorf in 1868, for example, Polizeisergeanten earned an average of 300 talers (900 marks) a year. By 1874, they were making an average of 1,125 marks.[48] In Krefeld in 1871, Polizeisergeanten were paid from 270 to 300 talers (810 to 900 marks) for a year's service. By 1876, they earned a minimum of 1,200 marks.[49]

In an effort to retain the men they recruited, cities offered increased premiums for seniority. In Barmen in 1876, Polizeisergeanten earning a minimum of 1,125 marks a year, plus a clothing allowance of 125 marks, received an additional 15 marks for each year of service, to a maximum salary of 1,275 marks.[50] And in Düsseldorf in 1877, Polizeisergeanten—who earned a minimum of 1,200 marks a year—received seniority premiums of 80 marks every four years, to a maximum salary of 1,600 marks.[51]

But even though their nominal wages were rising, policemen in the early 1870s found to their dismay that their pay increases were often outstripped by raises offered to industrial workers. The average annual earnings of a Ruhr miner, for example, rose from 793 marks in 1870 to 1,111 marks in 1873. If policemen could have looked into the immediate future, however, they might have been somewhat comforted. The miners' escalating wages in the early 1870s were followed by sharp drops after 1874, to an average 701 marks in 1879.[52] Police personnel were spared such downward wage adjustments.

That some of the strongest and most skilled miners and other laborers in the district's heavy industry actually made more than they, at least during the period of peak prosperity, caused discontent among rank-and-file policemen. In Essen in 1871, Polizeisergeanten, noting as in the 1850s how difficult it was to keep their uniforms looking presentable, complained that workers made fun of any shabbiness in their appearance. Though many laborers went to work in what the Polizeisergeanten contemptuously described as "near rags," policemen felt a strong need to keep up appearances, irrespective of pressures from their superiors to do so.[53]

An 1877 regulation on the payment of Düsseldorf city employees indicates the relative standing of policemen compared to others in communal service. The regulation divided city employees into seven pay categories, excluding at the very top the mayor (earning 12,000 marks in 1875) and his immediate assistants. The Polizeiinspektor was ranked with the city treasurer and city clerk in the first category, which consisted of those earning at least 3,500 marks a year. Polizeikommissare were assigned to the second rank and earned at least 2,500 marks. Also included in that category were supervisors for the city's waterworks, gasworks, and slaughterhouse. Polizeiwachtmeister, along with market supervisors and various administrative assistants, were in the fourth category and earned a minimum 1,500 marks a year. Polizeisergeanten and building and street inspectors earned a minimum of 1,200 marks and were placed in the fifth category. *Schutzleute,* full-time patrolmen for night duty, were in the seventh and lowest category and earned a minimum of 900 marks a year.[54] By comparison, in 1877 wages in a local piping factory ranged from 780 marks a year for a day laborer to 2,600 marks a year for a welder.[55]

The Schutzleute mentioned above represented a new departure in Düsseldorf, replacing at last the institution of part-time night watchmen. Krefeld took the same step in the mid-1870s, with the district's other major cities soon following.[56] Night watches, despite frequent reorganization in the middle decades of the nineteenth century, had long lacked credibility. The disparity between daytime and nighttime policing reflected at least in part the much greater interest the state took in the former. Night watchmen tended primarily to matters of local interest such as reporting fires, checking doors and windows to make sure they were locked, and keeping the streets quiet. The day force, as already indicated, performed a broad array of services for the state as well as for local administration. Since the state paid little attention to problems of nighttime patrol, impetus for major change in such matters came only when local property-owning citizens, increasingly concerned about the security of their possessions from fire and theft and about guaranteeing a good night's sleep for respectable residents, became supportive of allocating more resources for that purpose.

The newly established full-time night patrolmen proved, however, even more difficult to recruit than were men for the better paying and more respected daytime service. Krefeld's administration reported that men with long years of military service (the kind of recruits who staffed the day forces) could not be induced to apply for the night positions. As a consequence the men hired, although they had been in the army, fell far short of having served twelve years.[57] Once recruited, night patrolmen were regarded by their superiors as being generally less dependable than were those who served by day. In Düsseldorf between 1877 and 1881, for example, twenty-one of thirty-five departures (60 percent) from the new full-time night force were the result of dismissals. For the day force, only six of twenty-eight departures (21 percent) were dismissals (see Appendix, table A-2).

Hiring *Militäranwärter* for the day force, however, provided no guarantee against serious discipline problems. In 1876 the mayor of Essen listed his many grievances against such recruits, grievances leading to frequent dismissals. According to the mayor, those men who entered civilian service after many years in the military looked upon their new posts as rewards for their past efforts, not as the beginning of demanding new careers. The mayor complained that many of the former noncommissioned officers turned policemen became self-indulgent and inclined to drunkenness. Worse yet, he believed, their long military experience predisposed them to treat civilians in a brusque, even brutal manner. The mayor, like many other local administrators, worried about the consequences of an excessively militarized police. Although himself harboring a low opinion of industrial workers, he did not wish to see them further alienated from established authority as a result of needlessly harsh police behavior.[58] He realized that policemen, given their frequent face-to-face encounters with the public in often emotionally charged situations, had a special capacity for embarrassing their superiors by acting in a crude and capricious fashion.

Developments in Duisburg in 1868 provide an example of the kind of disruptive and demoralizing scandal that resulted when police behavior became the center of controversy. The Duisburg police were accused of routine physical abuse of their prisoners. Police critics called public meetings to discuss the issue. Although the meetings were disbanded by local authorities and Duisburg's police chief, Adolf Zöller, kept his job, officials could not prevent newspapers in south Germany and other parts of Europe from publicizing events in Duisburg. Critics interpreted these developments as additional evidence of the harsh, militarized character of the Hohenzollern monarchy. The charges, easy for many to believe because of Prussia's reputation in such matters, hardly represented the kind of publicity Prussian leaders desired on the eve of national unification.[59]

State officials, although aware of problems involved in turning noncommissioned officers into dispassionate and approachable public servants, continued to regard the hiring of anyone with less than twelve years of military service as permissible only as a last resort. The interests of the armed forces had to be safeguarded.[60] To induce adequate numbers of reliable noncommissioned officers to apply for communal police service and to stay on the job once recruited, urban administrations in the 1870s had recourse to a number of expedients. In adding benefits, they took the state administrative bureaucracy as their model. In particular, they sought to make police service more attractive by offering greater security to those men willing to commit their remaining working lives to municipal employment.

The offer of greater security came in two forms. One was to grant permanent appointments to Polizeisergeanten after satisfactory completion of two years of service. Elberfeld and Barmen both took this step in 1875. During the first six months of employment, recruits in those two cities could be dismissed at any time. During the next year and a half, they could be dismissed with three months' notice. Thereafter, their positions were secure. Formerly, such lifelong appointments had been reserved for the Polizeiinspektoren and Polizeikommissare.[61]

Cities offered further security by guaranteeing pensions. Previously discretionary, pensions were a matter of particular concern to police recruits because of their age. The requirement of twelve years of military service meant that communal policemen typically did not begin their civilian careers until they were in their late twenties or early thirties. For twenty-one Polizeisergeanten employed by Essen in 1873, for example, average age upon joining the force was 30.2 years.[62] In making their case for guaranteed pensions, Krefeld's policemen in 1875 pointed not only to age but also to their modest salaries. They acknowledged that recent improvements in their pay had lessened their daily worries but argued that they were still unable to provide adequately for future disability.[63]

The district's cities, in guaranteeing pensions for their policemen, decided to follow both state precedent and the wishes of their employees by agreeing to count years of military as well as civilian service toward retirement.[64] Retirement, however, continued to be dependent upon disability rather than age. And until the end of the century, policemen were more likely to die in service than to receive a pension. In Düsseldorf from 1877 to 1896, for instance, police deaths outnumbered retirements 38 to 15 (see table A–2).

But if, by the mid-1870s, cities were prepared to offer their policemen more financial security, they found themselves unable to make significant improvement with regard to the continuing sore point of excessive hours. No matter what elaborate schemes of personnel rotation were developed, the problem remained one of inadequate manpower to meet the workload of rapidly expanding cities and rising expectations regarding the proper level of urban decorum. In Essen, for example, Polizeisergeanten faced, in addition to their daytime responsibilities, patrol duty every other evening lasting until close to one o'clock in the morning. Sundays and holidays meant not free time but rather extra assignments for all available men. During strikes and other potentially turbulent situations, round-the-clock service might be required.[65] The continuing requirement that policemen live in the neighborhoods they patrolled was dictated not only by the wish that they be familiar with local conditions and readily accessible at all times but also by the simple lack of time for long walks to and from work.[66] Even more than most of Prussia's public servants, policemen were expected to devote their whole lives to their jobs, jobs that national and local elites had come by the 1870s to see as significantly more important than in the past.

CHAPTER FOUR

Policing Urban Life, 1850–1878

PATROLLING CITY STREETS

In the years leading up to the antisocialist law, as urban elites in the Düsseldorf district began to support the allocation of increased local resources to policing, many unanswered questions remained as to what exactly expanded police forces could and should do. If the use of communal police personnel in any but the most meager numbers was still a very recent development, so too were many of the social relationships the police were expected to monitor. As industrial capitalism, in the wake of two unprecedented entrepreneurial surges in the 1850s and 1870s, consolidated its dominance in the district's growing cities, the earlier society of ranks and orders was quickly fading into memory. With it went many previously utilized informal, personalized, and corporate means of regulating relations among urban residents. Thus, the role of the police as an expression of the power and authority of the state in everyday life loomed ever larger. And expectations of what policemen should be able to accomplish rose.

The district's liberals, despite their earlier suspicion of the police as repressive and intrusive, became increasingly appreciative of the promise of such forces for helping guarantee a more uniform, predictable, and tranquil urban order. Especially attractive in a society becoming less deferential and more heterogeneous was the prospect that the police would shift much of the onus of the day-to-day safeguarding of established relationships from individuals, particularly employers, to an ostensibly impersonal and impartial state-sanctioned agency. Conspicuously distributed throughout the community, however unevenly, policemen represented a welcome recourse for those who felt threatened, challenged, or offended by others. By the end of the 1870s, the National

Liberal *Düsseldorfer Zeitung*, in an article entitled "A Burning Local Question," assured its readers that if any luxury in municipal spending was justifiable it was expenditure for policemen. In fact, the paper asserted, trying to save on the police was actually a great evil. A dozen well-trained policemen, its editorialist concluded, could do more for public morals than a hundred preachers.[1]

As already indicated in chapter 3, those who appropriated local money for urban police forces and those who oversaw such forces in the name of the state were not always of one mind as to the uses to be made of police personnel. One emerging point of agreement, however, was the central importance of the systematic patrol of public spaces. A common criticism by upholders of the status quo of Prussian policemen in the midnineteenth century was that they were too sedentary, too inclined to prefer service behind a desk to the rigors of the street. Desk duty was attractive to communal policemen not only because it was less physically taxing than patrolling but also because it made their work seem more like prestigious employment in the administrative bureaucracy.

Property-owning taxpayers complained that policemen were often nowhere to be found when needed.[2] Local supporters of strengthened urban forces wanted policemen who were readily available when called and who between calls for assistance circulated as highly visible and reassuring symbols of state-approved order. Emphasis on the policing of public spaces would also, bourgeois citizens assumed, help reduce unwanted police intervention in their private affairs.

While making their rounds, policemen were under orders from their superiors not only to take action against the perpetrators of crimes and misdemeanors but also to keep a watchful eye on particular categories of individuals deemed inherently subversive of well-regulated city life.[3] Who such individuals were depended on time and place. Where industry had not yet made major inroads, vagabonds and beggars—anyone without a fixed residence and a readily identifiable source of income— remained the foremost focus of concern. Such persons were viewed by property owners both as probable thieves and as corrupting examples of undisciplined life without labor. In the early 1850s Düsseldorf's Polizeiinspektor Falderen identified the indigent as a central problem. He reminded city leaders that "necessity knows no law," adding that poor relief had to be as much a part of the answer as rigorous police patrol.[4] At the same time, Krefeld's Polizeiinspektor Walther, in a more industrial context, was drawing attention to young, male wage earners as a growing threat to urban order. The problem, he believed, was more and more one of too much rather than too little income for the city's propertyless residents. Wages above the subsistence level, he warned, encouraged rough and unruly youths to squander the surplus on drink and riotous living, transforming themselves from an asset to the local economy into a nuisance or worse for Krefeld's more respectable residents.[5]

In responding to complaints from their superiors and from influential citizens about the unwelcome presence of vagrants, beggars, and other elements of the itinerant poor, the police had the choice of either arresting such individuals or of unceremoniously hastening their departure from town. The second option often seemed the simplest and most expeditious. Non-Prussians, in particular, were readily dismissed.[6] The Duisburg police in 1864, concerned about the presence of a band of Dutch broom makers, simply raided their encampment and transported the sixty-two individuals over the frontier.[7] Such transports also took place between Prussian towns but could lead to resistance on the receiving end. Elberfeld's Polizeiinspektor reported in 1873 that a troop of gypsies had arrived accompanied by two Barmen Polizeisergeanten. The gypsies were immediately returned to Barmen in the company of Elberfeld policemen.[8]

Clearing the streets of vagrants remained one of the chief responsibilities of night watches. Homelessness often exceeded disorderly conduct as the chief justification given for nighttime arrests, accounting in Duisburg in 1876, for example, for 203 of 292 such actions.[9] Frequent inspections of boardinghouses also resulted in numerous arrests of those who had no credible means of support. In 1883–84 the Düsseldorf police reported making 1,318 inspections of six boardinghouses and arresting 364 presumed beggars.[10] Among individuals arrested for vagrancy and begging, those deemed most incorrigible were consigned, along with recalcitrant prostitutes, to the provincial workhouse in Brauweiler. The great majority, however, were released after being held briefly by the police with the injunction to find employment and lodging or to leave town.

The late 1870s, a time of increased unemployment following a period of unprecedented economic growth, were characterized by especially keen police attention to the activities of the homeless poor.[11] In Düsseldorf, combined arrests for vagrancy and begging rose dramatically from 462 in 1877–78 to a peak of 1,700 in 1880–81, before dropping back to the earlier level by the mid-1880s.[12] In Krefeld the peak year for such arrests was 1879–80.[13] This pronounced crackdown on vagrancy reflected heightened official concern with public order during the uneasy years at the close of the decade.

If much of the emphasis in dealing with vagrants and beggars remained, as in the past, on getting them to move on, a different approach was called for in response to the perceived problem of regulating the behavior of growing numbers of youthful workers. No matter how much disruption they were believed to cause, wage earners represented an important economic resource whose removal would constitute a loss to the community. Part of the answer, in the view of local authorities and property owners, was more rigorous police supervision of daily life, which would lead to the creation and maintenance of a more orderly urban environment. Such an environment was expected to foster more orderly living by all urban residents, especially young laborers.

Expanding police forces and growing official concern with the day-to-day disciplining of city life in the 1860s and 1870s were reflected in an upsurge of penalties imposed for minor contraventions (*Übertretungen*). Many of the ordinances violated had been formulated by the police themselves, subject to revision by administrative authorities and the courts. The Prussian police law of 11 March 1850 empowered the local police to be rule makers as well as rule enforcers. According to the 1850 law, local police ordinances could be promulgated to protect persons and property, to regulate traffic, markets, construction projects, public assemblies, innkeeping, and the sale of alcohol, to foster health and safety, and to order "everything else of particular interest to the community and its inhabitants."[14] The abundance of ordinances on the books in Prussian municipalities gave the police myriad excuses for detaining virtually any individual who aroused their suspicion or displeasure in any way.

Penalties imposed for contraventions consisted of either small fines or, less commonly, of brief jail sentences. For those of modest means who could not or would not pay, jail sentences were substituted for fines. In Düsseldorf, for instance, with a population of 80,695 in 1875, substitutions of jail time for the fines originally specified took place in 2,322 cases in that year. Spending time in jail (even if only briefly) for a minor violation was, as a consequence, a common experience for the poorest urban residents.[15]

As Ralph Jessen has noted in his study of policing in the Westphalian portion of the Ruhr industrial region, the incidence of penalties imposed for different kinds of petty violations varied greatly among the different elements of the urban population.[16] Young, single, male workers were, for example, particularly liable to be judged guilty of disorderly conduct or of having failed to comply with registration of residence requirements. Working-class parents were those most commonly accused of failure to abide by regulations relating to school attendance and vaccination. And carters and other transport workers received a disproportionate share of citations for traffic violations, the regulation of traffic representing an area of growing concern in industrializing cities whose narrow streets had never been intended to accommodate the vastly increased number of vehicles they now carried.[17] In addition, penalties were frequently imposed upon tavern keepers (especially for violations of curfews and for disturbing neighbors), peddlers and street musicians (for being nuisances and for intruding on the prerogatives of resident merchants), small tradesmen (for misuse of weights and measures and for violations of Sunday trading ordinances), and building contractors (for failure to keep streets and sidewalks clear of debris and for failure to procure required permits from the police).

For the frequency of penalties for Übertretungen, Duisburg is the best documented of the cities of the Düsseldorf district (see Appendix, table A–3). In that emerging center of Ruhr shipping and heavy industry, the enforcement of local ordinances underwent a dramatic intensification from 1866 to 1867. The number of penalties imposed (not counting those for truancy) jumped from 318.9 to 648.2 per 10,000 population in a single year. Around the same time, penalties for truancy also soared, apparently as the result of a decision to prosecute parents of persistent truants weekly instead of monthly as in the past.[18]

Not coincidentally, 1867 marked the advent of a new police chief in Duisburg. Certainly the significant change in practice inaugurated by Polizeiinspektor Zöller must have been a major cause of the contentious public meetings on the police question (already mentioned in chapter 3) that took place in that city in 1868. In spite of the meetings, penalties for minor violations were imposed at an augmented rate into the next decade, especially during the depression years of the late 1870s.

As the enforcement rate for violations of all kinds in Duisburg peaked in the late 1870s, so too did arrests for disorderly conduct. Among common offenses, disorderly conduct attracted particular attention and was viewed as a barometer of urban disruption. Actually, disorderly conduct was a very poor indicator of changes in popular behavior because of the great latitude the police had in defining the offense.

In terms of sheer numbers processed by the authorities, no offense came close to truancy, it too being prosecuted with particular rigor in the mid- and late 1870s. In most years, penalties for truancy outnumbered those for all other violations combined. And the number of individuals penalized for the failure of their children to attend school was in turn only a fraction of the much larger number who were called in and questioned before being either excused or dismissed with a warning. In Düsseldorf in 1879–80, for example, 3,287 parents were penalized for their children's truancy. But the total number questioned was 13,496, in a city with a population then numbering approximately 91,000. That same year, policemen escorted 1,085 Düsseldorf children to school.[19]

The involvement of the police in the enforcement of school attendance, in a way that directly impinged upon the lives of a large segment of the urban population—especially the working-class portion—reflects the great importance upholders of the established order attached to schooling as a means of creating a more disciplined populace. Local authorities and urban elites were far from placing all their hopes for an orderly future on a more numerous and vigorous police. A self-disciplined population, fostered by institutions of indoctrination like the schools, was recognized as preferable to one held in check solely by the threat of force. Yet, to achieve the goal of a schooled and presumably more disciplined working class, large-scale police intervention was deemed a necessary transitional stage.

Compared to penalties for minor violations, reports of felonies and misdemeanors were much less frequent. In Duisburg in 1872, for instance, penalties handed down for minor offenses numbered 2,507, plus 3,031 penalties for truancy, compared with 599 crimes and misdemeanors reported and 442 alleged perpetrators apprehended.[20] But if crimes and misdemeanors were much less common than the relatively petty incidents that occupied most policemen, they were of great importance as potent symbols of the feared potential breakdown of order in rapidly growing industrial cities.

Official perception of the incidence and seriousness of crime was shaped in large measure by police, as well as court, reporting. Indeed, a crucial function of an expanded police was to collect information on the urban condition that would help to shape official policy and public attitudes. And what the district's urban police reported was generally rising rates for both property and violent crime into the late 1870s. Thereafter, rates for crimes against property leveled off, while crimes against persons continued to climb.[21] In Duisburg, for example, reported property crime peaked dramatically toward the end of the 1870s, with rates not to be seen again for the rest of the century. But the city's violent crime rate for the late 1870s, while significantly higher than in the past, was still much lower than it would be during most of the next two decades (see Appendix, table A–4).

For the state, the growth of urban crime in the second half of the nineteenth century provided a convenient rationale for extending the influence of the central government in local affairs. In addressing the bourgeois public, officials could use concerns about mounting criminal activity as an effective argument for accepting the increased cost and intrusiveness of more policing. To this end, the Düsseldorf district administration recommended to all Landräte that they see to the broadest possible dissemination of a brochure reproducing a lecture given in 1878 before the Rhenish-Westphalian Prison Society by Prison Chaplain H. Stursberg of Düsseldorf.[22]

Stursberg began his discussion by pointing to an almost 50 percent rise in the number of individuals imprisoned in Prussia from 1871 to 1876. Interpreting this increase as indicative of a massive surge in criminal activity, while ignoring the part played by changes in enforcement and adjudication, Stursberg listed as causes several recent developments he regarded as socially disruptive. The chaplain ascribed particular significance to the prosperity of the early 1870s, leading to growing materialism and rising expectations. The consequence for workers, he believed, was a demoralizing pursuit of pleasure, further encouraged by a marked increase in the number of taverns and "low" entertainments. Stursberg also bemoaned increasing geographic mobility and the practice of young workers living as lodgers in working-class households rather than in the households of their masters. Finally, he believed that declining clerical influence over the workers was undermining public morality.[23]

The executive committee of the well-known and long-established organization Stursberg represented consisted of government officials, clergymen, and businessmen—individuals drawn from those segments of urban society who felt most threatened or affronted by criminal behavior and were most interested in law enforcement. Such men were not, however, the only ones to turn to the police for help. A list of the victims of theft in Düsseldorf between 15 February and 31 August 1860, for example, indicates that although business and professional men were greatly overrepresented, significant numbers of craftsmen and laborers had also reported losses to the police. Among the victims were fifty-two business and professional men, thirty-two craftsmen and skilled workers, and twenty-seven unskilled workers (almost half of them domestic servants), plus "several" soldiers, four farmers, three religious institutions, the city of Düsseldorf, and the Prussian state itself as local landlord.[24]

Although reports of property crimes outnumbered those relating to violent acts, the latter, as judged from official correspondence, occasioned more concern than did the former.[25] Assaults, especially those involving weapons (occasionally firearms but more often knives or work tools that anyone might legitimately carry), were interpreted as symptomatic of the increasingly "brutal" character of a significant segment of the urban proletariat. In this context, tavern brawls were perceived not as relatively harmless releases of interpersonal tension and high spirits, of little interest to any but the immediate participants, but as serious threats to efforts to create a social order respectful of established authority and geared to the needs of commercial and industrial development.

Officials and concerned citizens typically agreed that working-class "excesses" were the product of the erosion of traditional restraints on behavior, the ready availability of alcohol, and the nefarious influence of oppositional ideologies. In an 1877 report, the Düsseldorf Regierungspräsident, citing factory inspectors as witnesses, painted a lurid picture of bands of "drunken socialists" armed with revolvers and knives, who were invading factories in Barmen and enticing honest workers away from their labor. Such individuals, he feared, were capable of doing great harm to both the economic and the political order.[26] What he judged to be dangerous propensities for violent and irresponsible working-class carousing on the one hand and for political protest on the other were seen as merging.

Those who harbored fears for the future of urban order could take some comfort from reports that showed police in the 1860s and 1870s were usually able to secure arrests in a majority of reported cases of property crime and in almost all cases involving crimes against persons, since victims in these latter incidents usually knew their assailants. In Duisburg, for example, between 1864 and 1879, the number of arrests for property crimes equaled 69.5 percent of incidents reported. For the same years, the number of arrests for violent crimes in Duisburg equaled 86.9 percent of reported cases (see Appendix, table A–4). Instances of police failing to live up to these norms resulted in official inquiries, demand for remedial action, and follow-up reports until the situation was corrected.[27]

In the 1870s, those concerned about heightening the effectiveness of the police in what seemed more dangerous times considered whether patrolmen needed the protection of firearms, in addition to the bayonets and truncheons they typically carried. By the end of the decade the official consensus was that police personnel should not carry revolvers on routine patrol, but that guns could be issued when there was a special reason for doing so. Such special reasons included preparation to arrest a particularly dangerous criminal, or assignment to patrol an isolated and threatening area, such as nighttime harbor patrol.[28]

REGULATING POPULAR AMUSEMENTS

In the various laments about the condition of Germany's emergent urban proletariat, a recurrent theme (already encountered in Chaplain

Stursberg's commentary) was the allegedly corrupting and destabilizing influence of alcohol and of the entertainments associated with its consumption. As it happened, the formation of an industrial working class overlapped chronologically with economic changes fostering the widespread availability of cheap distilled spirits. How much alcohol laborers actually consumed was, however, less important than how much their social superiors believed they consumed and what they feared would be the consequences of worker intoxication. Although teetotalism and prohibitionism failed to make much headway in central Europe, would-be reformers of working-class life looked to regulation of proletarian drinking as crucial to guaranteeing urban order.[29]

Official concern during the reactionary 1850s with taverns as breeding places for both political discussion and demoralizing behavior had found expression in stepped-up police surveillance and extensive use of licensing powers to enforce conformity with the wishes of the state. Where workers were present in substantial numbers, establishments catering to their needs were singled out for particularly close attention. Such was the case in Elberfeld. In that city, however, rigorous police efforts to limit the number of purveyors of drink encountered resistance from individuals reportedly prepared to accept payment of fines as part of the cost of doing business. In response Elberfeld's royal police director, Hermann Hirsch, ordered patrolmen to raid suspected premises three or four times a day. Not only the proprietor but patrons as well were cited and compelled to report to police headquarters. Hirsch reasoned that the most effective way of eliminating unauthorized establishments was by frightening away their customers.[30] In a further effort to curtail drinking, this time by limiting temptation, Hirsch ordered taverns to keep their doors closed and their wares out of sight of passersby.[31]

Although anxious to curb excessive and unregulated drinking, Hirsch believed that workers did have a legitimate claim to wholesome recreation in their limited hours of leisure. In 1856 Hirsch, the state-appointed outsider, defended a popular beer hall against accusations of impropriety, which he believed originated from the Wuppertal's "fanatical" Protestant establishment. Better, he claimed, for workers to have a place where they could sit and drink beer and listen to music than for them to resort to consuming distilled spirits in disreputable dives.[32]

Among approaches to controlling proletarian drinking was prohibition of the sale of spirits to individuals designated by the police as drunkards. Prohibited sales led to fines of from one to three talers for each violation, with three contraventions resulting in a revoked liquor license. One such list distributed by the Düsseldorf police on 6 October 1854 had sixty-four entries. Of these, occupations were given for fifty-three, thirty-two being listed as day laborers and other unskilled workers and twenty identified as craftsmen or skilled workers. The list also included one shopkeeper.[33] A list distributed by the Essen police in February 1861 named forty-eight workers and one mining foreman (*Steiger*).[34] Bourgeois alcoholics, compared with their working-class counterparts, were less likely to drink in public and were as a consequence usually spared the indignity of being officially identified by the police as problem drinkers.

Another way to regulate drinking was through strict enforcement of closing hours. One difficulty with closing-hour ordinances, however, was that they cut short bourgeois as well as working-class night life.[35] The city administration in Essen attempted to get around this difficulty by instructing the police that the curfew should be enforced for taverns serving beer and spirits but not for establishments that served only wine. Since wine was more expensive than other commonly available alcoholic beverages, workers did not frequent the places where it was served. In 1871, however, the Düsseldorf district administration informed the city that this kind of discrimination was impermissible; it undermined the credibility of claims of impartial law enforcement. The mayor of Essen characterized this decision as a "slap in the face" for the city's "educated and well-to-do public," that is, that segment of the population whose collaboration he deemed crucial in controlling a "restless" proletariat.[36] The state, however, increasingly challenged in the 1870s by the emergence of organized labor, had to worry about maintaining its legitimacy in the eyes of as many citizens as possible, even workers.

Police use of licensing powers as a major instrument for the control of drinking establishments was significantly curtailed by the liberalized trade legislation passed by the North German Reichstag in 1869. In particular, elimination of the requirement of periodic license renewal lessened the potential for police intervention. Within a decade, however, the government, pointing to the growing number of taverns and taking advantage of the more conservative tenor of the times and the changed composition of the Reichstag, was able to secure a revision of the 1869 commercial code in favor of a return to stricter controls.[37]

Much as defenders of the existing social and political order fretted about proletarian drinking, they were even more concerned about entertainments that could serve to disseminate immoral or subversive ideas among workers. They were especially suspicious of innovations in leisure activities. New enticements that seemed in any way to invite further departures from an idealized frugal, hard-working, family-oriented life-style always seemed more threatening to upholders of the status quo than did those disapproved activities that had been long practiced. Defenders of respectability therefore reacted strongly when tavern keepers attempted to expand their business by offering what was called *Tingel-Tangel*, a form of variety theater combining songs, skits, and recitations. Tingel-Tangel was not against the law and so could not be prohibited outright. Nevertheless, in 1878 and 1879—a time of general tightening of enforcement in many areas of urban life—the authorities called upon the police to launch a major campaign designed to discourage the practice.[38] In subsequent years complaints from influential citizens prompted periodic government demands for renewed police crackdowns.[39]

Among police powers used against Tingel-Tangel was the setting of an eleven o'clock closing time, to be strictly enforced. In Krefeld, for example, the number of prosecutions for curfew violations rose from 157 in 1877–78 to 530 in 1878–79.[40] At the same time, a substantial tax was levied on Tingel-Tangel performances. In Düsseldorf, as a result, amusement tax revenue soared from 9,558 marks in 1877–78 to 22,798 marks in 1878–79.[41] In addition, the lyrics of all songs and the text of all skits had to be submitted for police approval to make certain they did not offend against religion, morality, state institutions, or public order and decency. Also, all female performers had to be validated as being of good reputation. The police were ordered to make certain the women did not appear in indecent costumes or mingle with the public.[42] And as noted by the mayor of Elberfeld, the presence of increased numbers of policemen at Tingel-Tangel performances served to discourage patronage.[43]

The suspicion evident in police relations with women performers in Tingel-Tangel extended to all female personnel associated with public entertainments and establishments selling alcohol. The authorities desired to prevent such employment from serving as a front for prostitution, especially where it could spread into previously unaffected urban districts.[44] The police preferred to keep prostitution as inconspicuous as possible by confining it to the back streets of older, less desirable neighborhoods.[45] In spite of fluctuations in official policy, the police proved generally resistant to moving much beyond containment toward efforts to achieve actual reduction in incidence.[46]

In 1880, for example, Duisburg's Polizeiinspektor Frankfurth admitted that a prostitute in his city would normally be little troubled by the police as long as she did not create a public scandal. Frankfurth attributed this low-key approach not only to lack of police manpower necessary to undertake a rigorous crusade of eradication but also to the desire to avoid drawing attention to the presence and activities of prostitutes.[47] Such a live-and-let-live attitude would, however, periodically run afoul of orders for stricter enforcement from higher authorities, themselves reacting to public complaints or responding to their own fears of the spread of disease, especially among present and future soldiers.[48]

INTERVENING IN LABOR DISPUTES

Beyond the surveillance and disciplining of individual behavior, urban police forces were, of course, expected to hold themselves ready at all times to counter collective actions deemed threatening by the supporters of the established order. In the industrializing cities of the Düsseldorf district in the third quarter of the nineteenth century, increasing concern focused on confrontations of employers and employees. The police, although not wishing to be cast as partisans of either side to such disputes, found their efforts to appear impartial severely hampered by their legal obligation to protect private property and strikebreakers and to suppress initiatives that could in any way be construed as subversive challenges to existing social, political, and economic relationships.[49]

During the reactionary 1850s, worker associations of any kind were regarded by the state with great suspicion and only those judged to serve completely innocuous self-help, convivial, or religious purposes were tolerated. Official vigilance against the mobilization of collective action by wage earners could not, however, totally prevent illegal strikes from occurring in the emerging industrial centers of the Düsseldorf district. A noteworthy example of how the Prussian government and its uniformed forces responded to such provocations is provided by the strikes of journeymen dyers in Barmen and Elberfeld in 1855 and 1857.

Involving close to one thousand workers in each instance, the two Wuppertal strikes were among the largest German work stoppages of the decade.[50] The 1855 strike aroused enough official concern that Berlin Police President Carl Ludwig von Hinckeldey decided to send one of his officers to investigate. The resulting report proved sympathetic to the plight of the workers and ascribed much of the blame for social unrest in Elberfeld and Barmen to employer greed.[51]

Primary responsibility for implementing all aspects of official response to the Wuppertal strikes devolved upon the local police director and his men.[52] Failing in his initial efforts to persuade the dyers to return to work, Police Director Hirsch used both paid informants and employer-provided lists to identify strike organizers. Known leaders were arrested; non-Prussian strikers were threatened with deportation. Taverns were closed and worker assemblies and street crowds disbanded. In the aftermath of the strike, those dyers who were refused reemployment turned to the police director to intercede for them with their former employers. But efforts to win their reinstatement proved fruitless, with the police director sharing the employers' belief that strikers should be taught a lesson.[53]

When confronted with the 1855 strike, Hirsch doubted the ability of his handful of policemen to maintain order and immediately requested the dispatch of a military force of one hundred men. He argued that the mere presence of even a small army detachment would chasten the strikers in a way that the less prestigious police could not.[54] His superiors, however, refused to comply with his request, arguing that the authority of the police would be greatly strengthened if they could handle the situation without the help of the army. Therefore, while sending in extra police and gendarmes to bring the local force to over thirty men for the duration of the strike, the Regierungspräsident held the military in reserve, pointing out that in case of need troops could be brought into the Wuppertal by railroad in less than an hour and a half.[55] The army continued to represent the ultimate defense of the monarchy, but if the police fulfilled their designated role, provocative military intervention could be avoided.[56]

In the late 1850s and early 1860s, a lessening of political repression in Prussia permitted a revival of more open organizational activity, including efforts directed toward workers. Noteworthy was the formation of Ferdinand Lassalle's General German Workers' Association in 1863. Early centers of that organization and subsequently of the Social Democratic party included the predominantly Protestant industrial cities of the Wuppertal and of the surrounding Bergisches Land. In the largely Catholic cities of the rest of the Düsseldorf district, however, the influence of the church would long preclude significant social democratic inroads.[57] But in such settings the state often found itself confronted with the rise of political Catholicism and Christian-Social initiatives. Where worker organization—whether socialist or Catholic—developed, authorities regarded such activity as a sufficient argument for heightened vigilance and for increasing allocation of resources to urban policing.[58]

In addition to increased political mobilization, the years from the late 1860s to the mid-1870s witnessed a dramatic surge in strike action as well as early experiments with unionization in the newly forming German Empire. Unleashing these initiatives were the legalization of worker combinations by the North German Reichstag in 1869 as well as the booming economy that accompanied unification.[59] In the Düsseldorf district, official concern centered first and foremost on strike activity among Ruhr miners, especially in and around Essen. Not only were the late 1860s and early 1870s a period of unprecedented growth for Ruhr heavy industry but at that time miners and their employers also had to adapt themselves to the end of state direction of mining and the establishment of direct entrepreneurial control of labor relations.

Early efforts to mobilize Essen miners led in 1868 and 1869 to confrontations between stone-throwing crowds and bayonet-wielding policemen and gendarmes. In this context, the police used the 1850 Prussian law of association to its fullest to disband worker assemblies. Placards posted or handbills distributed by strikers without police permission were subject to seizure. Any irregularity in the conduct of a meeting or any statement deemed improper or inflammatory by the police officer in attendance provided an excuse for halting proceedings, although at times such police pronouncements proved difficult to implement for officers who found themselves surrounded by a large gathering of determined miners. Following worker assemblies, the police often made use of their powers to license and inspect taverns to take action against the owners of premises where such meetings had been held. Any noncompliance with the building codes could provide a convenient excuse for prohibiting future use of a room for assemblies.[60]

Largest by far of the work stoppages of the turbulent early 1870s was the Ruhr miners' strike of 1872. Focused primarily on pits in and around Essen, the strike at its peak saw approximately 21,000 men lay down their tools. The mine operators, determined to make no concessions, demanded and received from the authorities extra police protection for strikebreakers and vulnerable mine property. Paydays that fell during the strike aroused particular concern. Strike organizers, in the interests of winning over public opinion and to avoid providing excuses for armed suppression, did their best to maintain order, but their attempts were little appreciated by either employers or state officials. Spokesmen for the coal industry, anxious for a show of strength beyond the capacity of the police, called for troops to be sent into the Ruhr. Government officials were, however, divided on this question. Düsseldorf Regierungs-präsident von Ende prevailed in resisting the dispatch of army units but did send in fifty-five gendarmes to supplement local police.[61]

After the failure of the 1872 miners' strike and with the coming of the socially tense depression years of the middle and end of the decade, employers and government authorities throughout the district collaborated closely in their efforts to counter the growth of organized labor. Rising rates of unemployment strengthened the hand of employers, giving them the opportunity to cull their work forces of individuals suspected of association with disapproved groups. Industrialists received police help in identifying such employees. Organized workers had legitimate grounds for fearing that membership and subscription lists that came into the possession of the police would be passed on to bosses.

Düsseldorf Regierungspräsident von Hagemeister, reporting to the minister of the interior in the troubled summer of 1878, apparently saw nothing wrong with such partisan police initiatives. Indeed, his chief concern was that with the return of prosperity, some of the weaker industrialists would be tempted to take any workers they could find, regardless of known political or trade union associations. As a consequence, Hagemeister regarded a strengthening of the legal arsenal against socialism as essential.[62] That many influential Germans agreed with the chief administrator of the Düsseldorf district would be confirmed by the passage of the antisocialist law in 1878. Earlier in the decade, exceptional legislation directed against Catholics had already shown the way.

The Empire and Its Internal Enemies, 1871–1890

POLICE AND THE CATHOLIC CHURCH

In the history of German policing, the achievement of national unification in 1871 did not in itself mark important new departures. Law enforcement remained the responsibility of the individual states. Other major political initiatives of the 1870s, however, most notably the Kulturkampf and the antisocialist law, were of much greater significance for police forces. New laws discriminating against Catholics and workers brought additional onerous responsibilities for the police. Efforts to implement regulations whose legitimacy was emphatically denied by significant portions of the population increased tensions between police and public and even, in some instances, within police departments themselves.

Since Catholics comprised approximately three-fifths of the inhabitants of the Düsseldorf Regierungsbezirk, the Kulturkampf necessarily had a major impact on the district. Class differences reinforced religious divisions in cities such as Krefeld, Düsseldorf, and Essen where an influential minority of Protestant entrepreneurs and government officials confronted predominantly Catholic populations.[1] For the district's Catholics, the unsettling experience of Protestant Prussia's war against Catholic Austria in 1866 was followed by the opening of new opportunities for popular political participation through the creation of a democratically elected Reichstag.

Urban liberals perceived the prospect of clerically led political mobilization of Catholic artisans, shopkeepers, workers, and peasants as a serious challenge. In the 1860s, even in strongly Catholic cities, liberal notables had dominated local politics through the plutocratic three-class system of voting used for both municipal and Landtag elections. But in Reichstag elections in the 1870s, those same notables were shocked when liberal candidates were defeated by Catholic outsiders.[2] As the prospect of an era of mass politics dawned, with the Catholic church as an early practitioner, liberal business and professional men joined with Bismarck's government in the campaign to reduce clerical influence.

The Catholic faithful were not prepared to accept the government's hostile initiatives passively. One noteworthy confrontation, already alluded to in chapter 3, took place in Essen in August 1872. In that city, recently shaken by the mass miners' strike of June and July, the Landrat's pronouncement of the explusion of the local Jesuits led to angry crowd scenes and attacks on the persons and property of those associated with the implementation of anticlerical legislation. Those policemen ordered to contain public expressions of popular dissatisfaction were met with insults and stone throwing. The authorities, perceiving that bayonet-wielding policemen were inadequate to the task, called in extra gendarmes and the military to preside over the departure of Essen's Jesuits.[3]

Within the context of the Kulturkampf, Catholic organizations of all kinds—whether ostensibly political or not—were subjected to close police surveillance. According to Klaus Tenfelde, of 609 known Catholic associations in the Düsseldorf district, 59 were closed. Special attention focused on the Association of German Catholics (*Verein deutscher Katholiken*), a mass organization formed in 1872 with a membership reaching close to 200,000 by the middle of the decade. Although the Verein deutscher Katholiken was commonly referred to as the Mainz Association because it had its headquarters in that Hessian city, over 90 percent of its membership resided in the Prussian provinces of Rhineland and Westphalia. The choice of a non-Prussian city as headquarters had been determined by the desire to circumvent the restrictions of Prussia's 1850 association law. Despite such precautions, however, by 1876 the organization had succumbed to the combined pressures of the Prussian police and courts.[4]

During the Kulturkampf the police in the Düsseldorf district not only had to keep watch over the meetings of Catholic associations (in the process enduring snubs from the participants, who knew how to make policemen feel unwelcome)[5] but also were expected to monitor religious observances to make certain they did not serve political purposes. Police officers and other officially designated observers were sent to monitor sermons and to report clerical comments that might be construed as subversive or inflammatory. In 1875, for example, a Düsseldorf chaplain was sentenced to a month's confinement (*Festungshaft*) because, according to the city's

Polizeiinspektor, he had preached a sermon focusing on the theme of persecution of the church through the ages.[6]

Purely religious celebrations could not be prohibited, but anything interpreted as a secular innovation with possible political significance was subject to police intervention.[7] Processions and festivals sponsored by the church were closely scrutinized. Particular attention focused on Pius Day observances. The choice of the Catholic population to celebrate the 16 June anniversary of the election of Pius IX as pope and to ignore the 2 September observance of the nationalist Sedan Day, commemorating victory over Catholic France, reflected the bitter divisions within the new German Empire.[8] Such divisions would find further expression in the development of alternative worker festivals, especially May Day. The failure of Sedan Day or some other national holiday to become a unifying observance says much about the nature of Imperial Germany. Nowhere was this more apparent than in the Rhine province.

The discriminatory measures of the Kulturkampf were not only an affront to Catholic communities but also a cruel test for Catholic civil servants, including Catholic policemen, some of whom lost their jobs for failing to follow orders. Reports of patrolmen who continued their memberships in Catholic associations, who passed warnings of impending police actions to the clergy, or who distributed Catholic publications while making their rounds infuriated royal officials and raised questions about the reliability of local enforcement.[9]

Available sources do not indicate the percentage of Catholic policemen in the Düsseldorf district in the 1870s or how many of them lost their jobs during the Kulturkampf. In the case of night watchmen, who were recruited locally because their positions were not attractive enough to interest outsiders, their religious affiliation probably mirrored that of the local lower classes. A listing of forty-six members of the Düsseldorf night watch in 1858, for example, identified only five as Protestants.[10] However, for the day forces whose members at Berlin's insistence were recruited from a statewide pool of former noncommissioned army officers, the percentage of Catholics employed was doubtless less than that of Catholics in the district's general population. Nevertheless, scattered personnel records suggest that a substantial number of patrolmen were Catholic. At century's end, for instance, in lists of policemen being honored for thirty or more years of service in the Düsseldorf district, that is, men whose careers extended back to the Kulturkampf era, the names of Catholics appear about as frequently as do those of Protestants. Of fifty-six listed from 1899 to 1902, religious affiliation was given for thirty. Of those thirty men, sixteen were Catholics and fourteen were Protestants.[11]

For the religiously divided police forces of the Düsseldorf district, dispensation from enforcement of the anticlerical legislation of the 1870s must have come as a relief. While failing in its goal of weakening political Catholicism, the Kulturkampf had often placed the police in embarrassing and frustrating situations. Also, or so the critics of the Kulturkampf argued, the police by aiding in the campaign against the church were helping to undermine an institution that saw itself as their natural ally against crime, immorality, and "godless" socialism.[12]

In the aftermath of the Kulturkampf, the police returned, as they had in the 1850s, to a role more supportive of the interests of both Catholic and Protestant church authorities. Among the services the clergy wanted from the police was rigorous enforcement of the laws relating to Sunday trading. According to a district police ordinance of 1853, shops were to be closed during the hours set aside for religious services and their windows were to be covered so that no salable wares were on public display during the forbidden times. This ordinance proved both widely unpopular and difficult to enforce.[13]

Shopkeepers complained that the ordinance caused them great inconvenience and loss of business. They stressed the plight of laborers who often had only Sundays free to make necessary purchases. Small entrepreneurs claimed that the rules were inconsistently applied, resulting in lost sales for businesses in cities with the strictest police and unfair advantage for those who operated where enforcement was lax. Shopkeepers argued that such restrictive practices were increasingly inappropriate in an ever more urbanized and business-oriented society.[14] In the long run this argument carried the day, and the provisions of the 1853 ordinance relating to shop windows were rescinded in 1908.[15] In the 1880s, however, stepped-up enforcement was in order.[16]

Another issue eliciting police support for established Christianity, whether Catholic or Protestant, was the containment of missionary activity by proselytizing outsiders. Religious assemblies not sanctioned by recognized clerical authorities were watched carefully by the police. In particular, they were to make certain that children were not present at such meetings unless accompanied by their parents.[17] Any disturbances caused by the presence of the missionaries, even though in no way initiated by them but rather by hostile elements of the local population, could be used as an excuse to forbid or sharply restrict future activity. Such, for example, was to be the result of several riotous encounters involving the Salvation Army, local residents, and the police in various district cities in 1890.[18]

ENFORCING THE ANTISOCIALIST LAW

As noted in instructions from the Düsseldorf district administration to local authorities in 1874, repressive tactics used at the time against

Catholic organizational efforts were equally applicable to socialist initiatives.[19] For the district's police, the mission of combating socialism would ultimately prove both more demanding and more enduring than the struggle against political Catholicism. But the antisocialist campaign would be no more successful than the Kulturkampf and would do more lasting damage to police-community relations.

With the passage of the antisocialist law in 1878, police responsibilities moved beyond surveillance and harassment of working-class associations to enforcement of their dissolution. The police were given such difficult and frustrating tasks as making certain that social democratic organizations did not reconstitute themselves in some ostensibly innocuous guise (perhaps as a singing society), that socialist activists did not infiltrate nonsocialist associations, that funerals of working-class leaders did not become demonstrations, and that worker outings in the countryside did not turn into open-air meetings.[20] Taverns were watched with heightened vigilance in an effort to make certain that rooms were not let to disapproved groups. Known socialists were kept under close watch and their houses searched repeatedly. For example, over five hundred house searches took place in the Bergisches Land before the mass socialist trials of 1888–89.[21]

Information collected by the police about socialist and anarchist activities was reported to Berlin. Such information, given the direst interpretation, was used to defend continued repression. In particular, it helped justify the renewal of the antisocialist law every two years. In certain instances, police agents manufactured some of the most provocative evidence themselves, on at least one occasion composing fiery articles for anarchist publications. At an international anarchist congress in 1889, the only German delegate was someone sent by Elberfeld's Polizeikommissar Otto Kammhoff. At the congress, this delegate presented a plan to assassinate the German emperor.[22]

As social democrats were forced by the antisocialist law into clandestine activities, such as the smuggling of party publications, police responded with stepped-up reliance upon informers. They even—with varying results depending upon the individuals approached—called upon postal officials to infringe upon the confidentiality of the mail entrusted to them. The postal director in Essen chose to comply, whereas the Düsseldorf postal director refused to cooperate.[23]

Actually, as already noted in the previous chapter, in most of the cities of the Düsseldorf Regierungsbezirk, Catholicism, as an alternative set of loyalties, turned out to be a much more effective bulwark than were the police against the spread of socialism.[24] Although the Lassalleans had been able to achieve some success in predominantly Catholic

Essen in the late 1860s, they were soon displaced by Christian-Socialist organizers.[25] Elsewhere in the district, social democratic inroads through the 1870s and 1880s were largely limited to the Wuppertal and the surrounding Bergisches Land, areas where Catholics were a minority.

In the Reichstag election of 30 July 1878, for instance, the total social democratic vote in the Düsseldorf Regierungsbezirk was 21,225. Of that number, 18,865 or 88.9 percent came from only three of twelve electoral districts: Elberfeld-Barmen (11,325 votes), Solingen (5,067 votes), and Lennep-Mettmann (2,473 votes).[26] The subsequent runoff election in Elberfeld-Barmen not only sent a social democrat to the Reichstag but was also accompanied by demonstrations and attacks upon the police.[27] In the Reichstag elections during the years of the antisocialist law, social democratic votes from the Düsseldorf Regierungsbezirk continued to be overwhelmingly concentrated in the same three neighboring electoral districts.

With the Catholic communities of the Düsseldorf Regierungsbezirk proving largely inhospitable to the social democratic movement in its earliest decades, efforts to enforce the antisocialist law focused first and foremost on Elberfeld and Barmen. By the mid-1880s, both cities exceeded one hundred thousand in population and continued to represent the largest industrial concentration in the Rhine province.[28] Official conviction during the 1870s and 1880s that a strong need existed to combat socialist influence among workers in the Wuppertal led to closer scrutiny of the local police forces and generally negative evaluations of their adequacy for the tasks assigned them. Among those rendering such evaluations, in addition to the district administration, were the state prosecutor in Elberfeld and representatives of the political police sent from Berlin.[29]

In 1883 the state prosecutor in Elberfeld had been given supervisory powers over the local police in their antisocialist efforts.[30] In addition, the Berlin police president was responsible for overseeing the implementation of the antisocialist law throughout Germany. This increased intervention by outside observers was resented by local police officials. One Barmen Polizeikommissar even went so far as to omit the word "obediently" from reports submitted to the state prosecutor.[31] Both the prosecutor and agents from Berlin complained of a lack of cooperation.[32]

At the beginning of 1882, in response to critical inquiries from the state prosecutor, Elberfeld's Polizeiinspektor Daum outlined how "all conceivable means" were being utilized to counter social democracy. In addition to gathering information from a paid informant in the ranks of local socialists, Elberfeld police officers were detailed to prepare weekly reports on the activities of socialist leaders and to maintain surveillance over all public meetings to make certain that socialists were excluded from participation. On Sundays and Mondays, days of leisure among local workers, eight plainclothes policemen were assigned to scour the wooded hills outside town to prevent secret meetings. Taverns frequented by laborers were watched with care and were subjected to a strict 10 P.M. curfew. And every evening three Polizeiwachtmeister and three Polizeisergeanten, dressed in civilian clothes and disguised with false beards and wigs, presented themselves as patrons in establishments suspected of being socialist meeting places.[33]

All this reported antisocialist activity, however, failed to silence official critics of the police in Elberfeld, Barmen, and surrounding communities. The decline of the local socialist vote in the 1881 Reichstag election proved only temporary and was reversed in the next national balloting. A dynamite attack on an Elberfeld tavern in 1883 provided an additional argument for those who believed that stronger repressive measures were needed in the Wuppertal. The 1883 incident in Elberfeld was but one of a brief spate of anarchist deeds in Germany in the early 1880s. Significantly, the majority of such attacks were aimed against the police, who were prime symbols of an authoritarian state. Among the victims were two policemen in the Ruhr town of Wattenscheid.[34]

Police officials in the Wuppertal wanted the government to exercise the option provided by the antisocialist law of imposing a partial state of siege in the area, which would permit the expulsion of individuals believed to be subversive agitators. The lists of those to be expelled included twenty individuals identified as anarchists and sixteen as social democrats in Barmen and ten classified as anarchists and fourteen as social democrats in Elberfeld.[35] An agent of the political police from Berlin and the state prosecutor in Elberfeld argued, however, that the local police were inadequate both in numbers and prestige to the task of containing the disturbances likely to result.[36]

Elberfeld's state prosecutor elaborated on what he saw as serious deficiencies of the police in Elberfeld and Barmen. He linked their poor quality to poor pay. The prosecutor believed insufficient salaries made the police susceptible to petty bribery and he cited several recent cases as examples. He also believed that communal policemen were subject to unwelcome influence by the city council, a body too liberal in its composition to satisfy him. Although the mayor administered the police as an agent of the state rather than of the city council, the wishes of that body could never be completely ignored. While the state prosecutor believed the communal police distressingly ready to curry favor with well-to-do citizens, especially city councilmen, he saw them inclined to treat the lower classes, who had little to offer, with brutality, which resulted in increased popular alienation.[37]

Düsseldorf's Regierungspräsident von Berlepsch agreed with the assessment of the state prosecutor and joined him in arguing that the answer to the perceived inadequacies of the communal police in the Wuppertal was their replacement with a royal police force. According to Berlepsch, not only would a royal Schutzmannschaft be completely free of local influence, but it would also have better qualified and better disciplined manpower. Berlepsch argued that mayors were too preoccupied with other matters to give communal police the close oversight they needed. He also believed mayors to be too sensitive to local politics to demand truly rigorous policing.[38]

From the perspective of the state, Berlepsch believed that another important advantage of a royal force with authority for the entire Wuppertal was that it would not be limited by conflicting municipal jurisdictions. Socialists had proven themselves adept at making use of narrow jurisdictional restrictions on local police forces by moving political gatherings back and forth across city limits.[39] A strong and lasting argument for increased centralization of policing in industrialized areas was that maintaining order and enforcing laws in such environments were increasingly perceived by informed observers as essentially regional, not municipal tasks.

Berlepsch went beyond endorsing the proposal for state police in the Wuppertal and argued in addition for establishing a military garrison in or near Elberfeld and Barmen. Berlepsch regarded even the most efficient and best-led police as inadequate to the task of guaranteeing order in an industrial center with a largely proletarian population of over two hundred thousand, a population he believed included a significant politically unreliable component. Berlepsch stressed that keeping strict control of the political and social situation in the Wuppertal was vital not only for the sake of local interests but also because of the valley's proximity to the great concentrations of capital increasingly represented by Ruhr heavy industry, the Ruhr also being as yet without a garrison of its own.[40] In calling for the stationing of troops in the Wuppertal, Berlepsch was supporting a request that had been presented repeatedly since the 1850s by manufacturing interests and their representatives on city councils in Elberfeld and Barmen. Such men typically saw their interests much better protected by soldiers than by the police, whether state or communal.[41]

The much-discussed provision of the Wuppertal with a state police force, a military garrison, or both failed to materialize. Berlin, although sympathetic, had to consider competing demands for limited money and manpower.⁴² Rather than being displaced, the communal police forces in the Wuppertal were subjected to strong pressures to reconstitute themselves as more credible representatives of the Prussian state, capable of operating effectively in an emergency without the prospect of immediate outside aid.

The district administration was convinced that the communal police needed stricter supervision to meet the challenges of the embittered years of the antisocialist law. The mayor of Elberfeld was instructed to make certain that the city's Polizeiinspektor concentrated less on paperwork and more on directly observing his men at their jobs. In particular, the police chief was enjoined to see that his subordinates spent less time in taverns, unless present as official observers. Drunkenness was a recurrent cause for complaint about the behavior of rank-and-file policemen.⁴³

Official attention focused primarily on police personnel who did their drinking in taverns frequented by social democrats. Such suspicious associations provided grounds for dismissal.⁴⁴ Indeed, any sign of willingness to accommodate the socialists led to removal from the police. One noteworthy case from 1887 involved an Elberfeld police official accused of too readily granting associations with suspected socialist connections permission to sponsor public festivities. Not only was the official in question forced to find alternative employment in Aachen but also the mayor's assistant (Beigeordneter) for police affairs was, as a consequence of his failure to prevent the scandal, transferred to oversight of commercial matters.⁴⁵

Official concern in the 1880s about the credibility of the Wuppertal police forces made local police chiefs increasingly sensitive to criticism from any outside source. In particular, they paid close attention to the press. From bourgeois newspapers came complaints about policemen who were not available when needed or who were insufficiently deferential in their interactions with well-to-do citizens. Questions were also raised about the adequacy of the police for preserving order. In 1886, for example, the Elberfelder Zeitung recounted the difficulties the police had in controlling—with curses and blows—the crowd at a military funeral. Since the spectators were reported to have been mainly women and children, the newspaper's editorialist pointedly wondered how the police would manage if confronted with an unruly crowd of men.⁴⁶

From working-class newspapers came not only the expected complaints about police brutality, bias, and intrusiveness but also reports of petty corruption and immorality designed to embarrass the police by documenting their failure to live up to the professedly high standards of the Prussian bureaucracy. Favorite targets for such accusations of wrongdoing were those police officers assigned a leading role in the antisocialist campaign.⁴⁷ Otherwise-powerless individuals might seek redress from policemen by threatening them with publication of their misdeeds in opposition newspapers. In Elberfeld, for instance, a barber so threatened a patrolman who reportedly refused to pay for his shaves and cigars.[48]

Although the police stressed the hostile bias of complaints in socialist publications, such information was not simply ignored because it came from an allegedly questionable source. Not only did police officials believe they had to set the record straight by countering socialist accusations, but they also sometimes acted on such information, revealing as it did abuses that otherwise might have remained unknown to them. In 1882, for example, two of Elberfeld's Polizeikommissare and a Polizeiwachtmeister were forced to resign as a result of investigations initiated after reports of bribe taking had appeared in the Sozialdemokrat.[49]

For officials desiring to purge the communal police of personnel likely to undercut the credibility of law enforcement, the most difficult decisions were those involving accusations of police brutality. In Barmen in 1888, for example, two night patrolmen were brought to trial for having used excessive force against a coppersmith. The court sentenced the two to jail, one for a term of three months and the other for six months. The judge argued that if the public was to be expected to respect the police, then policemen had to act in a reasonable manner. The mayor of Barmen noted that the sensational case had divided opinion in the city. Opposed to residents who approved the sentences were others who argued that the provocativeness of a working-class population given to "excesses" made it understandable that policemen at times overstepped the bounds.[50] Disagreements about the relative weight to be given to claims of police brutality on the one hand and worker provocation on the other occur many times in the disciplinary records of the district's forces.

Serving a sentence for brutal on-the-job behavior did not necessarily disqualify a policeman from further service. In Duisburg in 1889, Mayor Lehr considered the future employment of a Polizeisergeant who had been sentenced to three jail terms, ranging from two weeks to three-and-a-half months, for mishandling a shop clerk, an apprentice, and a factory worker. The mayor decided that since the Polizeisergeant had acted not out of personal animosity against the men he had abused but rather from an excess of zeal, and since large cities needed "energetic" policemen, it would be a shame to dismiss the man.[51]

RESPONDING TO STRIKES

Implementation of the antisocialist law meant not only outlawing working-class political organizations but also banning most labor unions in existence in 1878. Thereafter, as long as the law remained in effect, restructured unions, designed to circumvent the law's provisions, struggled to survive in an environment of official hostility. Furthermore, during the 1880s worker mobilization in the Düsseldorf district was also hampered by often unfavorable economic conditions. Brief recoveries were overtaken by renewed slumps. At the end of the decade, however, a vigorous business upturn set the stage for revival of strike activity on an unprecedented scale.

Far overshadowing all other work stoppages in the strike wave of the late 1880s and early 1890s was the massive strike of Ruhr coal miners in May 1889. At its peak, the strike was supported by some 90,000 Ruhr miners. Work stoppages in other German mining districts brought the number of striking miners in 1889 to nearly 150,000. Confronted with this unparalleled challenge, the powerful and well-organized coal industrialists called upon the government, although without success, to declare a state of siege in areas of strike activity.[52]

Although they failed to secure the declaration of a state of siege, the mine operators were successful in persuading the state to use its armed might in other ways to chasten the contentious workers. That the strike began among young, poorly paid haulers and horse drivers and was initially accompanied by violent clashes with mine officials and local police strengthened the employers' argument. In the eastern or Westphalian half of the Ruhr, authorities complied with the wishes of the bosses by securing the early dispatch of military forces, along with extra gendarmes. The presence of the troops, however, merely served to heighten tensions. During the resulting confrontations, soldiers shot several miners and innocent bystanders.[53]

For the western half of the Ruhr, the portion lying within the Düsseldorf administrative district, Regierungspräsident von Berlepsch resisted the call for troops but sent additional gendarmes into the areas of strike activity. It did not escape official notice that where the military was not used, the strike took a less bloody course. As older, more established miners joined the work action, the strike moved of its own accord in a more peaceful direction.

The magnitude and bloodiness of the 1889 coal strike inevitably prompted a reconsideration of the appropriateness of the government's response. Among those considering how the state might best respond to similar situations in the future was General Emil von Albedyll, commander of the VII Army Corps in Münster in Westphalia. Albedyll had commanded the troops sent into the eastern Ruhr in 1889. Unwilling to accommodate the leaders of industry by endorsing a sustained military presence in the coal basin, he argued instead for a strengthening of the police. In particular, he called for an increase in the number of gendarmes.[54]

According to Albrecht Funk, Prussia between 1892 and 1913 increased the size of its gendarmerie corps from 4,665 to 5,629 men, still significantly short of the 9,000-man force originally planned before 1820. More important than mere numbers, however, was the nature of deployment. Initially intended primarily for rural policing, a strengthened gendarmerie would, in the last prewar decades, assume an increasingly important role in patrolling the new and poorly policed industrial settlements springing up between and beyond the established cities, especially in the fastest-growing parts of the Ruhr.[55] The realization was gaining ground among those responsible for the maintenance of public order that reinforced police forces in the major cities could only be effective if the surrounding areas were adequately patrolled.

The 1889 coal strike played out against the background of rising tension between the new emperor, William II, and the now-aged chancellor Otto von Bismarck. The two men held differing views of how the government should react to the Ruhr strike. The emperor agreed with those of his advisors who believed that socialists, although not responsible for the strike, might take advantage of the situation if it were allowed to continue and escalate. Anxious to avoid a major bloodbath, William sought to encourage some employer accommodation with the miners' demands for improved conditions.[56] Employers were dismayed by the emperor's decision to meet with a miners' delegation. For his part, Bismarck apparently saw in a prolonged and bitter strike a means of preparing bourgeois public opinion for stronger antisocialist measures, possibly even for changes in the political structure of the empire that would serve to enhance his own power.[57] Bismarck's days in office were, however, numbered and so too were the days of the antisocialist law.

The lapsing of the antisocialist law and the inauguration of what initially promised to be a more flexible and conciliatory "New Course" did not, however, signal any significant lessening of governmental determination to contain the spread of social democracy, using heavy-handed means whenever they seemed necessary. In the summer of 1890, Minister of the Interior Ernst Ludwig Herrfurth explained to Prussia's administrative hierarchy what he believed needed to be done to make up for the coming loss of the antisocialist law. In industrial areas, he admonished, urban police forces and the gendarmerie would have to be strengthened in both numbers and quality. Local councils reluctant to provide the necessary financial resources would have to be forced to do so. Those responsible for oversight of the police were to see to it that all remaining antisocialist options were used to their fullest, up to the very limits of the law. As Herrfurth's instructions indicated, the end of the antisocialist law opened up the prospect of an increased rather than diminished political role for the police.[58]

CHAPTER SIX

Big-City Police, 1890–1914

RECRUITMENT

The economic resurgence of the late 1880s that had set the stage for the massive Ruhr coal strike of 1889 was followed by renewed economic difficulties early in the next decade. Before the end of the century, however, the economy recovered and then entered a period of sometimes hectic expansion. The last two prewar decades were a time of general, although far from uninterrupted, prosperity for Imperial Germany.[1]

For the Düsseldorf administrative district, especially in the portion that extended into the Ruhr, rapid urban development accompanied impressive industrial growth. Large proletarian settlements such as Hamborn and Oberhausen mushroomed into existence from tiny beginnings. Among the district's more established municipalities, Düsseldorf, Essen, and Duisburg approximately tripled their populations through a combination of births, in-migration, and the large-scale incorporation of surrounding communities.[2] By comparison, major textile cities such as Barmen, Elberfeld, and Krefeld, while still growing, failed to match this frantic pace (see table 4). As a consequence, the centers of textile manufacturing increasingly fell behind the district's faster-growing heavy-industrial areas as a focus of official concern in matters relating to public order.

The extremely rapid expansion of many of the district's leading municipalities was accompanied by the even faster growth of police departments. Prussian officials and local elites were determined to continue strengthening civilian forces available to contain possible proletarian unrest and to meet bourgeois expectations relating to urban order and security.[3] By March 1914, Düsseldorf, now the largest city in the Regierungsbezirk with a population of 413,027, had 545 policemen,

TABLE 4

Police Personnel, 1890–1913

Police District	Population	Policemen (Day and Night)	Inhabitants per Policeman
Barmen			
1890	116,000	116	1000
1898	126,992	157	809
1905	141,947	190	747
1913	169,101	216	783
Duisburg			
1890	55,853	36	1551
1898	80,000	82	976
1905	110,103	119	925
1913	248,313	322	771
Düsseldorf			
1890	142,496	126	1131
1898	196,700	226	870
1905	253,767	302	840
1913	400,000	545	734
Elberfeld			
1890	125,000	149	839
1898	139,337	191	729
1905	156,937	237	662
1913	170,195	248	686
Essen			
1890	76,118	61	1248
1898	106,867	130	1120
1905	230,000	275	836
1913		State Police[a]	
Krefeld			
1890	107,485	96	1120
1898	107,279	121	887
1905	109,084	140	779
1913	129,406	153	846

Sources: Reports from individual cities, July and August 1890, Staatsarchiv Düsseldorf, Regierung Düsseldorf 8611; Nachweisung über den Zahl und die Verhältnisse der Gemeindepolizeiexecutivbeamten, 1898, Staatsarchiv Düsseldorf, Regierung Düsseldorf 8612; Nachweisung, 1905, Staatsarchiv Düsseldorf, Regierung Düsseldorf 30267; Nachweisung, 1913, Staatsarchiv Düsseldorf, Regierung Düsseldorf 30268.

[a]State police were established for Essen and surrounding communities in 1909 (see chapter 9).

or one for every 758 inhabitants. At the beginning of the 1890s, Düsseldorf had only 126 policemen, or one for every 1,131 residents.[4] In Krefeld, per capita expenditure on the police increased more than twice as fast as inflation, rising from 2.60 marks in 1890 to 4.21 marks in 1913, even though in the meantime the cost of both firefighting and streetlighting had been transferred out of the police budget (see Appendix, table A-1).

The substantial growth in absolute terms of communal resources allocated to policing during the Wilhelmian era, however, did not represent any significant increase in the percentage of municipal budgets expended on law enforcement. Rather, policing at best was only more or less keeping pace with a general marked expansion of communal services.[5] In Düsseldorf, for example, the city's total budget in 1908 was 5.55 times and the police budget 5.92 times greater than they had been in 1888. In Duisburg during the same period, the total municipal budget increased 6.26 times, the police budget 6.07 times. And in Elberfeld, whereas the total budget was 7.89 times larger in 1908 than it had been in 1888, the police budget was only 3.41 times larger.[6] In Düsseldorf in the first half of the nineteenth century, policing had represented the second biggest expense in the city's budget, surpassed only by the cost of poor relief.[7] By 1860 policing ranked fourth among six categories of municipal expenditure. By 1870 it had fallen to fifth place. In 1880, 1890, and 1900, it ranked seventh among seven categories, coming behind public works, education, debt payment, general administration, poor relief, and communal enterprises.[8]

The expanded and better-financed communal police departments of the prewar years became the focus of heightened governmental and public debate about how they should be organized, how they should function, and how they should be monitored. But of most immediate concern to those responsible for these enlarged law enforcement agencies was how they should be staffed. As far as the state was concerned, the first priority was the hiring of as many candidates as possible who were holders of the *Zivilversorgungsschein* awarded to noncommissioned officers in good standing at the end of twelve years in the armed forces. Also entitled to special consideration in hiring were military invalids. Police recruiters, however, often deemed invalids unequal to the physical demands of big-city policing and in addition considered them less desirable than the twelve-year veterans because of their more limited military experience.[9]

During the last prewar decades, the state's expectation that the communal police should consist first and foremost of former noncommissioned officers with long years of military service frequently confronted the lack of qualified men willing to present themselves as candidates for employment as patrolmen by the district's industrial cities. As noted in chapter 3, *Militäranwärter*—men who had qualified through extended military enlistment for preferential employment in lower-level public service positions—had seldom been willing to apply for nighttime police duty. This remained true even when full-time night forces increasingly replaced part-time night watches in the 1870s and 1880s. In 1883, for example, the mayor of Düsseldorf, responding to inquiries from the district administration, gave notice to the city's twenty-seven night patrolmen because they all lacked the proper military credentials. The mayor took this step even though eighteen of the twenty-seven men had held their positions for at least five years.[10]

In response to the advertisement of the soon-to-be-vacant twenty-seven nighttime positions in Düsseldorf, only fourteen men applied. Of these, four were without the Zivilversorgungsschein; the remaining ten were deemed unacceptable because they were either too old (past their mid-thirties), had been given negative references by previous employers, or had failed to respond to follow-up correspondence from the city. Having demonstrated the unavailability of suitable replacements, the mayor retained the men to whom he had given notice.[11]

Throughout the district, cities, despite their frequently expressed preference for experienced noncommissioned officers, had no choice but to hire mostly local workers for their night forces. In Krefeld, for example, ten new night patrolmen, ranging in age from twenty-six to thirty-seven, were hired in 1887. Of the ten, five were weavers and one a dyer, reflecting the primacy of the textile industry in Krefeld. The other four gave their former occupations as shipbuider, shoemaker, brakeman, and tailor.[12]

By the 1880s, and much more so after 1890, the district's fastest-growing cities were finding it increasingly difficult to recruit holders of the Zivilversorgungsschein not just for night service but also for the better-paying and more-respected day service as well. According to the mayor of Krefeld, writing in 1883, the only way he had been able to secure an otherwise qualified man to fill a vacant position as Polizei-sergeant was to hire someone who was forty-five years old, ten years past the usual upper age limit for new recruits.[13] In 1891, while Krefeld and Elberfeld reported that they were still managing to staff their Polizeisergeanten positions with holders of the Zivilversorgungsschein, Düsseldorf, Duisburg, and Essen found the supply of candidates with the requisite military experience falling ever more short of their needs.[14] By 1911 the Düsseldorf department with forty-six Polizeisergeanten positions to fill, reported that of 500 to 600 applicants, only 22 were qualified by reason of military service. And most of the 22 were invalids, not twelve-year veterans.[15]

As early as 1898 Düsseldorf had modified its stated expectations, stipulating that Polizeisergeanten could be recruited from among former noncommissioned officers with as little as five years of military service. But while reducing the number of years of military experience required, the city's police department indicated a continuing preference for men coming directly from the army, such recruits presumably having experienced minimal contamination with civilian values and associations.[16] By 1904 most of the 258 Polizeisergeanten employed by Düsseldorf had spent substantially less than the five years with the military proposed as a standard in 1898. Eighty-five had served enlistments of two years and seventy-three had served three years.[17] Only fifteen had served twelve years with the army, and these were men who had typically joined the police before 1890 when the Zivilversorgungsschein was still the norm.[18]

By the beginning of the First World War, rank-and-file policemen with the Zivilversorgungsschein had become a rarity in the Düsseldorf district. In Barmen in 1913, they represented only 9 of 169 Polizeisergeanten, in Krefeld 12 of 125.[19] During the last prewar decades, the kind of men officially sought for police service had too many alternative employment opportunities available to them to choose communal policing as a career. If they wished to remain in state employment, they could turn to the postal or customs services or to the railroads.[20] Private employers sought former noncommissioned officers as reputedly rigorous supervisory personnel. And for those men interested in policing, the royal Schutzmannschaft was often short of militarily qualified recruits and offered the greater prestige of state over communal employment. Also, noncommissioned officers who were a few years short of earning a Zivilversorgungsschein had the opportunity to continue to work toward it in the royal Schutzmannschaft (or in the gendarmerie) but not in the communal police.[21]

Thus, despite persistent pressure from above to seek out experienced noncommissioned officers for police service, the cities in the Düsseldorf district turned increasingly to the local wage-earning population for recruits. Urban administrators usually did so reluctantly, continuing to perceive the ideal policeman not just as someone shaped by long years of military discipline but also as someone from the outside, preferably of rural or small town origin. But the reality was that most applicants were local residents with only minimal military experience. As a consequence, the specter of policemen having personal contacts with organized workers loomed ever more threatening.[22]

Insight into the prior occupations of police recruits is provided by a list of the 258 Polizeisergeanten employed by Düsseldorf in 1904. No prior occupation is given for 1 individual; only the military is cited for 3 others. Thirty-five are described as having been employed in agriculture. One hundred nine claimed to have been craftsmen or skilled workers. A significant number of these men, especially many of the 36 trained in various metal trades, had doubtless been employed in factories rather than in craft shops, but that number cannot be determined on the basis of occupational titles alone. Of the remaining recruits, 63 were unskilled or semiskilled industrial or transport workers and 48 were clerical workers and shopkeepers. The overall impression is of a group of modest wage earners, although one generally excluding casual laborers and the poorest of the poor.[23]

Lists prepared by the Essen police in 1908 in anticipation of the establishment of a royal Schutzmannschaft in the Ruhr provide further information about the kind of men employed. On one list of 253 Polizeisergeanten, ages given ranged from twenty-four to fifty-six.[24] The requirement of prior military experience and official assumptions that policemen should have some measure of maturity account for the absence of men under age twenty-four. By way of comparison, the mean age of entrance into the London police before the First World War was only twenty-three.[25]

Most of Essen's rank-and-file policemen in 1908 were in their thirties (138) or late twenties (70). Only 41 were in their forties and 4 were in their fifties. That most members of the force were under forty years old reflects neither early retirement nor large numbers of promotions to higher rank but rather the relatively recent recruitment of most of these men. All but 35 had joined the force within the previous ten years of rapid growth.

Polizeisergeanten were typically family men. Of the 253 Essen Polizeisergeanten already mentioned, all but 27 were married, with 21 of the bachelors being young men under thirty years old. And all but 18 of the married men had children. Large families were common. Sixty-four had four or more children. The largest family had nine. Family status, along with age and secure employment, helped set policemen apart from the young, unmarried industrial workers who were a primary target of routine police surveillance of streets and taverns.

All 253 men had some military experience, but for 133 service had been limited to two years. A further 73 had three years of service. Only 3 had spent a full twelve years with the army. Perhaps more worrisome for the state, only 53 had been noncommissioned officers, attaining the rank of *Unteroffizier* or higher. The highest rank achieved by almost exactly half the men (127) was private first class (*Gefreiter*).[26]

A second list from 1908, this one enumerating 276 Essen Polizeisergeanten, includes information about education and religion. With regard to schooling, the situation was quite simple. All the men were listed as having an elementary (*Volksschule*) education. Religiously, they divided into 157 Catholics and 119 Protestants, a ratio almost exactly mirroring that of the city's general population. Whatever prejudices against the employment of Catholics as Polizeisergeanten may have survived at higher levels, the limited availability of suitable recruits permitted little or no discrimination on the basis of religion.[27]

Judging from this second Essen list, education and religion played virtually no role in determining promotion of Polizeisergeanten to the next higher rank of Wachtmeister. Of twenty-three Essen Polizeiwachtmeister listed, all but one had only an elementary education. The single exception was a man who had attended a secondary school (*Oberschule*) and was employed in criminal investigation, a specialty assumed to be more intellectually demanding than routine police patrol. Among the twenty-three Wachtmeister, Catholics outnumbered Protestants by thirteen to ten.[28]

Not surprisingly the Essen Wachtmeister, who ranged in age from thirty to sixty-three, with all but two in their thirties and forties, were on average slightly older than the Polizeisergeanten. They also had somewhat more police experience, even though half of them had been recruited within the past ten years. The big difference between the Polizeisergeanten and the Wachtmeister was in years of military service and highest military rank achieved. Of twenty-six Wachtmeister included in the first of the two lists mentioned, fourteen had served twelve or more years. Only three had served three years or less. The average length of military service for the twenty-six Wachtmeister was 9.77 years, compared with an average of 3.57 years for the 253 Polizeisergeanten. Of the twenty-six Polizeiwachtmeister, twenty-two had been noncommissioned officers, most of them at a rank (Sergeant, Wachtmeister, *Feldwebel*) higher than Unteroffizier.[29]

Whereas holders of the Zivilversorgungsschein had become a rarity among communal police recruits before World War I, they were still the norm among men chosen to become Wachtmeister.[30] Polizeiwachtmeister were well aware of this distinction and used it to argue, unsuccessfully, that they should be reclassified from lower-level to middle-ranking (*subaltern*) public servants. They resented being lumped together with the Polizeisergeanten, whose military superiors they were likely to have been.[31]

If Polizeiwachtmeister were usually men promoted from the ranks, further advancement was rare and officially discouraged, especially after the turn of the century.[32] In Düsseldorf, for instance, two Wachtmeister were promoted to Kommissar in 1893, but no further such appointments were reported in that department before the war.[33] As a general rule, the distinction between officers and men continued, as in the past, to be sharply maintained and began with separate recruitment and career paths. The Anglo-American practice of recruiting police officers from among rank-and-file policemen was not for Germany or other continental countries.[34]

The gulf between Polizeisergeanten and Wachtmeister on the one hand and Kommissare and Inspektoren on the other continued to be determined in large part by education. Officers in the communal police were normally expected to have secondary educations, not the Volksschule instruction nearly universal among Polizeisergeanten and Wachtmeister. In Essen in 1908, eleven of fourteen police officers had attended secondary schools (*Gymnasium, Realschule,* or Oberschule).[35] The importance attached to the distinction between elementary and secondary education in determining the future rank of communal police recruits closely paralleled similar distinctions made between the lower and middle levels of the state civil service.[36]

At least in Essen, police officers were further distinguished from their men by religion. Whereas the majority of Polizeisergeanten and Wachtmeister in Essen were Catholics, only two of their fourteen officers in 1908 shared this confessional identification.[37] To what extent this discrepancy resulted from deliberate discrimination against Catholic officer candidates or was merely the consequence of recruitment from a pool of applicants extending to all parts of predominantly Protestant Prussia is impossible to say with certainty, but discrimination probably played a significant role.

Ideally, the district's prewar police departments wished to recruit as officers men whose education had qualified them to enter the army as one-year volunteers and who subsequently became either regular or reserve officers. Where such candidates were lacking, the cities sought out holders of the Zivilversorgungsschein with twelve or more years of military service, provided they had some secondary education or its equivalent gained through various military courses and examinations intended for ambitious noncommissioned officers.[38] Would-be Kommissare could also work their way up through various clerical positions in police, court, and municipal administrations.

The desire of Prussian officials to add to the prestige of communal police forces by encouraging the recruitment of regular army or reserve officers as Kommissare was largely doomed to disappointment.[39] Of twenty-six Kommissare appointed to the Düsseldorf force between 1893 and 1912, only one had been an army lieutenant and two were reserve officers. Five had worked their way up through the civil administration. Aside from the two promoted Wachtmeister already mentioned and six recruits who had been Kommissare elsewhere, the remaining ten were former noncommissioned officers with long years of military service.[40] For six Düsseldorf Kommissare listed in 1900, their years with the military ranged from eleven to eighteen. For twelve Essen Kommissare listed in 1908, six had twelve or more years of military service. One had served eleven years, and the remaining five had served three years or less.[41]

In summary, on the eve of the First World War the ideal communal police force was one composed of officers who were recruited from among reserve officers or former regular army officers and patrolmen who were recruited from among former noncommissioned officers holding the Zivilversorgungsschein. The reality was different: police officers who were frequently former noncommissioned officers and patrolmen who were often local wage earners. In competition for manpower with the military, royal police forces, various government agencies, and burgeoning private industry, the communal police found themselves at a disadvantage. That the occupational origins and education of communal policemen at all ranks were more modest than Prussian authorities wished both reflected and reinforced the low prestige attached to policing compared to other kinds of public service.[42]

INTERNAL RESTRUCTURING

Closely linked to problems of recruitment was the major restructuring of communal police forces that took place during the last two prewar decades. The connection was particularly obvious with regard to the creation of integrated day-night forces for the district's largest cities.

The special difficulty of recruiting reliable men exclusively for night patrol was central to growing official dissatisfaction with the traditional separation of day and night personnel. Night policemen had a reputation for poor discipline. In Düsseldorf from 1877 to 1896, fifty-eight members of the night force but only seventeen members of the larger day force were dismissed (see Appendix, table A–2). In Essen in 1885, the daytime Polizeisergeanten complained that their reputations were suffering because of the repeated misdeeds of the men with night duty. The petitioners requested that clearly different insignia for the two bodies of men be introduced so that the Polizeisergeanten who worked by day would not be mistaken for the Schutzleute who patrolled at night.[43]

High turnover was a serious problem for the night forces. In Düsseldorf from 1877 to 1896, resignations among Schutzleute outnumbered those among the more numerous Polizeisergeanten by seventy-five to forty-six (see Appendix, table A–2). Of Düsseldorf's eighty Schutzleute in 1897, forty-seven had been recruited within the past two years.[44] Although employment as night patrolman was regarded as an entry-level position giving access to more desirable day service after perhaps four or five years, large numbers of Schutzleute were unable or unwilling to stay long enough to make the transition.

The biggest impediment was the work schedule.[45] Not only did night policemen typically patrol from nine, ten, or eleven o'clock at night until six in the morning, with no nights off, but they also were required to patrol two or three hours each afternoon while the men of the day force took their midday breaks. Night patrolmen also had to be available for extra duty relating to court appearances and for special events such as election days or local festivals, with no compensatory time off.[46] No wonder night patrolmen in Krefeld petitioned in 1903 for a change in their terms of service on the grounds of their endangered health, pointing out that they never had more than six or seven hours of unbroken rest available to them and often not even that.[47]

The problems caused by the separate organization of nighttime service were obvious and pressing, but authorities hesitated to advocate the establishment of integrated forces with personnel rotating on and off night duty. Police administrators feared that the serious problems encountered recruiting and retaining suitable night patrolmen might well extend to the whole force if all members faced regular employment at night.[48] But night policing was such an obvious source of discontent, both for the men who were employed in it and for the urban citizens who complained of the unsatisfactory performance of night personnel, that major restructuring became unavoidable. After the Berlin Schutzmannschaft assumed responsibility for night patrol in the capital in 1894–95, integrated day-night forces were established in Düsseldorf in 1897, in Essen in 1898, in Duisburg and Barmen in 1907, and in Elberfeld in 1911.[49]

As anticipated, the daytime Polizeisergeanten were greatly distressed to lose their previous exemption from regular night duty and to find their ranks now flooded by the wholesale inclusion of the former Schutzleute. They complained of departure from the long-established principle of reserving lighter (daytime) duties for older men so that their years of active service could be maximized.[50] In Barmen in 1907, twenty-four Polizeisergeanten hired an attorney to represent their grievances, a major departure from the highly deferential petitions rank-and-file police had submitted to their superiors in the nineteenth century. The twenty-four men in question had themselves served initially as nighttime patrolmen. After four years they had accepted new daytime positions, requiring them to start afresh after sacrificing their accumulated claims to pension benefits and lifetime tenure. They argued, unsuccessfully, that they had a right to continue to be employed on the terms offered them when they were recruited as Polizeisergeanten.[51]

Most Polizeisergeanten did not, of course, go so far as to hire a lawyer. Many, however, did express their unqualified opposition to the newly imposed terms of employment by resigning. In Düsseldorf in the first five years after the creation of an integrated day-night force in 1897, 109 men chose to resign (see Appendix, table A–2). This marked surge in resignations was almost certainly a direct consequence of restructuring.

At the same time that the old distinction between daytime and nighttime personnel was being eliminated in the name of creating presumably more efficient and better qualified round-the-clock police forces, important new distinctions on the basis of specialized function were being introduced that were supposed to serve the same end. Most significant was the creation of separate criminal divisions, staffed by men who went about their tasks in civilian attire and who concentrated on the investigation of crimes with unknown perpetrators.[52] Such divisions aided communal police departments in meeting their obligations to the state prosecutors and freed the district's cities from the need to call upon Berlin to send trained outside agents to help solve serious local crimes. Around the turn of the century, recently created criminal divisions existed in Düsseldorf, Elberfeld, Essen, Krefeld, and Duisburg.[53] Barmen parsimoniously held out against the innovation until 1907, finally succumbing to pressure from the district administration. The Regierungspräsident and judicial officials insisted that a separate criminal division was essential for a city of the size and importance of Barmen.[54]

The new criminal divisions were initially given responsibility not just for the investigation of crimes but also for the surveillance of activities relating to political movements and vice. Increasing police specialization before the war, however, led to the formation in the largest cities of separate units to assume these tasks. By 1911 the Essen police, given the importance of the local Krupp concern as a producer of arms, even believed they needed someone specially trained to investigate espionage.[55]

In Duisburg in 1912, the criminal division consisted of 1 of the city's 3 Inspektoren, 4 of its 18 Kommissare, 5 of its 36 Wachtmeister, but only 15 of its 247 Polizeisergeanten.[56] The disproportionate presence of men chosen from the higher ranks reflected the assumption that criminal investigation called for special skills and mature judgment and reliability beyond what could be expected of ordinary patrolmen.[57] In hiring personnel for the criminal division, the Elberfeld police in 1903 asked for permission to give preference to candidates with civilian rather than military backgrounds because the latter were unlikely to have the kind of education and experience deemed appropriate.[58] Introducing such innovations in the identification of suspects as photographs and fingerprints, the new criminal divisions would be in the forefront of those trying to give the police an increasingly desired aura of scientific expertise.

THE POLICEMAN'S LOT BEFORE 1914

In their efforts to recruit and retain increased numbers of policemen in an often tight prewar labor market, urban officials were under pressure to offer more attractive terms of employment. Nominal salaries rose significantly. In Essen the annual starting salary for Polizeisergeanten increased from 1,200 marks in 1888 to 1,300 marks by 1898 and then to 1,500 marks by 1902.[59] Already in 1897, the mayor of Essen was suggesting to his counterparts in neighboring cities that they should reach an agreement on police salaries to avoid a bidding war such as had occurred, he claimed, in the case of teachers.[60]

But mayors were unable to avoid further increases. In Düsseldorf, salaries paid to newly recruited Polizeisergeanten rose from 1,300 marks in 1891, to 1,400 marks by 1905, to 1,500 marks by 1909, and to 1,700 marks by 1913. These gains, however, were counterbalanced by increases in the cost of living, which were especially marked during the last decade before the war. According to Gerhard Bry, the cost of living in Germany rose from an index figure of 75 in 1890 to 100 in 1913. During those years, for example, the price of a ton of Ruhr coal increased from 7.96 to 11.01 marks. Food prices soared. In Düsseldorf the cost of a half kilogram of beef rose from .74 marks in 1908 to 1.06 marks in 1911–12.[61] To help police families cope with the sharp rise in prices, Elberfeld in 1913 offered allowances ranging from 4 marks a month for one child to 21 marks a month for seven or more children.[62]

As in previous periods of inflation and rapid industrial expansion, policemen in the Düsseldorf district lost some of the comparative advantage they enjoyed during years of declining prices. Between 1898 and 1913, for instance, average annual earnings for Ruhr miners rose from 1,175 to 1,755 marks, an increase of 49.4 percent. During those same years, starting salaries for Düsseldorf Polizeisergeanten rose only 30.8 percent, from 1,300 to 1,700 marks. Of course, part of the increased earnings of miners was attributable to extra shifts and longer hours, whereas the hours worked by policemen were unaffected by the business cycle. And policemen continued to be better paid than most workers. In Barmen, according to Wolfgang Köllmann, the average annual income of an adult male laborer was 720 marks in 1892 and 1,200 marks in 1912. Barmen Polizeisergeanten, however, earned from 1,200 to 1,650 marks a year in 1891 and from 1,850 to 2,400 marks a year in 1913.[63]

Those policemen who looked for extra sources of income in an effort to make ends meet confronted growing official suspicion of most such initiatives, especially those entailing involvement in the private economy.[64] These activities were viewed not only as distractions from official duties but also as potentially harmful to claims of police impartiality in the conflicts of daily life. Particularly frowned upon was the common practice of employing policemen to manage rental housing. Prussian officials feared that policemen acting in that capacity would be perceived by much of the public as misusing their authority in the interest of landlords, especially if patrolmen donned their uniforms to collect rents or evict tenants.[65] Also frowned upon was the acceptance by individual policemen of payment from newspapers for the preparation of reports about police activity.[66] As a general rule, during the last prewar decades, the state stepped up its demands for tighter control over all gifts and rewards given for police services by private groups or individuals.[67]

When communal policemen of the Wilhelmian era compared their terms of employment to those of industrial workers, they were more likely to feel agrieved about hours than about pay. As the average workweek for German workers declined by approximately one-third between 1860 and 1914,[68] the long hours still required of police personnel came to seem increasingly onerous. In 1893 Polizeisergeanten in Elberfeld complained of excessive demands on their time. In addition to regular weekday shifts that began between 6 and 8 o'clock in the morning and lasted until between 8 and 11 o'clock at night, with breaks, they worked six to twelve hours during the day on Sunday as well as Saturday and Sunday evenings.[69] When police service was reorganized in Krefeld in 1905, daily shifts were scheduled for ten to eleven hours, still without provision for regular days off.[70]

In their quest for leisure, rank-and-file policemen attached particular importance to securing for themselves regular days off and annual vacations. They used as arguments the supposedly health-endangering consequences of their stressful work and of being out in all kinds of weather, and also the precedent of the enjoyment of such benefits by other public servants, including their own officers. To those who reasoned that policemen did not need vacations because they worked outside in the fresh air, they countered that they spent their time in the midst of the nerve-wracking din and dirt of urban streets.[71]

Many police administrators had long recognized the legitimacy of demands from their subordinates for more leisure. With the substantial enlargement of urban police forces after 1890, officers had increasing flexibility in scheduling. Before 1914, the district's major cities had begun to provide their rank-and-file policemen with two to three days off per month, including one Sunday or holiday, plus an annual vacation of one to three weeks. Police personnel were, however, reminded that they had no legal claim to such privileges. Scheduling days off and vacations remained dependent upon the needs of the department. In addition, vacations were to be given only to those judged to have demonstrated good behavior.[72]

And whatever time off was granted to policemen, they were not completely free to spend it as they wished. Not only were they always on call for any emergency, but they were also expected to dedicate their leisure hours to preparing themselves for upcoming duty. In Essen in 1896, in an effort to prevent policemen from visiting taverns before work, night patrolmen were ordered not to leave their dwellings between 4 P.M. and the start of their shifts.[73] Forbidden from membership in political associations and discouraged from fraternizing extensively with the general public, policemen were encouraged to spend their limited leisure with their families or on such safe and health-giving activities as sports and gardening.[74]

TRAINING AND DISCIPLINE

Careful monitoring of the lives of policemen reflected the expectation of their superiors that such men should serve as models of state-approved behavior both on and off the job, such models being especially important for the most rapidly growing and most proletarian of the district's industrial cities. In the interests of enhancing their public credibility, communal policemen were enjoined to follow the behavioral guidelines that had been developed for the state civil service. Like more prestigious Prussian bureaucrats, policemen were expected to be above reproach personally as well as vocationally to avoid embarrassing the state they so conspicuously served. In particular, they were warned to avoid sexual improprieties and to abstain from making debts except in unavoidable cases of dire family illness or similar emergency.[75] General failure during the Wilhelmian era, however, to recruit the preferred types of candidates for the communal police meant that Prussian officials and local elites often doubted that their expectations in regard to police behavior would be reliably fulfilled.

For much of the nineteenth century, police officers could anticipate that most recruits would come to their new vocation extensively indoctrinated and tested by long years in the military. Already possessing the desired military bearing, such personnel, their superiors assumed, could readily learn on the job all they needed to know about police practice. Probationers were assigned to more experienced policemen, who were to instruct them in the fundamentals of policing. Later in the century, at least in larger departments, recruits joined other Polizeisergeanten and Wachtmeister in weekly classes taught by the Kommissare.[76] The Kommissare, for their part, had typically received their training by attaching themselves to a police department as unpaid interns for six months or more.[77]

By the end of the nineteenth century, questions about the adequacy of police training multiplied. Urban police departments were attempting to assimilate large numbers of recruits, often of working-class origin. At the same time, police misdeeds and misjudgments were receiving ever wider publicity in the press, especially in social democratic publications.[78] With hopes of being served by more reliable and well-informed policemen, capable of engendering more general public confidence in the reasonableness and expertise of law enforcement, the cities of the Düsseldorf district, encouraged by state officials, agreed to support the formation of a police school in Düsseldorf in 1901.[79] Similar institutions were being established in other Prussian districts as well at about the same time, beginning with Berlin in 1895.[80] Police schools were intended not only to impart necessary knowledge and approved attitudes but also to raise police prestige. Increased formal training (whatever its content) would help lessen the gulf between policemen and other more respected representatives of the Prussian state.[81]

In Düsseldorf the course for Polizeisergeanten lasted two months, that for Kommissare for three months. Students were required to live at the school so that its influence could prevail around the clock. The cities paid the costs for the Polizeisergeanten, fearing that if the men were required to use their own resources they would fall into debt, a condition policemen were strongly enjoined to avoid. The Kommissare, expected to come from somewhat more well-off families, had to pay for their own instruction, just as they were expected to support themselves during the internships that preceded their employment.[82]

Cities tried to protect their investment in the Polizeisergeanten by stipulating that those who left their departments after less than five years had to repay all or part of the costs of their schooling. Also, attendance at the school was typically reserved for those recruits who had already completed six to twelve months of service. As justification for this fiscally prudent move, police administrators argued that schooling was more meaningful if it followed a substantial period of practical experience.[83]

By 1906, the district administration had stipulated that in cities of ten thousand or more, Polizeisergeanten either had to attend the police school or pass an examination before being confirmed in their posts.[84] Supporters of the Düsseldorf school were dismayed to find that many communal police departments, to save the cost of instruction, either tried to hire recruits who had already attended a police school elsewhere or else encouraged the taking of the examination. To make certain that the Düsseldorf school had enough students to pay for itself, the provincial administration before the war was contemplating eliminating the examination option.[85]

As a step toward making communal policemen more credible as rule enforcers by increasing the likelihood that they knew and understood the rules, the Düsseldorf police school represented only a hesitant beginning. Much more official energy focused on the persistent problem of disciplining policemen on the job. As always, a serious obstacle to achievement of uniform and predictable performance remained the dispersed character of much police work. The official assumption that the military provided the most suitable model for police discipline failed to take into account the wide disparity between the conditions under which soldiers and policemen usually operated.

For administrators frustrated in their efforts to monitor as closely as they would like the routine activities of patrolmen, one possible approach was to use numbers of arrests made or violations reported as a measure of individual diligence. But if such an approach became public knowledge, the likely result was sharp criticism from liberals, social democrats, and even some conservatives who argued that Prussian policemen were already more intrusive and heavy-handed than they were helpful and supportive, and should certainly not be encouraged to impose even more penalties on the unwary for the sake of meeting some arbitrary quota.

A notable debate over this issue focused on a 1911 controversy in the fortress town of Wesel. Newspaper articles, presumably based on information initially leaked by disaffected Wesel policemen, recounted that the mayor intended to withhold vacations from ten members of the force for failing to report at least twenty violations each between 1

October 1910 and 20 May 1911 (reports per policeman during that period ranged from six to eighty).[86] The mayor argued that he had been driven to this expedient by the recalcitrance of a police force that resisted the efforts of a new Polizeiinspektor to undo the consequences of previously "lax" administration.

When representatives of the city's commercial interests protested the policy, the mayor responded that expecting policemen to issue at least a minimal number of citations was no different from expecting traveling salesmen to come back with a minimal number of orders. Responding to critics within the city council, the mayor reminded them that they had no say in how he administered the police. Reporting to the Landrat, the mayor argued that he could not rescind his punitive order without giving communal policemen the impression that they had only to turn to the press or the city council to get their way.[87] Although the Landrat in Wesel decided to back the decision to withhold vacations from the ten policemen, he believed that the mayor and Polizeiinspektor should have made their case on the basis of evidence against individuals collected by observation rather than by merely counting the number of violations reported. The latter approach aroused too much public disaffection.[88]

Withholding vacations represented an extreme penalty for wayward policemen. The standard departmental sanctions for misbehavior were written warnings and reprimands, fines, and detention. Being a few minutes late for duty could result, at least for those who had a record of such behavior, in a fine equivalent to about a day's wages.[89] Drinking, sleeping, and conversing about unofficial matters while on duty were frequent causes for warnings and fines, as were any hints of disrespecct in the presence of superiors.[90]

Preoccupation with replicating strict military-style discipline found symbolic expression in the loving attention given to police uniforms. Each rank sought to ensure that its uniform would be conspicuously different from and more impressive than that of the ranks below it. Even men at the bottom of the police hierarchy considered an elaborate military-style uniform important as a means of raising police prestige and inspiring respect from a population accustomed to showing deference to the army.[91] Police officials prized a militarized uniform as a constant reminder to the men wearing it of the kind of discipline expected. Before the war, increasing importance attached to wearing the uncomfortable, conspicuous, and provocative spiked helmet.[92]

Despite official preoccupation with discipline, police behavior far short of the ideal did not necessarily disqualify an individual from continuing employment.[93] Take the case of Polizeisergeant Aloysius

Brun of Elberfeld. Joining the police in 1890 after twelve years with the military, he remained on the force until 1902. His record for that period included forty-three disciplinary actions: sixteen warnings and reprimands, twenty-three fines ranging from one to nine marks, and four detentions ranging from one to three days. The infractions noted included drinking or entering a tavern while on duty (fifteen times), failure to carry out an assignment (ten times), leaving his post without permission (eight times), idle talk while on duty (four times), smoking in uniform in public (two times), possession of a watch taken from a prisoner (once), and insubordination (once). The insubordination charge drew the heaviest penalty—three days of detention. By 1902 the decision had finally been made to dismiss Brun, but in view of his long military and police service and his current health problems, he was pensioned off instead.[94]

Of all police disciplinary problems, brutality continued to attract the greatest public and judicial attention. Of twenty-nine convictions of policemen in the Düsseldorf district handed down by the courts in 1892 and 1893, sixteen were for inflicting bodily harm. The court-determined sentences in these cases ranged from one to nine months in jail but usually were commuted by higher authorities to no more than two months of fortress arrest.[95] As in the past, such incarceration for brutality did not necessarily preclude further police employment. One Essen Polizeiwachtmeister, for example, served a ten-week sentence in 1903, yet continued on the force until judged unacceptable—because of his drinking—for transfer to the new royal Schutzmannschaft created in 1909.[96]

Police supervisors who had typically served many years in the military were predisposed to regard subordinates who could claim only minimal military service as seriously lacking in discipline. For their part, at least some rank-and-file communal policemen questioned the appropriateness of military-style discipline for a civilian force and resented being subject to punishments not applied to other city employees. Among such punishments was detention (*Arreststrafe*), which was objected to as bringing public discredit to individual policemen and their families.[97] Although detention was seldom used (usually only from one to four times a year in Düsseldorf and Elberfeld during the first decade of the twentieth century and not at all in Duisburg during that same period), police administrators insisted that the option should be retained as a deterrent and as an alternative to dismissal.[98] In Elberfeld, Polizeisergeanten objected to the practice of recording penalties in the police reports. Although names were indicated by first letter only, discovery of individual identities was easy enough, leading to the humiliation of those involved.[99]

Expected by their officers to embody both military honor and bureaucratic rectitude and confronted by a proletariat that often met police efforts with ridicule as well as distrust, policemen were sensitive to insult. In 1913, for example, Duisburg's approximately 250-man force reported 103 instances in which they claimed to have been slandered, usually by workers.[100] Policemen frequently turned to the courts for redress, and punishment of those found guilty could be harsh. A drunken or excited worker heard to compare a patrolman to one of the lower members of the animal kingdom, a common occurrence, could expect to pay a fine equivalent to several days' wages or spend that number of days in jail.[101] A Düsseldorf policeman even brought suit in 1900 against a mason's apprentice for proposing that an assembly being observed by the policeman close with a cheer for that official.[102] In one noteworthy case, a bookseller in Kattowitz in Silesia was fined fifty marks plus court costs in 1912 because he had sent a social democratic election flier to a Polizeisergeant. The court ruled it slanderous to assume that a policeman could possibly be interested in social democracy. The Düsseldorf Regierungspräsident was so impressed by this decision that he encouraged all Landräte and mayors to inform local policemen of its nature.[103]

Although police personnel were expected to guard their honor, some police administrators feared that the readiness of some patrolmen to take offense at the slightest mutterings of irate citizens into whose lives they intruded made the police appear ridiculous. In addition, police officers were concerned that court cases carried with them the danger of making public police misdeeds that had provoked the insults in the first place. Cases involving confrontations between policemen and shopkeepers or building contractors were especially likely to lead to accusations of police solicitation of gifts or favors in exchange for more lenient regulation. Therefore, police grievances against members of the public were preferably investigated by the department first before turning to the courts.[104]

In their efforts to create more disciplined and reliable police forces to patrol burgeoning industrial cities, Prussian officials during the last prewar years were especially concerned that communal policemen, emulating local organized workers, might form organizations of their own. Police administrators were instructed to move immediately to crush any such efforts. Even regional conferences of communal Polizeiinspektoren, begun in the 1890s and intended to permit the exchange of professional experience, were not completely above suspicion and were subject to discreet surveillance.[105] The Polizeiinspektoren, for their part, refused to recognize any organizational activity by their subordinates as legitimate, even in those instances where the stated goals were sociability and mutual aid. Rank-and-file policemen, their officers believed, lacked the education and insight needed to recognize the limits that could not be exceeded without damaging police discipline.[106]

Recruitment drives launched by organizations such as the *Bund kommunaler Polizeibeamten Preussens* (League of Prussian Communal Policemen), founded in 1909, met scant success in the Düsseldorf district. By the end of 1912, the Bund had reportedly garnered a mere sixty-nine members in the Regierungsbezirk, and local police administrations were moving quickly to reverse even those modest gains. In this campaign, unrelenting opposition to organizational freedom for policemen was repeatedly justified on the basis of the inconsistency of such activity with the military character of police discipline. Officials argued that only malcontents would be drawn to the organizations, and they would in turn use them as vehicles for undermining the discipline and internal cohesion regarded as essential to policing.[107] Policemen who persisted in advocating any type of organizational activity faced dismissal.[108]

Those who administered the Düsseldorf district's urban police insisted so rigidly on preserving the forms of militarized discipline in part because they had serious doubts about many of the rank-and-file policemen they employed, doubts fed by the major prewar changes that had taken place in both the environment and personnel of policing. Policemen who argued that they and their fellows would give better service if treated with more respect met general incomprehension from superiors who regarded them as a generally rough, poorly educated, and potentially unreliable lot, of questionable worthiness of the proud traditions of either the Prussian military or the administrative bureaucracy.

CHAPTER SEVEN

Police and Daily Life, 1890–1914

PROVIDING SERVICES

As indicated in chapter 3, as early as the 1850s at least some police officials in the Düsseldorf district were questioning the broad array of tasks assigned to their men, responsibilities above and beyond those directly relating to law enforcement and public safety. More than half a century later, the successors of those questioners found themselves confronted by a situation that had not changed greatly. On the eve of the First World War, communal policemen still spent much of their time carrying out such miscellaneous routine duties as distributing tax and registration forms, enumerating buildings and animals, keeping lists of children to be vaccinated and of horses and men liable to military service, providing a variety of identity papers needed by citizens, making certain various fees were paid, and licensing and inspecting a wide range of enterprises and activities.[1]

To be sure, by the beginning of the twentieth century numerous older police responsibilities had either lapsed or been transferred to newly emergent, specialized agencies. Fire fighting and street lighting, for example, were removed from police budgets. In Duisburg in 1901 and in Krefeld in 1908, shelters for the homeless were established as an alternative to accepting overnight lodgers in the jails. This departure from previous practice was, however, limited, as oversight of these new institutions was assigned to Polizeisergeanten living on the premises.[2]

As urban service providers became more diverse and specialized, social welfare workers began to assume some functions policemen had performed in the past. In Duisburg in 1907 a deaconess was employed by the city, joined shortly thereafter by a second. The two, in cooperation with local women's and religious associations, took over from the police the placement and supervision of foster children as well as the counseling of "morally endangered" women and girls and of unmarried couples living together. The city administration hoped that in such cases the woman's touch would prove more beneficial than the heavy hand of the police, although the threat of police intervention remained if feminine solicitude failed.[3] At the same time, however, that the police cooperated with the new social workers in regulating the behavior of those who were poor, transient, or otherwise outside the limits of respectable society, they strongly discouraged what remained of the more boisterous traditional customs of community self-policing. To counter the long-established practice of *Katzenmusik* (noisy public demonstrations staged three nights in a row before the residence of offenders against local mores), the police, if possible, dispersed the crowd in the process of formation and penalized the ringleaders.[4] The police and their superiors insisted that public authorities, not self-generated popular groups, should decide what sanctions were to be imposed for misdeeds and against whom. Determining what behavior was permissible and what forbidden was a critical prerogative of the state.

In the cities of the Düsseldorf district up to 1914, despite reassignment of duties, little overall narrowing of police function occurred. The shedding of some older police assignments was counterbalanced by the imposition of new ones. Communal policemen remained deeply enmeshed in many aspects of the daily lives of their fellow citizens, especially those of modest means.

Among police responsibilities were those arising from official concern with public health and sanitation. Before the First World War more and more health-related monitoring was transferred to technically trained specialized personnel,[5] but much remained for the police to do. In Duisburg in 1893, for example, the city, following an outbreak of cholera, provided a disinfection service. For a fee, policemen would pick up and deliver items to be disinfected.[6] In addition, policemen inspected latrines and monitored the removal of wastes. Continued police responsibility for the regulation of stray and unmuzzled dogs was also in part a health measure, linked to prevention of rabies.

Furthermore, concern with public health could be used as one justification for the inspection of housing, another major task for the police, even where specialized urban housing inspectors had been appointed. In Düsseldorf in 1909, the police inspected 16,828 dwellings, whereas the city's housing inspectors examined only 2,891. In 1902 the comparable figures had been 6,165 inspections by the police and 4,228 by the housing inspectors. The city administration described inspections by the police as a service to tenants, making it possible for renters to bring pressure on their landlords to correct deficiencies.[7] At the same time, however, inspections of rental housing provided the authorities with an excuse for increased police observation of the private lives of poorer citizens. Special attention was paid to households including boarders, since worried bourgeois observers of working-class life saw the presence of outsiders in a family setting as fraught with potential for increased immorality. However, efforts to prevent overcrowding and thereby presumably to lessen temptations to promiscuity often proved impossible to enforce because of the lack of alternative accommodations in rapidly growing industrial cities.[8]

As in the past, many new tasks devolved upon the police simply because they represented a widely dispersed body of public servants, available on an around-the-clock, seven-days-a-week basis and with closer contact to the daily life of the general populace than most public employees had. In addition, utilization of the communal police for a wide variety of highly visible services helped legitimate their costly and intrusive presence in the eyes of city councilmen and local taxpayers. Representative of the catchall nature of many new responsibilities assigned to the police was the decision to entrust them with the maintenance of lost-and-found services. In Elberfeld the police also took the initiative in establishing and staffing facilities enabling the public to call taxis, with operating costs being paid by the taxi owners. In their expanding regulation of markets, local transport, and insurance contracts, the police cast themselves as the guardians of consumer interests, often arousing the resentment of small traders, carters, and cab drivers in the process.[9]

Among services businessmen sought from the police was increased access to the masses of information collected on urban residents. In 1900 and 1902 the minister of the interior ordered the police to supply businesses with the names, addresses, and birthdates of individuals sought as debtors.[10] Before the First World War, police in the district's major cities were also providing advertising agencies with lists of names, addresses, and occupations of well-to-do potential customers.[11]

Among the most troublesome of requests for assistance that came to the police were those linked to master-servant relations. Until 1918, police remained responsible for monitoring contracts entered into by domestic servants. When difficulties arose, both sides to a dispute might turn to the police for support. The police could try to mediate or impose fines to force compliance with their decisions, but they could not really make someone work in a household who refused to do so. Disputes between landlords and tenants and among neighbors often proved equally intractable.[12]

With requests for intervention and assistance coming from so many sources, the communal police tried to free themselves from some of their most menial and irksome tasks. But their successes remained limited. In Elberfeld in 1906, for instance, the police informed the local continuation school that they could not, without detracting from "real police responsibilities," repeatedly delegate patrolmen to conduct truants to school.[13] In that same year, however, Düsseldorf policemen accompanied 567 reluctant boys and girls to schools of various kinds.[14]

MAKING ARRESTS

In the public reporting of their activities, the district's police dwelt less upon the hodgepodge of routine services they performed for state and municipal administrators and local citizens than upon situations involving use of their powers to arrest and penalize. During the Wilhelmian era, calls for the urban police to respond to crimes against both persons and property increased, and official action against individuals who had merely violated police ordinances lessened somewhat.

Police departments in the Düsseldorf district perceived the most worrisome increases in prewar crime in those communities experiencing the most rapid urban and industrial development: especially in and around Düsseldorf, Duisburg, and Essen.[15] In Duisburg, reported property crime soared from 63.3 cases per 10,000 population in 1890–91 to 209 in 1913. During that same period, violent crimes reported in that city climbed from 29.4 to 51.9 per 10,000 population (see Appendix, table A–4). This dramatic increase was closely linked to the annexation of surrounding proletarian communities by the city during the first decade of the new century. As a result of such annexations, Duisburg's population rose from 92,731 in 1902 to 203,436 in 1906. By 1906, the city's police department confronted a situation that had been transformed both quantitatively and qualitatively.

For the elites of the district's fastest growing municipalities, any rise in reported crime rates was likely to be interpreted as the result of an influx of working–class outsiders, especially those coming long distances from Prussia's eastern provinces or even from foreign countries to seek jobs in heavy industry.[16] In the Oberhausen mining district located between Essen and Duisburg, to take an extreme example, of 29,352 coal miners employed in 1904, 7,977 had arrived from the Prussian east and 5,903 were foreigners, mostly from Austria-Hungary, the Netherlands, and Italy.[17]

The newcomers of the last prewar decades were disproportionately young males, including many who did not speak German. Between

1900 and 1912, the Düsseldorf district's Polish-speaking population increased from 27,105 to 75,341. In Hamborn in 1910, 17.1 percent of the population consisted of Polish speakers.[18] Settled residents were inclined to view these new arrivals as prone to lawless, often violent, acts.[19] Hamborn had a "wild west" reputation. According to Erhard Lucas, formidable gangs of forty to fifty miners carrying their pickaxes were to be encountered in Hamborn's streets.[20]

The newcomers were considered particularly likely to be implicated in incidents involving the use of weapons. The bloody 1899 strike of young Polish-speaking miners in Herne in neighboring Westphalia heightened fears of the supposed gun-toting, knife-wielding ways of recent migrants.[21] The district Polizeikommissar in Düsseldorf, commenting on miners coming to the Ruhr from the Prussian east, reported in 1904 the widely held assumption that such individuals acquired first watches, then revolvers, as soon as possible after their arrival.[22]

Understandably, the concern of the police and their superiors about violent acts committed in proletarian settings was especially great when policemen themselves were the targets. Policemen were well aware of their widespread unpopularity, which found expression in the readiness of working-class bystanders to jeer and obstruct patrolmen attempting to make arrests.[23] In Duisburg, the number of reported incidents involving resistance to public authority increased from an average 2.14 per year per ten thousand population in the 1880s to 6.24 in the 1890s and 6.16 in the first decade of the twentieth century.[24]

During the first six months of 1900, Düsseldorf policemen reported suffering seven serious, twenty-one moderate, and six minor injuries as a result of encounters with the populace. How police wounds were inflicted provides some indication of how and to what extent offenders were armed. Of forty-nine serious injuries sustained by Düsseldorf policemen between 1890 and the first half of 1900, nineteen were caused by knives, fourteen resulted from blows from a variety of objects at hand (e.g., stones, bottles, work tools, household implements), and seven were the result of being kicked or punched. In addition, five of the policemen were assaulted with clubs, walking sticks, or brass knuckles, and three were cut by bayonets (presumably wrested from the policemen themselves). Despite official concern about firearms, only one policeman suffered a gunshot wound.[25]

In the Düsseldorf district, the fears harbored by government officials and local property owners of an increasingly armed and violence-prone population translated into demands for greater limitation of workers' access to weapons. In Prussia's western industrial areas, police ordinances in 1872 and 1894 had already made carrying a broad range of weapons dependent upon possession of a license.[26] Such licenses were to be granted only to individuals with a proven need and of known reliability. Automatically excluded were workers, especially those who were young and foreign.[27] The police were even hesitant about permitting watchmen employed by private companies to carry weapons, seeing their arms as an infringement of a police prerogative as well as a potential source of troublesome incidents.[28]

From 1898 to 1900, over three-fourths of all reported violations of the district's ordinances relating to the possession and use of weapons were recorded in the Ruhr or in and around Düsseldorf, clearly indicating the areas that were the prime focus of official concerns about violence. Particularly noteworthy in this regard were the city and county of Essen. With 1,339 prosecutions for weapons violations during the three years up to and including 1900, Essen and its surrounding industrial settlements accounted for 42.8 percent of all such cases in the district.[29]

In the aftermath of the 1899 Herne strike, demands for stricter limitations on access to weapons multiplied. In particular, police officials wished to permit the sale of arms only to individuals who already possessed licenses to carry them. However, proposals to issue such an ordinance for the entire Rhine province encountered effective resistance. The minister of the interior explained that responsible citizens who desired weapons for their own protection would be inconvenienced and the arms trade would be damaged.[30]

But what was not possible for the whole Rhine province proved feasible for the Düsseldorf administrative district. In 1905 a stricter police ordinance regulating the sale and possession of weapons was issued specifically for that highly industrialized area, while more permissive ordinances remained in place for the rest of the province. The advantage of using district-level police ordinances rather than statewide legislation to regulate access to arms was that restrictions could be tailored to particular areas where the need was deemed greatest without forcing unpopular change in less sensitive Prussian lands.

Paralleling the campaign to contain the spread of weapons among the working-class population of the Düsseldorf district were efforts to put more firearms in the hands of its urban police. Until the end of the nineteenth century, government officials and local elites hesitated to entrust rank-and-file patrolmen with guns, fearing that such men lacked the sophistication to make wise use of deadly weapons. As late as 1897, when Polizeiinspektor Terpe in Duisburg had secured approval from the minister of the interior to arm men patrolling outlying areas with revolvers, the city council objected on the grounds of possible misuse of such weapons.[31] By contrast, as noted by Wilbur Miller, American policemen were allowed much more individual discretion than their transatlantic counterparts and started carrying firearms at an early date. In New York patrolmen began, unofficially, to carry revolvers in 1857. In Boston, the city council provided for the routine arming of all patrolmen with revolvers beginning in 1884.[32]

As the twentieth century began, resistance to equipping Prussian patrolmen with firearms finally dissipated, not because of growing confidence in the reliability of ordinary policemen but because of increased fears in the areas of fastest industrial growth of a highly mobile and increasingly alien working class. The first to receive revolvers were men assigned to especially dangerous areas and also members of the newly created criminal divisions. The argument for arming the detectives ahead of most patrolmen was not only their more frequent contact with criminals but also the supposedly greater reliability of this more select body.[33] By 1905 the arming of policemen in the Ruhr had proceeded far enough that the Landrat in Essen could express dismay when royal Schutzmänner, sent from Cologne to provide supplemental support during that year's Ruhr coal strike, arrived without revolvers. The Landrat argued that miners armed with guns could hardly be expected to respect policemen not similarly equipped.[34]

In the new century the argument in favor of deadlier arms for the police shifted significantly from the danger of random attacks on individual patrolmen to the need to contain strikes and mass protest. In the aftermath of the bloody Moabit demonstrations in Berlin in 1910 that left two dead and over two hundred injured, the interior ministry stepped up its support for more heavily armed policemen.[35] In this context, requests for rifles began to supplement, but not displace, pleas for more revolvers. Both types of firearms were increasingly seen as necessary: rifles for subduing unruly crowds, revolvers for subduing unruly individuals.[36]

Yet, at the same time that arming policemen was becoming more common, at least some of the district's police officials were exchanging ideas about alternatives to deadly force. They were aware that killing or wounding citizens was likely to increase antipolice sentiment. Also the capture and safe delivery of prisoners without recourse to firearms would bolster a desired image of bureaucratic efficiency and adherence to proper procedure. Police departments sought to demonstrate how up-to-date and scientific they were by introducing new techniques for dealing with resistance to their commands. Speaking to his colleagues from other industrial cities in 1913, Polizeiinspektor Adolph of Elberfeld optimistically surveyed the most promising possibilities. In particular, he recommended greater use of armor and shields, tear gas, and police dogs.[37]

The introduction of police dogs was an especially favored innovation at the beginning of the twentieth century. They were perceived first and foremost as a means of protecting patrolmen in isolated areas. Two-man patrols, designed to discourage attacks on policemen in dangerous settings, could be displaced by individual policemen with dogs.[38] At the same time, police departments also made increased use of horses in the patrol of outlying areas. Not only could more ground be covered by men on horseback, but also mounted policemen were deemed more intimidating than those on foot.[39]

MAINTAINING ORDER

Even in cities that aroused the greatest official concern, most day-to-day police work did not involve confrontations with dangerous criminals or armed workers running amok. Reports of assaults and thefts remained far fewer than police-identified violations of local ordinances. Most police actions continued to be the result of police initiative rather than a response to calls for help from victims of crime. The police of the German states, especially Prussia, had long had an unenviable reputation for excessive concentration on the petty.[40] Perceived overreaction to minor violations not only elicited annoyance or animosity from the individuals affected but also often made the police appear absurd. Newspapers representing a variety of political viewpoints delighted in reporting instances of police overzealousness.

Officials responsible for overseeing the police were not oblivious to the problem. In 1907 and 1908, for example, the Düsseldorf Regierungspräsident advised the district's police administrators that their men should largely ignore violations that were not regarded as such by most of the public. He had in mind especially drunkenness. Drunks, he believed, should be left alone unless they represented a danger to themselves or others. He also warned against actions harsher than the situation demanded. He referred specifically to an embarrassing incident in Düsseldorf where the police held a man in jail overnight (deprived for that period of his clothes and suspenders) for riding his bicycle after dark without a light, even though the man had volunteered to leave his bicycle and twenty marks as a guarantee of his return on the following day.[41]

The police were ordered to exercise particular restraint when dealing with individuals in military uniform. Rather than offend the army or provide the public with the spectacle of an open confrontation of policemen and soldiers, patrolmen were advised to refrain from taking action except in the most serious circumstances. Instead they were supposed to report incidents to the superiors of the men involved and allow military authorities to take whatever steps they deemed appropriate.[42]

Among the police departments of the Düsseldorf district, Duisburg's force published the most comprehensive reports concerning violations of ordinances. In that city, as noted in chapter 4, enforcement of local police ordinances had been especially strict in the troubled years leading up to the antisocialist law. Thereafter, the incidence of penalties fell off substantially to a level that did not fluctuate greatly from the 1880s into the next century. Neither the sharp rise in the number of police ordinances to be enforced nor the mass incorporation of largely proletarian suburbs after the turn of the century led to a marked surge in penalties handed down by the Duisburg police (see Appendix, table A–3).

But if the overall number of penalties did not change dramatically, the recorded frequency of specific violations did. A comparison of the five most commonly recorded violations of 1890–91 with those of 1909 (the last year for which comparable figures are available) reveals truancy in first place in both instances, but by a much narrower margin in 1909. This relative decline probably reflects both changes in enforcement policy and an actual decrease over time in truant behavior. Disorderly conduct continued in a modestly strengthened second place. The relative importance of enforcing ordinances relating to keeping streets clean and unobstructed as well as those relating to the ownership of dogs declined. Meanwhile, registration of residence, regarded as vital for keeping track of a mobile and expanding proletarian population, received much more attention. At the same time, the growing number of penalties imposed on owners of bicycles in 1909 pointed to the increasing significance that traffic-related functions would have for the urban police in the twentieth century (see table 5).

A bewildering and expanding multiplicity of police ordinances served not only such ostensible purposes as protecting public health, discouraging fraud, and regulating traffic, but also provided the authorities with convenient justification for restricting the activities of individuals or groups who were deemed suspect by their very nature. Thus, for example, health and safety regulations could be used to deny access to halls engaged for political meetings. Traffic ordinances could serve as grounds for disrupting legal picketing.[43] And as the minister of the interior explained to his subordinates in 1911, the police could always find a reason for denying a travel permit to gypsies because they had

TABLE 5

Most Commony Recorded Ordinance Violations in Duisburg

Violation	Number Penalties Imposed	Percent of Total
1890–91[a]		
Truancy	1,936	40.4
Disorderly Conduct	696	14.5
Street Ordinances	416	8.7
Dog Ordinances	334	7.0
Registration of Residence	295	6.1
1909[b]		
Truancy	5,315	25.2
Disorderly Conduct	3,575	17.0
Registration of Residence	3,294	15.7
Street Ordinances	1,033	4.9
Bicycle Ordinances	1,024	4.9

Source: *Bericht über den Stand und die Verwaltung der Gemeinde-Angelegenheiten der Stadt Duisburg* (Duisburg, 1891), pp. 118–19, and (1909), pp. 151–53.
[a]Total penalties in 1890–91: 4,795 (1 for every 12 residents)
[b]Total penalties in 1909: 21,043 (1 for every 10 residents)

invariably infringed some local ordinance. Among likely violations were failure of gypsies to provide adequately for the education of their children, failure to secure lodging, begging, commission of an immoral act, damage to property, resistance to authority, disturbing the peace, and spreading human and animal diseases.[44]

Gypsies were among those groups whose very existence was an affront to settled, respectable society. Although few in number, their appearance in or near the district's cities was always cause for concern. The police responded by escorting newly arrived gypsies to the city limits and tried to make certain that their visit was unpleasant enough to discourage return in the future.[45] In 1912, following prompting by the minister of the interior, a police ordinance for the Rhine province outlawed group travel by gypsies and those who lived like gypsies.[46]

Beggars and vagrants were accorded much the same reception as gypsies. The police continued their frequent inspections of disreputable lodging places, and in Düsseldorf they instituted regular "beggar patrols" by plainclothes patrolmen to round up offenders, especially those who frequented busy downtown streets.[47] In 1907 the Düsseldorf Polizeiinspektor sought to stimulate the beggar patrols to greater efforts by making seniority pay increments dependent upon the arrest of at least five beggars a month. This policy, leaked to the press (probably by a disgruntled policeman), was publicized throughout Germany, much to the embarrassment of the superiors of the police official responsible.[48]

MONITORING LEISURE AND MORALS

Among local police ordinances were several relating to the regulation of popular amusements. As the ten-hour day and early closing on Saturday became standard in many factories before the First World War, workers found themselves with increased—though still very limited—free time.[49] How laborers used their greater leisure was a matter of serious concern to those above them in the urban hierarchy. The police were called upon to ensure that workers at play neither offended those who did not share their notion of fun nor damaged society's prospects for future stability and productivity by undermining values of thrift, hard work, and family obligation.

During the last prewar decades, chambers of commerce and other organizations representing employer interests were in the forefront of the campaign for government action to reduce the number of public dances and other festivities (especially Kirmessen) appealing to a working-class clientele.[50] In Düsseldorf the chamber of commerce claimed that its 1908 survey indicated seventy-two days a year customarily given over to Kirmessen in one or another part of the city or its neighboring county.[51] Employers argued that improved transportation and urban growth meant that workers were easily lured to increasing numbers of celebrations. Although more and more employers came to recognize that workers needed at least some leisure, if only to allow them to revive their energies for renewed labor, businessmen wanted their employees to use their free time for such wholesome pursuits as gardening, walks, family visits, or company-sponsored recreations, not for sporadic bouts of all-out celebration. Although police and local officials in the Düsseldorf administrative district were far from insensitive to the employers' concerns, efforts to comply with their wishes by significantly reducing the number of Kirmessen and other popular festivals often resulted in a strong public outcry. Tavern owners, brewers, butchers, bakers, and musicians pointed to the business they stood to lose. Would-be celebrants and upholders of local traditions complained of the threat to customary practice. Caught in the middle, the police and their immediate superiors looked for compromises.[52]

While the Prussian government did move to eliminate some of the traditional fairs, Kirmessen, and other festivals, especially in highly industrialized areas, it proved generally willing over time to permit increased numbers of public entertainments, at least those not entailing the display of opposition symbols or the proclamation of dissident ideas. In particular, government regulations allowed the holding of more, not fewer, public dances. In 1860 in the Düsseldorf district, approved tavern keepers could sponsor dances for Kirmes, carnival, the day after Christmas, New Year's Eve, and the king's birthday. By 1905 the number of permissible dates had risen to twenty-six. And by 1909, public dances could be held on any Sunday as well as on specified special occasions, provided the local police consented.[53]

One important reason for this greater permissiveness was the growing number of dances and other entertainments being organized by private associations for their members. Many sponsoring associations, authorities believed, existed only to circumvent police controls on amusements.[54] The proliferation of such organizations made government authorities, if grudgingly, more tolerant of public entertainments. They strongly preferred amusements open to the public and under police supervision to ostensibly private celebrations beyond their direct observation.

In this context, government officials came to see the growing entertainment business in major cities of the Düsseldorf district as at least partly beneficial. Among its merits was the substantial economic contribution from out-of-town visitors and the provision of employment. Another perceived merit was the potential of commercial amusements to function as counterattractions to the recreational activities offered by organizations linked to opposition movements. The lapsing of the antisocialist law in 1890 had opened the way for increased numbers of such associations. Authorities definitely preferred to see worker leisure spent on commercial amusements rather than on socialist or union activities. To be sure, many would-be reformers of working-class life held up such new amenities as parks, city forests, playing fields, and museums as worthy claimants for the free time of urban inhabitants, but other bourgeois residents were less than enthusiastic about seeing workers—especially those who were young and unmarried—actually make use of those facilities.

Commercial establishments offered relative ease of surveillance by scheduling amusements for specified times and places. In addition, the entrepreneurs of entertainment, with much to lose through noncompliance, could usually be prevailed upon to collaborate with the police in maintaining order. Policies relating to the enforcement of closing hours reveal how cooperation by owners of places of entertainment could be fostered. In 1896, police responses to a government survey about closing hours indicated that in most of the district's biggest cities the official eleven o'clock curfew was not being enforced for most licensed establishments, particularly those in downtown entertainment districts. As long as operators stayed on the good side of the police, they were allowed to remain open at least until midnight. But for those who did not cooperate, the curfew was strictly enforced. Police departments argued forcefully against revising closing-hour ordinances to bring them into line with actual practice because then they would lose the threat of selective enforcement against those who incurred their disfavor.[55]

By 1906 enforcement of closing hours for the majority of big-city establishments had become even more permissive. In justifying such flexibility the Barmen police pointed to the difficulty of rigorous enforcement and the frequency of court decisions reversing police efforts to secure compliance, thereby undermining police prestige.[56] In Barmen and elsewhere during the last prewar years, premises approved by the police were permitted to stay open to one or two in the morning, even all night in some instances. The police still argued, however, for leaving the official curfew at eleven o'clock, as a threat to those not inclined to cooperate.[57]

One exception the police typically made to their general tolerance of later closings was for establishments employing women to serve drinks. Where women worked at night, especially if, as was common, their income derived totally or in large part from tips or from a commission on sales, police assumed they were employed to entice customers to drink and spend more than they otherwise would. As a result of the police decision to enforce closings of 10:00, 9:00, or even 8:00 P.M. where bar hostesses were involved, the number of businesses conspicuously employing women, on the rise in the first years of the new century, declined. In Duisburg, for instance, the number of such establishments (so-called *Animierkneipen*) reportedly rose from five to fifteen after the turn of the century, then plunged to two by 1911 as a consequence of restrictive police ordinances. Lynn Abrams has suggested that such regulatory successes were at least in part the result of using a narrow definition of Animierkneipe, which permitted questionable practices to survive untroubled at many establishments that had not been targeted for special surveillance.[58]

The police also attempted to enforce restrictive hours in relationship to opening times for drinking establishments with working-class clienteles. The police were supposed to prevent the sale of spirits before 8:00 A.M. The purpose of such a ban was to keep workers from drinking while on their way to a day shift or while returning from a night shift. The assumption was that most laborers were at work or at home by 8:00 A.M., thus making it safe to lift restrictions on the sale of alcohol. To ensure that such ordinances did not unduly inconvenience bourgeois travelers, establishments serving railway passengers and hotels serving their overnight guests were exempted.[59]

Regulations relating to opening hours proved difficult to enforce. Tavern operators and customers engaged in mutually agreeable transactions. Side doors were used while main entrances remained locked. Efforts by the police to collect evidence of infractions by having plainclothesmen order spirits before 8:00 A.M. aroused widespread indignation. The publicity generated by such efforts was so unfavorable that the police often abandoned them. The Elberfeld force did so in 1905. The Düsseldorf police, however, were still using plainclothesmen for this purpose in 1913.[60]

Whatever problems the police encountered in attempting to regulate establishments offering such time-honored pastimes as drinking and dancing, they worried most about entertainments that were new, that had a predominantly youthful or working-class clientele, or that could be used for the dissemination of ideas. Especially noteworthy on all three counts was the advent of motion picture theaters.

The new theaters were immediately popular. In Elberfeld, for instance, annual attendance soared from 126,000 in 1906 to 880,650 in 1911. Like live theater, films were subject to precensorship by the police, with emphasis upon removing all politically, religiously, or morally controversial subject matter. By 1912 this function had become centralized for all of Prussia as a responsibility of the Berlin police. In line with mounting official concern for protecting the morality of the young, attendance by children and adolescents was strictly regulated.[61]

At the same time, in the struggle to safeguard the future by preserving the morals of the younger generation, officials expected the police to report to parents and teachers those youngsters caught singing objectionable carnival songs, to root out provocative new dance crazes, to discourage the sale of popular fiction of questionable content, and to monitor the amount of flesh that could be exposed during mixed bathing. While acknowledging, for instance, that bathing trunks, rather than the less revealing bathing costumes, could be worn at pools and beaches in and around Berlin, the Barmen police administration saw no reason why such permissiveness should extend to the Wuppertal.[62] In Bottrop, north of Essen, according to Franz Brüggemeier and Lutz

Niethammer, the mayor charged the police with reporting children who spent more than fifty pfennige at Kirmes celebrations, the assumption being that larger sums were unlikely to have been acquired honestly.[63] Campaigns to protect youth and their families from the corrupting temptations of the modern urban world proved, however, difficult to implement and had the potential for making the police appear ridiculous and bothersome to many.

In their efforts to protect the next generation, the police even encountered some legal barriers. For example, a 1902 district police ordinance forbade the sale of distilled spirits to schoolchildren for transport to some other site. In 1908, however, a Duisburg innkeeper successfully appealed his conviction on this charge. The court ruled that the ordinance represented an unwarranted intrusion into private interests. Parents and other adults were not to be deprived of their right to send children to fetch refreshments, even if the result was to make youthful access to alcohol easier.[64]

Of all issues relating to the policing of public morals, the most troublesome remained prostitution. The police, who continued to regard prostitution as inevitable, were under recurring pressure from local residents who did not wish to have prostitutes as neighbors, and from clergy, associations of moral reformers, and newspapers advocating a cleansing of urban life. One common reason residents objected to the presence of prostitutes was the increased police intrusion it brought into their neighborhoods.[65] Confronting prostitution could motivate neighbors to undertake self-policing. In Barmen in 1900, for instance, the mayor reported that the city had only four registered women. He attributed this low number to the unwillingness of community members to tolerate the presence of prostitutes.[66]

For their part, the police remained convinced that, aside from enforcement of medical examinations, too vigorous implementation of ordinances relating to prostitution would be counterproductive. In Krefeld, for example, known prostitutes were confined to houses on two shabby streets. Police oversight extended to such matters as who could be employed as a cleaning woman in such domiciles. The Krefeld police believed centralization eased supervision and reduced streetwalking, and they hesitated to make life too difficult for the women and their customers for fear of causing them to disperse.[67] In Düsseldorf the police argued for a degree of tolerance for street prostitution in areas already affected, believing that attempted suppression would only result in increased opportunities for pimps. In addition, certain bars and cafes that sheltered prostitutes were permitted to operate freely, in the interests of having a focus for police surveillance, of keeping other entertainment establishments from being troubled with an unwanted clientele, and finally of keeping prostitutes as much as possible off the streets.[68]

For the police, the registration of prostitutes had the advantage not only of making possible the monitoring of their health and their activities but also of providing an incentive to those outside the system to behave more discreetly than they might without the threat of being placed under police supervision.[69] As a general rule, on the eve of the First World War, police authorities in the largest cities of the Düsseldorf administrative district were more convinced than ever that regulation and segregation were preferable to outright prohibition not just for prostitution but also for most leisure activities, especially those offered to adults by commercial enterprises in central entertainment districts. The massive expansion of big-city police departments in the last quarter of the nineteenth century and the first years of the twentieth century had provided the resources needed for close surveillance of such establishments.[70]

Small towns and villages remained much less intensively policed, and there, authorities reasoned, more prohibitions were in order. In particular, taverns were compelled to close at an early hour. As in the case of restrictions on the leisure pursuits of the young, officials hoped to shield the inhabitants of small town and countryside from the supposedly corrupting influence of big-city ways.

Also less intensively policed were rapidly expanding industrial suburbs and new cities springing into existence in areas only recently opened to industrial development. With high infrastructure costs and tax bases limited by the low incomes of mostly proletarian populations, the newest industrial centers had the fewest resources to spare for policing. With populations that were overwhelmingly young, working class, recently arrived, and sometimes ethnically diverse, such settlements represented a special challenge to notions of urban decorum developed in older cities in the course of the nineteenth century. These areas had comparatively few bourgeois inhabitants to voice complaints, but they were viewed with alarm from more established centers. The proliferation of these new rough-and-ready proletarian settlements seemed to officials and men of property to call for stricter policing. One police response was to use their licensing powers to keep the number of taverns in such areas to a minimum.

But if the defenders of the existing order believed more vigilance was needed in newer industrial centers, they remained content to endorse generally more relaxed policies relating to leisure activities in established cities. An important argument in favor of increased flexibility was the desire not to alienate large numbers of citizens by interfering excessively in their recreations, even those that were less than edifying.[71] Because of the continued extensive utilization of the Prussian police for the systematic harassment of opposition groups, as discussed in the next chapter, police relations with much of the population were often characterized by bitterness. There seemed little reason to add unnecessarily to these grievances. Also the police feared that too-vigorous campaigns against forbidden pleasures would only drive such activities underground and make them more difficult to oversee.

Although, on the eve of the war, employers complained as much or more than ever about amusements they believed tempted workers to use their free time for debauchery rather than for the regeneration of their strength, and clergymen and moral reformers continued to call for support in their crusades against the feared corruption of urban life, the police and their superiors had increasingly come to see big-city entertainments and recreations as more diversion than threat and reacted accordingly. They had found that routine surveillance of the kind large urban police forces were well suited to provide, backed by the extensive powers of the bureaucratic state to license, tax, and to set hours as well as health and safety standards, frequently represented the most effective and least disruptive means of responding to changes in daily life.

CHAPTER EIGHT

Police and Organized Workers, 1890–1914

POLITICAL SURVEILLANCE

The routine daily tasks of the police described in chapter 7, although important in their own right, also served the essential function of keeping much enlarged urban police forces occupied and visible to broad segments of the public while waiting to be called upon to respond to possible collective challenges to established authority. The lapsing of the antisocialist law and the growth and increased activity of organized labor, in conjunction with the investment of far greater resources in big-city police departments, translated into official expectations that the police would play an ever greater role in suppressing any significant disruptions of urban life that might occur. In 1905, the mayoral assistant (*Beigeordneter*) responsible for administering the Düsseldorf police boasted that he could, if a threatening situation materialized, assemble 120 policemen at any point in the city within 20 to 30 minutes.[1] Conceivably, if police forces were formidable enough, their very presence would help prevent minor incidents from escalating into serious confrontations. Demoralizing recourse to the military would become less frequent, as does indeed seem to have been the case for the German Empire in the last decades before the First World War.[2] This did not, however, prevent the army from devising and continuously reviewing elaborate plans for intervening to quell civil disturbances, should the need arise.

Government authorities during the Wilhelmian era emphasized continued careful police surveillance of opposition movements as a crucial first step in keeping potential popular unrest in check. In the early

1890s, memories of the recent 1889 coal strike, along with the demise of the antisocialist law, socialist electoral successes, and sensational news of anarchist assassinations in other parts of Europe combined to make close political oversight seem especially important.[3] The Reichstag's failure to pass such repressive legislation as the antirevolution bill (*Umsturzvorlage*) of 1894–95 and the penitentiary bill (*Zuchthausvorlage*) of 1899 heightened official determination to make maximum use of the extensive and flexible powers of the police to conduct an ongoing guerrilla war against those classified as the empire's internal enemies.[4] In this campaign, increasing concern focused on Prussia's fastest growing industrial cities, of which the Düsseldorf district had a disproportionate share.

Mayors of important cities received subsidies from the state for political policing.[5] In their oversight of urban affairs, state officials questioned, however, whether communal policemen were equal to the sensitive and demanding task of monitoring political activity. In the interest of ensuring greater expertise, increased zeal, and more centralized direction of political policing, six state-supported district Polizeikommissare were appointed in 1896 for Prussia's western industrial heartland: three for Westphalian and three for Rhenish areas. In the Rhine province, the three district Kommisare were headquartered in Düsseldorf, Elberfeld, and Essen.[6] To avoid the impression of introducing a secret police presence in these cities, the state ordered the new civilian-clad appointees to be as unobtrusive as possible.[7] Organized workers were, however, soon aware who these men were. The institution of the district Polizeikommissare, plagued by controversy throughout its existence, survived until absorbed by the royal police forces formed in the Ruhr in 1909.

The new district Polizeikommissare, to justify their existence and to gain a more complete overview of local political activity, called on communal police forces to make increased use of the rights of surveillance conferred on them by the Prussian Law of Association of 11 March 1850 and to submit numerous detailed reports of their observations. City-appointed police officials grumbled about the heavier work load. In Düsseldorf the mayor protested that drawing up the requested list of the city's 5,000 to 6,000 foreign residents would take the local police four to six weeks. For their part, the district Polizeikommissare complained that the communal police, especially the region's Polizeiinspektoren, resisted providing the required information.[8]

Given the proliferation of working-class associations after 1890, communal police officers were hard pressed to allocate enough personnel to monitor all the meetings that were potentially subject to police oversight. As the Elberfeld police noted in 1905 in response to demands from above for a police presence at all public and private meetings of Polish and socialist associations and trade unions, fulfilling this responsibility would mean delegating uniformed observers to endless routine and often poorly attended gatherings of sixty-one different organizations. Elberfeld's police chief argued for adhering to the established practice of monitoring only those meetings that seemed to warrant special attention because of the identity of the scheduled speaker, the topics to be discussed, or the probable attendance.[9] Police in the Düsseldorf district's other major cities joined in arguing that only selective surveillance was necessary or feasible.[10]

Complicating the problem of delegating adequate personnel for overseeing all working-class political meetings was the assumption that only policemen of the rank of Wachtmeister or above were qualified for this task. Their superiors considered Polizeisergeanten to be too poorly educated, unsophisticated, and sometimes politically unreliable to match wits with socialist spokesmen.[11]

Prussian officials expected local police departments during the Wilhelmian era to be especially vigilant in monitoring open-air meetings, marches, and demonstrations by opposition groups. Because demonstrators sought to attract as much attention as possible, carrying signs and symbols and congregating in busy and conspicuous urban locations, how the police responded was widely noted and discussed by many segments of urban society. For state authorities, prohibition was often the preferred manner of dealing with planned demonstrations. Events associated with May Day celebrations or processions organized by Polish associations were, for example, frequently prohibited on the grounds that they were inherently provocative and therefore constituted a threat to public order, assurances to the contrary notwithstanding.[12] Any display of opposition symbols, especially anything red, could also provide grounds for police intervention. Even ribbons on funeral wreaths were not exempt.[13] In Barmen the outcome of a court case hinged on deciding whether a flag displayed in the streets was actually red or merely a faded violet.[14]

Prior to the First World War, the largest socialist street demonstrations were those associated with the movement for Prussian suffrage reform. In 1906, in the wake of the previous year's revolution in Russia, Prussian officials banned planned marches, setting the stage for a noteworthy clash of police and demonstrators in Hamburg.[15] In Düsseldorf in 1910, however, thousands of demonstrators were allowed to march through the heart of the city, with the police taking a wait-and-see attitude.[16]

In those prewar instances involving confrontations between the police and protesters, the police were aware that their superiors were more likely to criticize them for being too lenient than for acting too harshly. In contending with mass protest, the police drew reassurance from their increased numbers and improved arms and equipment. The availability of horses, dogs, tear gas, armor, and firearms, including rifles, had strengthened the ascendancy of the police in crowd control. Mass arrests had been made easier by the introduction of patrol wagons, which eliminated the necessity for the often troublesome marching of prisoners to the place where they were to be held. And if need be, fire departments could be called upon as well. Fire fighters not only represented a reserve of auxiliary manpower but also could make effective use of their hoses for dispersing demonstrations, as in Remscheid in 1910.[17]

As in the past, police surveillance of the working-class movement during the last prewar decades extended beyond meetings and demonstrations to informal gatherings of all kinds. To this end, policemen were kept busy observing places where workers congregated away from the job. Taverns, as always, were the center of attention. Because of the continued importance of taverns as a primary focus of working-class associational life, the police and their superiors in the early 1890s were disturbed by the proliferation of *Schnapskasinos*, proletarian drinking establishments organized as private cooperatives with closed memberships. As private associations, Schnapskasinos were not subject to regular police surveillance and the enforcement of closing hours.

Schnapskasinos were concentrated in the towns and cities of the Ruhr coalfield. In the Ruhr the police, using licensing powers that had been significantly strengthened by Reichstag legislation in 1879, following a decade of liberalization, had succeeded in holding the granting of new licenses strictly in check, despite mushrooming urban populations. In Essen, for example, by 1898 there were 457 inhabitants per public drinking place compared with only 135 in Berlin. And in Hamborn, the newest of the Ruhr's major cities, the ratio by 1900 was 545; by 1910, there were 764 residents per drinking establishment.[18]

Licensed premises were relatively few and far between in many parts of the Ruhr, and they were largely unavailable to those laborers whose shifts kept them at work until after closing hours. Schnapskasinos provided an opportunity for after-hours drinking and socializing free from police surveillance, a privilege long enjoyed by the members of elite private clubs. Government authorities worried that the new Schnapskasinos not only circumvented normal regulations on taverns but that they also might easily serve as places of socialist and union agitation. This could not be permitted. Passage by the Reichstag in 1896 of a law requiring cooperatives that served alcohol to apply to the police for a concession brought the brief existence of the Schnapskasinos to an end, much to the relief of the police, employers, and those tavern operators who had suffered from the competition.[19]

As they strove to provide the government with required reports about the attitudes and activities of present or potential members of opposition movements, the district's police confronted a particular problem in monitoring growing numbers of Polish-speaking residents. Polish speakers from Prussia's eastern provinces were especially numerous in Ruhr mining. On the eve of World War I, they constituted more than a third of that industry's work force. According to District Polizeikommissar Hansch of Essen, in a report delivered to his colleagues in 1904, ethnic Polish workers who migrated to the Ruhr became demanding and restless in their new environment. They were encouraged, he believed, in this transformation by their contacts with organized German workers and also by the nationalist agitation of business and professional men within the Polish community.[20] So convinced was Hansch of the dangers of Polish nationalism in the Ruhr that he had even argued in 1899 against a proposal to translate temperance tracts from German to Polish so that they could be distributed to Polish-speaking workers. Hansch viewed the battle against excessive drinking as less important than the need to deny official, even if unintentional, sanction to the use of the Polish language in Prussia's western provinces.[21]

Official concern about an ever-greater Polish presence in the industrial west intensified when Polish miners joined their German colleagues in the massive Ruhr coal strike of 1905. In their growing efforts to monitor Polish associations, police in the Düsseldorf district were handicapped by the scarcity of personnel who had the necessary language skills. In Essen in 1908, for instance, none of the 12 Kommissare and only 2 of the 26 Wachtmeister and 6 of the 253 Polizeisergeanten could speak Polish.[22] And those few policemen who did know the language well enough to report on meetings of Polish organizations were usually themselves of Polish extraction and were therefore regarded by their superiors as politically suspect and of little use for surveillance.[23] Finally in 1909, a special office was established in Bochum in Westphalia to coordinate police observation of Polish associations and publications throughout the Rhenish-Westphalian industrial region.[24]

In 1908 Reichstag passage of an imperial law of association (*Reichsvereinsgesetz*) displaced existing relevant legislation of the federal states, including the much-used Prussian law of 11 March 1850.[25] Under the new imperial law, police in Prussia no longer had direct access to the nonpublic meetings of political organizations. And such organizations were no longer required to provide the police with membership lists. The 1908 legislation did not, however, grant greater freedom of association to all German citizens. Most notably, in line with rising governmental concern about efforts to organize Prussia's ethnic Polish population, the new law prescribed the use of German for political meetings. This language provision was designed both to discourage attendance at assemblies addressing non-German-speaking audiences and to ease police surveillance. In the Ruhr, Polish organizations responded initially by holding silent meetings, until these, too, were disbanded by the police. The Poles in turn established electoral associations, charging nominal dues. In the closed meetings of such associations, Polish could again be spoken.[26]

The imperial law of association lifted restrictions on participation by women in political associations, but youths under age eighteen were to be excluded. The prohibition against youthful political involvement, contained in the 1850 Prussian law on association, was thereby extended to the rest of Germany. This decision reflected Berlin's growing preoccupation with the indoctrination of young males during the years between completion of primary schooling and the beginning of military service. Official concern about the politicization of adolescents had been increasing significantly since 1904 as social democratic leaders turned greater attention to organizing young workers. In the Rhine-Ruhr region, the first socialist youth sections were initiated in 1907.[27]

As a consequence, while the 1908 law meant that in general the total number of political meetings to be monitored by the district's police would decline, Berlin expected policemen to step up their surveillance of gatherings of proletarian youth. In the last prewar years, most notably in 1911 and 1913, the central government instructed the police to monitor closely all assemblies, including hikes and excursions, of socialist adolescents and to disband them upon detecting any expression, no matter how oblique, of antipatriotic or antimilitary sentiment. Derek Linton, in his recent study of German prewar youth policy, notes that many municipal police officers (Düsseldorf's Polizeikommissar Gauer, for example) believed that the heavy-handed harassment mandated by Berlin did more harm than good. Opposition newspapers made effective use of stories of armed policemen dispersing assemblies of young boys and girls. Nevertheless, as far as organizations of working-class adolescents were concerned, district officials continued to demand strict vigilance and prompt action to the very limits of the law.[28] Not present threat to public order but prospects for the reliability of future recruits and citizens increasingly preoccupied the administrative bureaucracy.

In the Düsseldorf district, while some police officials were ambivalent about stepped-up surveillance of working-class youth, others questioned the wisdom of the 1908 association law as a whole. According to the district Polizeikommissar in Elberfeld, police officers welcomed the sharp reduction in the number of political meetings to be monitored. He believed most policemen would prefer street duty in the worst possible weather to being unwelcome guests at opposition gatherings where they were subject to open or implied insults.[29] But in Krefeld, Düsseldorf, Duisburg, and even in Elberfeld, although police administrators were pleased with the reduced work load, they fretted over the increased difficulty in keeping informed about the membership and activities of political organizations.[30] In particular, the Elberfeld police chief warned that police in the future would be less able to inform the army, navy, and civil service about opponents of the regime seeking appointment to or advancement within their ranks. In addition, he believed that to make up for the lost opportunities for direct observation of opposition groups the police would be forced to become more dependent upon informers. He reminded his superiors of the embarrassing consequences for the police that followed revelations of spying.[31] For their part, organized workers were doubtless relieved to be freed of an obligatory police presence at their nonpublic meetings and especially of the need to submit membership lists. At the same time, however, they faced a reduction of one means of keeping at least some police officers—not all of whom were unsympathetic—directly and extensively informed of their particular grievances and concerns.[32]

INTERVENING IN EMPLOYER-EMPLOYEE RELATIONS

The well-known enlistment of the Prussian police to monitor and harass opposition movements inevitably influenced the character of police involvement in confrontations between workers and their bosses. In the highly industrialized Düsseldorf administrative district, labor relations stood at the top of the list of possible sources of serious disruption of the social peace. How and to what extent the police intervened in industrial disputes was of vital importance to both labor and management and was watched with keen concern by much of the rest of urban society as a key indicator of the state's definition of order and social justice.

Since intervention by the police, given their obligation to protect property and strikebreakers, was usually to the advantage of the employers, labor organizers hoped it would be kept to a minimum. To this end they typically admonished striking workers to be as orderly as possible so as to deprive the authorities of excuses for repressive measures.[33] They reminded government officials of the often declared obligation of state agents to enforce the law impartially, without regard to the wealth or position of the parties involved, and publicized numerous instances known to them of police failure to live up to that commitment. From the viewpoint of the state, the strongest argument of union leaders and their sympathizers against excessive use of police repression was that it would further embitter workers and drive them into the arms of the most radical opponents of the regime.

With the growth of labor unions, employers more than ever expected the fullest and most energetic engagement of the police to protect their interests, which they defined as synonymous with preservation of the established order in Germany. And they had strong reasons for assuming that their expectations would be met. The Düsseldorf district was home to many of Germany's wealthiest and most influential industrialists, men with direct access to the highest officers of the state, including the emperor himself. Locally, they were major taxpayers and landowners, and given the plutocratic three-class franchise used in municipal elections, their interests were disproportionately represented in city councils.[34]

Not content with these advantages, the district's major employers fostered direct links between their companies and local policemen. The practice of large firms paying the salaries of communal policemen assigned to patrol in their vicinity continued to be common, with companies retaining the right to cancel such agreements when it suited them. According to Erhard Lucas, the Thyssen steelworks in Hamborn provided funds for the employment of eight police patrolmen in 1912.[35]

Employers also provided housing subsidies to police personnel whose services were deemed directly useful to corporate interests.[36] In some cases, individual policemen took the initiative and negotiated their own agreements. In 1909, for example, two Essen policemen arranged to move into dwellings belonging to the Arenberg mining company. The policemen received the advantage of the low rent charged for such accommodations. The Arenberg concern for its part believed that a police presence in company housing would aid in maintaining control over the lives of the other inhabitants.[37]

One common way for employers to foster the goodwill of the police was through the provision of gratuities to those who acted to protect their interests during strikes. For the state, however, toleration of this long-established practice carried with it the danger that activities of its representatives would appear to be determined by the prospect for immediate personal gain. The issue came to the fore in the aftermath of the Ruhr strike of 1912 as coal companies agreed among themselves on substantial payments to policemen. Rank-and-file personnel were to receive a bonus of three marks a day for every day of the strike. Police officers were offered lump sums of fifty to one hundred marks. Policemen who felt they were entitled but received no offer of payment from employer funds did not hesitate to present their claims.[38]

Informed of these gifts, the minister of the interior responded by forbidding the practice. Such direct payments by employers to policemen represented a far too easy point of attack for the opposition press.[39] The minister was willing to permit contributions by grateful industrialists to general police welfare funds, but employers found this a much less attractive option. They wanted their money to go directly to individual policemen who they had identified as having played an antistrike role.

The carefully tended contacts between policemen and employers found expression in the exchange of information. Labor spokesmen complained, for example, that in fulfilling their assigned task of collecting strike statistics, the police turned to employers but not to the unions for data.[40] Workers were aware that reports on union meetings and other worker assemblies, along with membership lists of working-class organizations and subscription lists of opposition publications, often found their way from police to corporate files.[41]

A particularly sensational case of police collaboration with employers in securing information became public knowledge in 1912. A jealous colleague of Polizeiassessor (formerly District Polizeikommissar) Hansch of Essen revealed that Hansch had used substantial funds procured from the Zechenverband, the employer organization of Ruhr mining, to arrange for the theft of the subscription list of the Steigerverband, an association of low-level mine supervisors formed in 1907.[42] In defending his action, Hansch explained that the cooperation of officials of the Ruhr mining industry over the years had been invaluable and added that government and industry had a common interest in keeping a close watch on employee associations. Hansch's only regret was that his efforts had not remained secret.[43] The Düsseldorf Regierungspräsident found himself in the embarrassing position of having to apologize to the chairman of the social-democratically inclined Steigerverband for Hansch's indiscretion.[44] This apology was, however, of little help to an organization that lost most of its members once their employers knew who they were. On the order of the minister of the interior, Hansch was fined ninety marks but kept his job.[45]

In coal mining, a significant form of state-sanctioned cooperation between employers and the police was the enrollment of company supervisory personnel as auxiliary policemen for use during work stoppages. Identified by the wearing of arm bands or police caps and typically armed with revolvers, these mine protection forces (*Zechenwehren*) were extensively deployed during the Ruhr coal strikes of 1905 and 1912. At the same time, however, Prussian officials refused to give official recognition to unarmed order-keeping personnel designated by the unions and denied them the right to wear identifying arm bands, viewing such individuals as pickets in disguise.[46]

State authorities and employers were not, however, always of one mind about the establishment of mine protection forces. Some government officials recognized that the use of mining supervisors as auxiliary police carried with it the danger both of unpredictable performance from men unfamiliar with police work and serious undermining of the state's claim to neutrality in industrial disputes.[47] And some coal industrialists, especially in the Rhenish half of the Ruhr, resisted the formation of Zechenwehren. They feared that public opinion would hold them responsible for excesses committed by their armed men and that relations between miners and their supervisors would become even more tense than they already were. Mine operators also did not want their supervisors diverted from efforts to keep production at its highest possible level during strikes and argued that maintaining law and order was the responsibility of the state, not of private industry. Better, they argued, to let the government bear the onus of any use of armed force against striking workers.[48]

Beyond safeguarding property, what employers subject to strike action most wanted from the police was protection of strikebreakers and the disruption of picketing.[49] Although picketing remained legal, despite stepped-up prewar employer campaigns to have it outlawed, the police were well equipped with options for forcing picketers to move on and for arresting those who failed to comply.[50] The many restrictions attached to the right to picket made it virtually meaningless whenever the police and their superiors chose to make it so, as they often—but not always—did.

In confronting picketers, the police could act on either their broadly defined obligation to preserve public order or their responsibility to guarantee the free flow of traffic.[51] Almost any interaction between strikebreakers and pickets could be interpreted as an infringement on the right to work, thereby providing grounds for action against picketers. Isolated pickets could inform newcomers that a strike was in progress, but anything more, including attempts to use moral suasion, was subject to prohibition. Any public display by word or gesture of disapproval of strikebreaking constituted grounds for arrest for slander or intimidation.[52] Penalties imposed in such cases could range to up to two weeks in jail.

Such proceedings were not peculiar to Prussian authoritarianism. Sidney Harring recounts, for example, the 1891 trial of strikers and their supporters in Grand Rapids, Michigan, for use of the epithet "scab." In England the 1906 Trade Disputes Act guaranteed the right of strikers to use "peaceful persuasion" but left unresolved the difficult issue of distinguishing between persuasion and intimidation. The gathering of a significant number of pickets in itself could be interpreted as intimidation.[53]

In policing the most serious of prewar strikes, the state confronted the crucial question of whether to call in the military. Especially in the mass strikes affecting Ruhr mining in 1905 (210,000 strikers, representing 85 percent participation) and 1912 (235,000 strikers, representing 61 percent participation), employers were insistent on the need for troops and used their multiple contacts with government officials at every level to press their case. In 1905 their pleas were resisted. For many Prussian authorities, memories of the bloody military intervention of 1889, the generally quiet course of events in 1905, the broad public sympathy the miners enjoyed in that year, and a desire to resolve the strike as peacefully and quickly as possible led to the dismissal of the employers' warnings as exaggerated.[54]

In 1912, however, with the Catholic miners' union refusing to support the strike and with frequent clashes between strikers and strikebreakers, Ruhr employers were more successful in making a case for military intervention. They viewed the combination of local police forces, plus 255 royal policemen sent from Cologne and 100 sent from Berlin, along with mounted and foot gendarmes from all over Prussia, as inadequate to the task. In the eastern, Westphalian half of the coalfield, advocates of the dispatch of troops achieved their goal with the arrival of approximately 5,000 soldiers.[55]

In the western half of the Ruhr, that portion lying within the Düsseldorf administrative district, Regierungspräsident Francis Kruse worried about the unpredictable and embittering consequences of calling in soldiers insufficiently familiar with the region and with legal procedures.[56] When sharp clashes between police and striking miners occurred, focusing on the Deutscher Kaiser mine in Hamborn, Kruse attributed his ability to resist demands for military intervention to the availability of a reserve of one hundred communal policemen from Düsseldorf. The police assigned to Hamborn were under instructions from the district administration to use their weapons as needed so that strikers would not come to the conclusion that they had little to fear.[57]

Kruse and his colleagues subsequently used their 1912 experience to bolster their call for the creation of even larger police reserves to meet future contingencies. Big-city police forces were increasingly expected to have the resources to cover both their local obligations and to provide substantial aid elsewhere in an emergency.[58]

The military, for its part, was ever more reluctant to become involved in domestic confrontations. In particular, the expansion of the army in 1912–13 brought with it the prospect of the induction of more social democrats, making military participation in civil conflict seem even less desirable.[59] Heightened international tensions also made the army more hesitant to become involved in domestic clashes that distracted attention from preparation for national defense.

For workers and those who sympathized with their plight, the Prussian police and their superiors seemed hopelessly biased in favor of employers in any confrontation between labor and management. The bias seemed all the more glaring, both to contemporaries and to later commentators, because of oft-repeated assertions that Prussian officials were impartial and above special interest. Scenes of policemen harassing picketers, conducting strikebreakers to work, or clearing the streets with truncheons and bayonets provided unforgettable (although far from peculiarly Prussian or German) images of the police acting in the service of the rich and powerful. During the 1912 Rhine ship workers' strike, for instance, the government made policemen available to accompany ships as far as Cologne, provided employers paid the cost.[60] But while labor spokesmen criticized the police for being too compliant with the wishes of the bosses and believed police repression greatly exceeded what was necessary to ensure reasonable order, employers were often scarcely less critical. Their complaints, however, typically focused on police inaction rather than action and took the form not of public pronouncements but of appeals to higher officials who had authority over the police.[61]

The communal police, cognizant of the great political and economic influence of employers in the cities of the Düsseldorf district, could hardly be indifferent to their complaints. Yet they were not always either willing or able to do as they were bid by management. Themselves of comparatively modest social origins and indoctrinated with an official creed of the state's obligation to maintain some sort of balance of competing interests, communal police officers were frequently suspicious of what seemed to be unbridled entrepreneurial greed and lack of concern for social harmony. Closer to the daily life of ordinary people than were most government agents, the police experienced firsthand the consequences of embittered social relations.

The more independent-minded police officers pointed out in response to employer complaints that too close identification of the state with especially harsh and sometimes dishonest managerial policies undermined the legitimacy of the established order and made the long-term peacekeeping tasks of the police more difficult. Such a position was easier to take in a major city with a reasonably diverse economy such as Düsseldorf than it was in the single-industry and sometimes single-company towns common in the Ruhr. In Ruhr coal towns, the influence over local affairs of a small group of powerful employers often proved irresistible and accusations of police bias and brutality were particularly frequent.[62]

The difference in perspective between employers and at least some communal police officials as well as the kind of pressure employers could bring to bear upon recalcitrant police departments is evidenced by developments during the strike at the Wortmann und Elbers enamel works in Düsseldorf in 1900. Initially the Düsseldorf police held aloof from the confrontation, arguing that the strikers were conducting themselves peacefully and that intervention would appear one-sided and do more harm than good. Dissatisfied factory owner Alfred Elbers thereupon went in person to complain to the Prussian minister of the interior. The minister was receptive, demanding that strikebreakers be given "every possible protection." Düsseldorf Polizeiinspektor Setzermann countered that the strikebreakers had apparently been recruited under false pretenses. Agents sent to Galicia to attract substitute workers had lied, assuring them that no strike was in progress. When the misinformed recruits arrived in Düsseldorf, their papers were taken from them by their new bosses, making it impossible for them to leave.[63]

The Düsseldorf Regierungspräsident, responding to inquiries from the minister of the interior, gave an account different from that of the Polizeiinspektor. He agreed with Elbers that the police had failed to provide needed protection for the strikebreakers. He argued that undue pressure against those who continued to work consisted not only in physical or verbal attacks but even in the presence of anything other than single, widely spaced pickets, remote from the actual workplace. Although he acknowledged that picketing was in principle allowable, he added that even the most isolated, minor infractions of the rules, such as inevitably arose, could and should be used to justify a ban. The minister of the interior concurred, arguing that while picketing was indeed legal, in the majority of cases it led to the endangering of public safety and order. Therefore the police were obligated to find an excuse to suppress it.[64]

Operating under such instructions, the police were never able to achieve widespread acceptance of their claim to be impartial enforcers of law and order in strike situations. Instances of heavy-handed police repression of strikers remained far more numerous and well publicized than were examples of police resistance to employer wishes. Nevertheless, police response to strikes was not always completely one-sided. The district's policemen and those who directed their efforts did have some awareness that the state had interests in fostering social peace and enhancing its own legitimacy that transcended the short-term goals of local businessmen. But the obstacles to acting on such insights were great.

For organized workers, and especially their leaders, repeated encounters with policemen (whether as the product of day-to-day surveillance of working-class life or in the crisis situations of strikes and demonstrations) fostered and sustained a strong sense of the state's unfairness and hostility to their deepest concerns. Dissidents were frequently reminded that they were regarded as enemies of the state and the values espoused by those who ruled. Most labor leaders, particularly editors and journalists, had experienced at some point in their lives arrest, conviction, and imprisonment as the price of their outspokenness and willingness to challenge established authorities.

And yet, on the more positive side, for organized labor post-1890 circumstances were to be greatly preferred to the prohibitions of the antisocialist law. Police interventions, although commonly a nuisance and sometimes a real hardship, could often be evaded in ways that made the police appear more blundering than menacing. The seriousness and bitterness of the issues involved notwithstanding, an element of game playing frequently characterized the interaction of organized workers and policemen. If, for instance, red banners were forbidden, socialists might try sporting red ties or handkerchiefs instead. Meetings or demonstrations announced for one site might actually be held elsewhere. That policing in the Prussian-German Empire, official protestations notwithstanding, so often favored the rich over the poor, bosses over employees, did not seriously impede the vigorous functioning of the world's largest working-class movement and wide dissemination of its critique of the existing order.

CHAPTER NINE

On the Eve of War and Beyond

URBAN POLITICS AND POLICE ADMINISTRATION

In the aftermath of the mass Ruhr coal strike in the spring of 1905 and in the context of accelerated urban and industrial growth and shifts in municipal politics, reorganization of the police of the Düsseldorf administrative district became a topic of intensified official and public debate. The crucial issue was whether the district's communal police forces, even if provided with more and better trained and better armed manpower, were capable of controlling rapidly expanding, highly mobile urban populations in an era of increasingly large-scale political mobilization and of expanded trade union and strike activity. If not, the proposed alternative was the establishment of royal Schutzmannschaften in areas deemed most in need of rigorous, centralized surveillance.

Until the early 1890s, sporadic discussion of introducing royal Schutzmänner into the Düsseldorf district had focused primarily on Elberfeld and Barmen as early centers of the social democratic movement. In response to such suggestions, the mayor of Elberfeld argued in 1892, as had other Wuppertal mayors before him, that what was really needed in the valley was not state policemen but rather a military garrison.[1] After the turn of the century, a stronger and ultimately successful drive for royal police forces shifted focus from the Wuppertal to the Ruhr. The discussion accompanying this campaign highlighted those aspects of the organization and performance of the district's communal police regarded as most troubling by those who looked to vigorous and reliable law enforcement as a vital component of the protection of established authority.

Leading proponents of more direct state control of policing came chiefly from the ranks of the Prussian bureaucracy. They claimed that existing communal police forces were neither sufficiently forceful nor, in the long run, politically reliable enough to meet the serious challenges to maintaining order that were expected by defenders of the status quo. Advocates of royal police forces saw the situation getting worse, not better, unless significant police reorganization was undertaken. In demanding new initiatives in policing, they assumed that state police were better than local police in virtually every way. Opposition came primarily from socialists, liberal democrats, and Catholics—groups that had little reason to welcome more centralized control of law enforcement by an authoritarian state.

Critics of the district's communal police forces typically had a low opinion of the men who were patrolling the streets.[2] Royal policemen, their supporters argued, were on average better qualified because of longer military service. They were assumed to be more reliable, more mature and experienced, and more likely to enjoy public respect than were members of local departments.[3] The state's forces were even said to look more presentable because they were provided with better quality uniforms.[4]

As discussed in chapter 6, local police departments were often unable to attract men with the desired extended years as noncommissioned army officers, so municipal recruiters were forced to accept large numbers of working-class applicants. Putting former workers into police uniforms was hardly welcomed by the many officials and employers who believed the primary role of the police was to monitor and restrain proletarian activities of all kinds. Essen's influential mayor Erich Zweigert realistically noted, however, that merely introducing royal police forces into the Ruhr would not guarantee a significant change in the type of men willing to apply for police work in the region's more rough-and-ready cities. Whatever their formal requirements, royal Schutzmannschaften, he accurately forecast, might well find themselves compelled to make some of the same recruitment compromises local police forces did.[5]

However royal Schutzmannschaften selected their recruits, proponents of such forces assumed that they would at the very least be better disciplined than were communal policemen. Especially important was the availability of transfer as a means of discipline. Royal policemen who formed politically or morally undesirable associations in the communities where they were assigned, or who aroused local resentment, could be relocated elsewhere within the system of Schutzmannschaften.[6]

Advocates of introducing royal police forces also assumed that they would be better led than were local departments. In communal forces, the ranking uniformed officers were the Inspektoren. Under the supervision of the mayor or his assistant, the Polizeiinspektoren were responsible for the daily management of police business. Although at the apex of the local uniformed police hierarchy, such men were, in the context of the Prussian bureaucracy, only middle-level officials. They lacked university education and elite social contacts. The introduction of a royal force in the district would mean the appointment of higher ranking, more prestigious police authorities.[7] At the top would be a police director and his assistants, men selected not from the police hierarchy but from Prussia's much more prestigious, legally trained administrative bureaucracy.

A strong argument for royal police forces in the Ruhr was the realization that many important tasks assigned to the police, such as keeping track of population movements, monitoring political associations, and pursuing criminals, could be tackled more effectively on a regional than on a local level. With more centralized direction, strict enforcement in one town or city would be less likely to be undercut by a more relaxed approach in a neighboring jurisdiction. Mayor Zweigert in particular argued the great importance of uniformity in policing, believing that variations in practice from place to place threatened to undermine public confidence in law enforcement. Uniformity, he claimed, was almost more important than fairness and its presence or absence easier to determine. Zweigert also pointed out that more and more of the region's workers and employers were joining regional organizations. The police, he believed, should be equally unified. In particular, they should be prepared to respond to strikes and lockouts spread over large areas.[8]

Those who argued for regional rather than communal organization of policing for the Ruhr pointed to improvements in communication and transportation that had made centralized supervision of ever-larger jurisdictions more feasible as well as more necessary. Telegraphs and telephones permitted the rapid transmission of orders. Railroads and streetcars allowed the speedy movement of men; the Ruhr was particularly well served in this regard. Growing numbers of bicycles and automobiles would also help knit together the components of a regional police.[9]

Debate over the relative merits of royal and communal police forces took place against a background of growing official concern about the long-term implications for law enforcement of changes in the scope and direction of urban politics and administration. In the middle of the nineteenth century, local regulation of policing in the Düsseldorf district had rested primarily with the Landräte, backed by the gendarmerie.

Mayors and communal policemen played a subordinate role. By the beginning of the twentieth century, however, more and more big-city mayors, administering much enlarged communal police forces, reported directly to the Regierungspräsident on law enforcement, not to a Landrat as intermediary. In the most highly industrialized and densely populated portions of the district, the Landräte, those stalwart representatives of both state power and local propertied elites, now played a greatly diminished role.[10]

As the district's industrial settlements grew dramatically during the late nineteenth and early twentieth centuries, increasing numbers of them sought and were granted the right of municipal self-administration. In the Rhine province, cities with more than forty thousand inhabitants could aspire to become *kreisfrei,* that is, administratively separate from the county in which they were located.[11] By 1914, the Düsseldorf district consisted of fifteen counties (*Landkreise*) administered by Landräte and fifteen kreisfrei cities (*Stadtkreise*) administered by mayors. Two-thirds of the district's prewar population lived in the Stadtkreise, many of which were recently swollen by large-scale annexations of surrounding industrial suburbs.[12] The prospect of more such annexations promised further to limit the portion of the district under Landrat oversight.

Royal officials were particularly concerned about the prospect of removing from Landrat administration the newest, most rapidly expanding, and most proletarian of Ruhr industrial concentrations. They dreaded granting increased self-administration, especially in police matters, to settlements whose populations included little in the way of an established business and professional elite. Large numbers of ethnically diverse migrant workers added to official conviction that such places were not ready for more autonomy. Hamborn, today part of Duisburg, represented the most noted of these cases. Its population, a mere 4,260 in 1890, topped 100,000 twenty years later. By 1910, fully one-quarter of its inhabitants were recent arrivals from Prussia's eastern provinces. An approximately equal number were foreigners. Because of the state's reluctance to grant municipal self-administration to such an entity, Hamborn held until 1910 the dubious distinction of being Prussia's largest rural commune.[13]

In the first decade of the twentieth century, state officials were similarly reluctant to see such mushrooming proletarian communities as Ruhrort, Meiderich, Sterkrade, Borbeck, and Altenessen removed from Landrat oversight.[14] The prospect appeared considerably less daunting, however, if much of the Ruhr were to be encompassed in the jurisdiction of a royal police force. Under those circumstances, granting municipal self-administration would not involve transfer of policing powers.

Official reluctance to see the role of the district's mayors in police administration enhanced at the expense of the Landräte reflected a twofold concern about the holders of municipal office. First, big-city mayors were assumed to be too overburdened by a multitude of pressing problems to give needed attention to policing.[15] Such men typically delegated responsibility for police administration to one of their assistants. Second and more important, mayors, elected by city councils and dependent upon council cooperation for smooth implementation of their programs, were believed by state authorities to be susceptible to local influence and therefore not to be safely entrusted in all instances with vital police powers.

Bureaucratic concern about shielding the police from local politics heightened as working-class city councillors began to emerge around the turn of the century. Mobilization of working-class voters, especially in newly incorporated industrial suburbs with almost exclusively proletarian populations, was beginning to make modest inroads, despite the continuing massive barriers represented by the plutocratic three-class system of voting and open ballots used in Prussia's municipal elections. Liberals, long the dominant force in the district's municipal politics, found themselves increasingly challenged by both Center and socialist candidates.[16]

For the Essen city council, for example, twenty-seven National Liberals and only three Centrists were elected in 1885, twenty-nine National Liberals and seven Centrists in 1895. However, as a result of the 1909 election, following the annexation of neighboring proletarian communities and enlargement of Essen's council, thirty-four National Liberals found themselves confronting twenty-two Centrists and two socialists. Whereas no workers sat in the Essen council in either 1885 or 1895, seven workers (five of them union secretaries) were members in 1909.[17] In Barmen, the first socialist was elected to council membership in 1901. In 1909, socialists won five of thirty-six seats in the Barmen council.[18] By 1912, ten of thirty-six members of the Elberfeld council were socialists, giving them enough votes to compel discussion of issues of their choice.[19]

Opponents of change in the apportionment of urban political power lamented the intrusion of party politics into municipal affairs and warned that democratized city councils might in future select democratically inclined mayors, not the kind of men to be entrusted with police administration. Also, the presence of even small numbers of working-class representatives on city councils increased the likelihood that embarrassing questions about policing would be raised and established practices would be challenged in that forum. As already noted, city councils officially had few rights relating to police matters, except in the realm of budgets.[20] But in practice, mayors had often allowed them some leeway to discuss issues relating to law enforcement. The council did, after all, vote the budget. And although councils could be overruled by the state, the cooperation of the council majority was politically preferable. Also, trying to prevent all discussion of the police by the city council could undermine the legitimacy of law enforcement by giving the appearance of a deliberate cover-up of improprieties. Socialists found it objectionable that such discussions of police matters were regarded by mayors as concessions to the council rather than a right of elected communal representatives.[21]

Despite the often strong hostility felt by organized labor toward the police, the product of bitter experience, socialist council members did not deny the need for strong, well-equipped police forces capable of controlling crime, regulating traffic, and protecting the interests of consumers. Social democrats, like every other organized interest of the time, had come to accept policing as an essential urban service. Socialist representatives were willing to vote for police budgets, sometimes even championing higher wages and better conditions for ordinary patrolmen. Socialist publications, while printing numerous reports of police misdeeds, also increasingly opened their columns to disgruntled policemen, permitting them to make a public case, through anonymous letters, for better treatment.[22]

Social democratic spokesmen, themselves typically disdainful of the criminal and disreputable, did not argue for less law enforcement but rather pointed out that the essential public safety functions of the police would be better served if the police adopted a less military tone and spent less time in petty and counterproductive harassment of socialists and trade unionists.[23] What socialists wanted was not fewer and less vigorous policemen but rather policemen who would treat workers and their organizations with the same respect and tact usually accorded bourgeois citizens and their associations. From that perspective, working-class spokesmen in the Düsseldorf district saw the formation of royal Schutzmannschaften as a step in the wrong direction, the introduction of such forces into the Ruhr being obviously aimed not at improved crime fighting and increased public safety but at the containment of organized labor in that vital area.

STATE AND COMMUNAL FORCES

The campaign for greater centralization and state control of policing in the Ruhr culminated in the formation of three regional police authorities in 1909, two in the Westphalian part of the coalfield and a third headquartered in Essen. The communities encompassed in the new Essen royal police district (Essen, Oberhausen, and ten rural communes of the Landkreis Essen) had a population of over six hundred thousand.[24] Proposals to create a fourth district to the west of Essen for Duisburg and surrounding settlements foundered on financial considerations.[25]

Before the First World War, the number of royal Schutzmannschaften in Prussia had risen to twenty-three: Frankfurt, Danzig, Königsberg, Breslau, Magdeburg, Wiesbaden, Koblenz, Cologne, Hanover, Potsdam, Stettin, Posen, Zabrze, Kiel, Geestemunde, Bochum, Gelsenkirchen, Kassel, Hanau, Fulda, Essen, Saarbrücken, and Aachen. Facilitating expansion during the last prewar years was Landtag passage of a new police financing law in 1908 that shifted more of the cost of royal forces from the state to the cities where they were established. But although cities now provided one-third of the necessary funds, Schutzmannschaften remained enough of a burden on the Prussian treasury that they were only initiated where the need was deemed pressing.[26] During the last prewar years, the areas chosen for the introduction of new royal police forces were the Ruhr and Upper Silesian coalfields. Fear of proletarian unrest, not of individual criminal activity, justified these costly initiatives.

The creation of royal police forces did not mean the complete elimination of communal departments in the chosen cities. An initial question that had to be resolved was which police functions would remain communal and which would be assumed by state forces. Since the Ruhr Schutzmannschaften were being created first and foremost in hopes of providing a more effective guarantee of state-approved order and to serve as the eyes and ears of the central government, they concentrated on security policing (*Sicherheitspolizei*) and associated duties. In addition to routine street patrol and criminal investigation, the royal police were charged with registration of the population, political policing, and suppression or containment of vice. In preliminary discussions, government officials emphasized that the functions of the new royal police forces in the Ruhr needed to be broadly defined so as to bolster their prestige and give them multiple avenues for influencing and keeping contact with local communities.[27]

Small communal police forces would continue to be responsible for a number of regulatory functions having to do with such matters as markets, streets, public health, school attendance, master-servant relations, and various trades. Urban spokesmen attached greatest importance to keeping control of the building police, since building contractors and real estate developers (and their critics) were an important element of the local elites of expanding industrial cities. Besides, the building police largely paid for themselves through the fees charged contractors.[28]

Municipalities strongly resisted the suggestion that they should assume responsibility for night policing, even if only for an initial transitional period. State officials made this proposal in an effort to reduce the financial and manpower resources that would have to be allocated for the new Schutzmannschaften. The cities prevailed on this question, pointing out how difficult it would be to recruit good men to serve as communal night policemen while most of the more desirable day positions were reserved for the state police. They argued that the reintroduction of a separate night police force would represent a step back to a discredited practice.[29]

In selecting administrators for the new Ruhr Schutzmannschaften, the state gave clear expression of its intent to create a substitute for the diminished presence of Landräte in the region by naming three of their number to fill the newly created police directorships. In Essen, the man chosen for the post was Landrat von Bemberg-Flamersheim from Mülheim an der Ruhr. In neighboring Westphalia, the individuals chosen as police directors for Gelsenkirchen and Bochum were the local Landräte. These two men combined their new, higher-paying offices with continuation of their Landrat duties. The two Westphalian cities fought such dual appointments with determination but without success.[30]

Most of the initial manpower for the new royal forces consisted of transfers from the communal police. The normal prerequisite for admission into the Schutzmannschaft was a minimum of nine years of military service and attainment of noncommissioned rank. The majority of communal policemen, as noted in chapter 6, could not meet these requirements. For those willing to transfer, however, the state agreed to make the necessary exceptions.[31] Of 260 Essen Polizeisergeanten and Wachtmeister willing to enter state employment, none was rejected because of inadequate military service or rank. Thirteen were, however, turned down because of questionable health and 7 because of poor disciplinary records, much to the displeasure of the city, which was forced to keep the rejects on its payroll.[32]

Although being in the employ of the Prussian state was more prestigious than communal service, not all local policemen, especially those at the higher ranks, took advantage of the opportunity of joining the Schutzmannschaft. That the district's major cities paid their policemen more than the state paid those who served it was an important consideration. The comparatively high communal salaries had resulted from the difficulty of attracting suitable recruits to the Ruhr and by competition for manpower with local industry. In Essen, rank-and-file communal policemen earned an annual salary ranging from 1,500 to 2,300 marks, whereas royal Schutzmänner earned 1,200 to 1,600 marks a year, plus a modest rent subsidy. At the other end of the scale, the city's Polizeiinspektoren earned from 4,900 to 6,100 marks a year, their royal counterparts only 2,700 to 4,500 marks.[33]

Of Essen's Polizeisergeanten and Wachtmeister, twelve indicated that they were unwilling to make the transition to state service. Of the twelve, one, a man of sixty-three with thirty-two years in the police, planned to retire, and another pleaded ill health. Two plainclothes detectives refused to transfer because they would be required to wear uniforms for their new assignments, thus losing the outward expression of their special status. Of twelve Kommissare, six declared themselves unprepared to join the Schutzmannschaft. Two of these men, ages sixty-three and fifty-nine, each with thirty-four years of police service, planned to retire.[34]

Most notably, one of Essen's two Polizeiinspektoren turned down the opportunity to join the royal police and instead became chief of Duisburg's still-communal force. This man, Polizeiinspektor Eduard Hapke, left Essen with a remarkable endorsement from local socialists. They saw in Hapke someone who had departed from the rigid military style of his predecessors and suggested that the Duisburg comrades might be pleasantly surprised if they suspended judgment about the man slated to lead the police force in their city.[35]

If communal policemen were not always anxious to put on the uniform of the royal Schutzmannschaft, policemen in state service were even more reluctant to don a communal uniform.[36] In 1908, for example, much to the delight of local satirists, three royal Polizeikommissare were assigned to Essen to help facilitate the transition to the new police authority. Essen officials demanded that during the transitional period the new men would wear the local uniform and subordinate themselves to communal directives. Two of the three absolutely refused to appear in communal uniform even for a few months. Recognizing that the men were within their rights, the interior minister agreed to their reassignment elsewhere.[37]

Even with the transfer of most of Essen's communal policemen to state service in 1909, the new Schutzmannschaft headquartered there faced the prospect of attracting substantial additional recruits from the outside to meet its expanded manpower needs. In 1908, 370 uniformed policemen and detectives had been in Essen's service. By 1911, Essen's royal force numbered 470, with another 35 policemen still working for the city.[38] As Mayor Zweigert had predicted, the Essen Schutzmann-schaft encountered recruitment problems similar to those that had troubled the city in its search for former noncommissioned officers with long years of military service.

Because inadequate numbers of former noncommissioned officers with the required nine years in the armed forces applied to become Schutzmänner in Essen and other cities, the interior ministry permitted the hiring of individuals with less than nine but more than four years of military service as auxiliary personnel (*Hilfsschutzmänner*).[39] By October 1909, 128 such appointments had been made in Essen. These 128 men had served an average 5.2 years with the military and ranged in age from 21 (exceptionally young for a Prussian policeman) to 33, with an average of 26.2 years.[40]

By October 1910 the Essen Schutzmannschaft employed 228 auxiliary policemen. Of the 228 men, 124 had only the minimum four years of military experience.[41] Given that the Essen police would be dependent in a major way upon such appointments for the foreseeable future, the police director recommended that auxiliary pesonnel should be eligible for regular appointment once they had completed a combined total of nine and a half years of military and police service.[42]

Although the new Essen Schutzmannschaft had to make significant concessions in recruitment, it nevertheless represented a notable depar-ture from the communal force it largely supplanted. All of the police-men hired by the state had attained the rank of Unteroffizier or higher. In the communal police in 1908, as noted in chapter 6, approximately half had never attained that rank. About the same number in the communal police had served no more than two years with the armed forces, compared to the minimum of four years required by the state even for auxiliary appointment.

Because the new Essen Schutzmannschaft was so much more reliant on the military's noncommissioned officer corps as a source of recruits than the local police had been, Schutzmänner had less in common with their fellow urban residents than had been true of communal policemen. They were more likely to be outsiders from distant parts of Prussia. The religious background of the new policemen illustrates this point. As noted in chapter 6, in 1908 Catholic rank-and-file policemen in Essen had outnumbered Protestants by 157 to 119, a ratio comparable to that of the city's population as a whole. Of 94 men hired by the Essen

Schutzmannschaft in the second half of 1910, however, 68 were Protestants and only 26 were Catholics, reflecting the preponderance of Protestants elsewhere in the Hohenzollern realm.[43]

More military experience for would-be policemen, stricter discipline, and a wider gap between the police and the local population—combined with more centralized direction removed from communal politics— were developments welcomed by those who had advocated the establishment of Schutzmannschaften in the Ruhr. The new forces had scarcely been created when they were called upon to play a major role during the suffrage demonstrations of 1910 and the Ruhr coal strike of 1912.[44] State officials were relieved in those instances to have immediate recourse to royal policemen in the coalfield area, claiming to find them more suitable for peacekeeping than were communal police. Convinced that the new Schutzmannschaften had proven their worth in these confrontations, their superiors pushed for their early expansion and renewed the call for a fourth Ruhr royal police force in and around Duisburg.

WAR AND REVOLUTION

The coming of war in August 1914 had immediate repercussions for policing. Prewar planning had called for the Prussian police to maintain lists of politically suspect individuals who were to be detained in the event of hostilities.[45] Confronted when the time came with organized labor's clear demonstration of loyalty to the national cause, however, authorities decided against the implementation of preemptive antisocialist measures. In the interests of preserving the spirit of national unity that characterized the early days of the war, Prussia's minister of the interior instructed state and communal officials to moderate earlier routine harassment of opposition movements. He recommended, for example, dropping pending cases involving such petty issues as the use of red ribbons on funeral wreaths.[46]

At the same time, the onset of war saw not only efforts to patch together a political truce inside Germany but also the suspension of many civil liberties through the proclamation of a state of siege. When invoked, the Prussian siege law of 1851, unmodified since its formulation, conferred near dictatorial powers upon the commanders of the state's military districts, giving them (or their deputies) primary responsibility for making certain that domestic order was maintained. Throughout the war, military and civilian authorities were empowered to use heightened censorship, strict limitation of the right of assembly, and arbitrary searches and arrests to squelch behavior perceived as either oppositional or disruptive.

Mobilization meant a drastic loss of the youngest and most vigorous policemen to the military. On 5 August 1914, for instance, the Düsseldorf police reported that 3 Kommissare and 25 Polizeisergeanten had already departed. By the ninth day of mobilization they anticipated the loss of 7 Kommissare and 146 Polizeisergeanten, and by the fourteenth day the further departure of 2 Kommissare, 2 Wachtmeister, and 104 Polizeisergeanten. Düsseldorf's police administration predicted that these losses would make impossible fulfillment of the department's normal obligations.[47]

One initial response to the problem was the creation of local volunteer forces to supplement shrunken police departments. Barmen, for example, had by 19 August 1914 a contingent of two hundred volunteers drawn from the ranks of the local gymnastic society. Armed with truncheons, they guarded bridges, viaducts, and other structures.[48] The minister of the interior suggested members of shooting clubs and veterans' organizations as also being likely candidates for such duty.[49] In Düsseldorf, volunteer auxiliaries numbered 438 during the early months of the war.[50] Enthusiasm for volunteer police service soon waned, however, both on the part of the volunteers and of the authorities. Amateur policing proved unsatisfactory to all concerned.[51]

During the war years, police departments filled their ranks as best they could with auxiliary appointments of men deemed unfit for military service because of age or physical condition. They also relied on invalided soldiers.[52] Diminished resources for routine policing, combined with the declaration of martial law, translated into reduced police enforcement of many minor regulations. In Düsseldorf the number of penalties for ordinance violations dropped sharply from 27,720 in 1913 to 14,978 in 1914, to 11,813 in 1915, to 8,363 in 1916, to 6,081 in 1917, and to a mere 4,657 in 1918.[53]

Meanwhile, however, the police had the added responsibility of enforcing a wide range of war-related economic regulations. In Düsseldorf the number of penalties imposed for infractions of such ordinances rose from 384 in 1914, to 1,234 in 1915, to 2,984 in 1916, and to a high of 4,637 during the hungry and turbulent months of 1917. The police also had to respond to increases in reported crime, especially theft. In Düsseldorf reports of grand and petty larceny doubled from a combined total of 5,798 in 1914 to 11,696 in 1918.[54] In addition, the police were called upon by the military and their conservative supporters to use the war as an opportunity for stricter policing of morals, especially those of young workers. In the cities of the Düsseldorf district, youths under age sixteen were forbidden to purchase tobacco and alcohol or to visit bars, movie theaters, and music halls. At the behest of the military, censorship of films and cheap popular fiction was tightened and the young were subjected to early curfews.[55]

Confronted at war's end with the challenge of revolutionary upheaval, the Prussian police—not really called upon to do otherwise—initially remained largely in the background, acquiescing in the change in regime. Deprived of the prospect of effective counterinsurrectionary support from the military, even the most conservative police officials saw little alternative to accommodation. Long-standing working-class resentment of the close identification of the police with political harassment and class justice found expression in demands for police disarmament and subordination to worker militias. In Düsseldorf, for instance, a militia formed in November 1918 by the workers' and soldiers' council patrolled the streets and supervised the police. On the eighteenth of that month, the city's political police division was disbanded and its leader was arrested. In the Ruhr, worker militias displaced urban police forces during the Red Army uprising in 1920.[56]

But such experiments were short lived. Anxious to restore order as quickly as possible, Germany's newly established republican government much preferred the reaffirmation of professional policing to unpredictable experiments. Republican ministers did depart in a number of cases from prewar practice by choosing party and union secretaries rather than legally trained administrative bureaucrats as police presidents. In the Rhine province, such political appointees were more likely to represent the Catholic Center rather than the social democrats. But in general, republican leaders proved no more ready than their monarchist predecessors had been to diminish police powers or to alter drastically their definition.[57] Even political policing, initially dropped, was quickly restored, with communists rather than socialists now the primary target.

Critics of policing in Imperial Germany had often raised the issue of the suitability of the army as a model for civilian forces. The prewar spike-helmeted Prussian patrolman, given to speaking and acting in a manner bred of barracks life, had been a frequently resented symbol of the old authoritarian order. Although spiked helmets had to go, efforts to demilitarize the police image and to make policemen seem more helpful and friendly and less intimidating and intrusive were counterbalanced by the republican government's extensive reliance upon the police for riot and crowd control. To meet this need, large cities were provided with special companies of police for riot duty. These men were heavily armed (to the extent allowed by the victorious Allies) and assigned to barracks where they were subject to strict discipline.[58] Such units were intended not only to guarantee order in turbulent times but also to indoctrinate young police recruits, providing them with a substitute for the kind of disciplinary experience their monarchical counterparts had gained through military service. Day-to-day indoctrination by often conservative officers worked against the lessons in republican principles the government mandated for police training.

During the years of the Weimar Republic, the prevalence of social and political unrest and the greatly reduced size of the armed forces resulted in a much enhanced and very conspicuous peacekeeping role for the police.[59] The disappearance of the conscript army also meant for the police the need to reconsider its preferred source of manpower. One important change in recruitment was the selection of younger men, presumably an advantage in meeting the strenuous challenges of the Weimar years. Young men no longer needed to be reserved for the military. What had been a minimum recruitment age under the empire (twenty-four years) now became a maximum. In a further move away from the sometimes superannuated policemen of the empire, most recruits could now look forward to no more than twelve years' employment with the police, not the lifetime appointments that had been offered before the war.[60]

In the short run, the police could draw upon a large body of demobilized soldiers and militiamen. Indeed, the republican government initially saw an expanded police force as a means of salvaging portions of disbanding military units. Former commissioned and noncommissioned army and free corps officers found alternative careers as police officers. Separate recruitment and careers for officers and men in the police remained the rule. Relations among ranks were, however, substantially altered when the government granted to police patrolmen the right to organize and bargain collectively. They were not, however, permitted to strike.[61]

Under the empire, Prussian authorities had always denied in the strongest possible terms the right of rank-and-file policemen to organize, holding such initiatives to be inconsistent with the militarized discipline expected of the police. Granting the right to form associations represented a significant departure from previous police practice, one paying dividends in the republican loyalties of the largest patrolmen's organization, the *Verband Preussischer Polizeibeamten*. Many of the patrolmen's officers, however, belonged to an association, the *Vereinigung Preussischer Polizeioffiziere*, of more questionable allegiance.[62]

Aside from unionization, however, most changes in policing under the Weimar Republic were in line with trends already apparent during the empire. In particular, trends toward greater centralization, specialization, and standardization continued. In 1922, thirteen new Prussian state police forces were created, to add to the eighteen then in existence.[63] In the Düsseldorf district, Elberfeld, Oberhausen, Düsseldorf, Duisburg, Gladbach-Reydt, and Krefeld received state forces during the 1920s, usually in the second half of the decade, earlier efforts having been blocked by the Allied occupation.[64]

With increased state direction, recruitment and training of policemen became more uniform. Municipal policing became more marginal, with prior state service becoming a prerequisite for employment by communal forces.[65] On these and other issues, republican leaders opted to build upon rather than repudiate Prussia's prior police experience. They, like their monarchist precursors, placed their hopes in increased expertise and adherence to rules and regulations determined in Berlin—now combined with expanded public relations initiatives—as the best guarantee of heightened police effectiveness and legitimacy.

Conclusion

In the last year before the First World War, American Raymond B. Fosdick toured major European cities and collected information for what became a still frequently cited book, *European Police Systems* (1915).[1] In Germany he interviewed police officers and observed operations in Berlin, Hamburg, Bremen, Dresden, Munich, Stuttgart, and Cologne. He compared his German observations with his findings on police forces in Great Britain, France, Italy, and the Habsburg Empire.

In the police of Imperial Germany, Fosdick found much to admire, especially the apparent low incidence of corruption, the utilization of the most up-to-date policing techniques, and the availability of the latest equipment.[2] But he also noted the German policeman's penchant for treating citizens like raw army recruits, and he commented on the strong antipolice sentiments of the lower classes.[3] From his well-informed comparative perspective, Fosdick further singled out Germany for the pervasiveness and intrusiveness of police intervention in daily life, the preoccupation with keeping track of the comings and goings of ordinary citizens, the omnipresence of *Verboten* signs, the lack of meaningful local control over policing, and the arming of patrolmen "as if for war."[4] Concentrating on Germany's largest cities and their state police forces, he referred in passing to the down-at-the-heels quality of municipal police, the result of strong competing demands on municipal finances in growing cities.[5]

Germans made their own international comparisons. In the decades predating World War I, would-be police reformers paid close attention to foreign models. When making comparisons, Germans did not view their police with the same pride that attached to the German military and administrative bureaucracies.[6] The German states were not in the forefront of developing credible police institutions, and informed observers acknowledged in particular the influence of French and British innovations. Unlike the armed forces, the German police could boast neither a socially prestigious officer corps nor glamorous deeds that had shaped national history.

Across the political spectrum, German commentators were especially likely to find cause for envy when comparisons were made to the much admired London Metropolitan Police. Many Germans, agreeing with Fosdick, perceived English policemen (perhaps somewhat rosily) as being generally more polite, more helpful to citizens, able to maintain order with a minimum of force, and enjoying as a consequence a degree of popular acceptance unknown in Germany.[7] As noted in chapter 2, liberal admiration for the London constable had led to direct, though largely abortive, imitation in Berlin at the time of the revolution of 1848.

During the years of reaction following 1848, London's police continued to be widely esteemed in German central Europe, even by conservatives. Visitors returning from the Crystal Palace Exhibition of 1851 reported enthusiastically on how effectively the London police had handled the vast crowds. During the 1850s, Prussians extolling the greater virtues of the London police ranged from Westphalian industrialist and liberal spokesman Friedrich Harkort to future chancellor Otto von Bismarck.[8]

In succeeding decades, commentary in the press and in Landtag and Reichstag debates returned repeatedly to the theme of the superior quality of London's patrolmen.[9] The chorus was even joined by Prussian minister of the interior Friedrich Graf zu Eulenberg. Responding in the Prussian Lower House on 11 January 1873 to unfavorable comparisons being made of German with English policemen, he accepted the validity of the complaints about the comportment of the police under his authority. He attempted to explain the perceived superiority of the London force as reflective of its earlier development. He hoped that in time improvements in Prussian policing would be possible and speculated that higher pay for patrolmen would make it less necessary for them to seek compensatory gratification by acting in a preemptory fashion in their contacts with the public.[10]

For Germany in general and Prussia in particular up to the First World War, the most important and lasting decisions about the nature of police institutions were those made in the immediate aftermath of the revolutions of 1848–49. Resurgent conservative regimes jettisoned proposals to give the police a more civilian demeanor and to make them locally accountable. In Prussia the police law of 11 March 1850 remained unaltered as long as the monarchy survived. This fundamental and frequently cited law, buttressed by legislation significantly restricting both the right of association (1850) and freedom of the press (1851), reaffirmed the wide-ranging and flexible powers of the police and the primacy of state control over all uniformed forces.

Between 1850 and the First World War, impetus for change in German policing came, first and foremost, from the state. In Prussia, Berlin repeatedly prodded parsimonious city governments to make more resources available and to bring their police into conformity with standards prevailing elsewhere in the monarchy. The state's demand for police contingents strong and reliable enough to constitute a credible first line of defense against civil disorder, thereby reducing dependence on military intervention, persistently outstripped locally generated demands for more policemen to deal with threats to the life and property of individuals and with the day-to-day confrontations and nuisances of urban life.

The state's demand for more resources characteristically coincided with periods of increased social and political challenges, especially those generated by the political and economic mobilization of labor. In the Düsseldorf administrative district, official arguments for more police were more often than not couched primarily in terms of the numbers of industrial workers, socialists, or foreigners and other long-distance migrants present, and only secondarily in terms of the amount of individualized criminal activity observed. Reported increases in crimes against persons and property were readily seized upon to give added justification for augmented police forces, but readiness to forestall or control civil disorder remained the primary concern of those responsible for the provision of policing.

But while demanding that cities do more to strengthen their police departments, the state consistently denied urban spokesmen, whether liberals, Catholics, or socialists, either in the Landtag or in city councils, a meaningful role in controlling law enforcement institutions. And democratically elected Reichstag deputies were conveniently excluded from most debates about the police because law enforcement remained a responsibility of state, not national, government.

During the prewar decades, demands for local accountability of the police fell on deaf ears. Actually, by the latter part of the nineteenth century, such demands had largely receded into the background. With the passage of time, urban elites were increasingly content to have the state take the lead, complaining only when proposed changes seemed too costly or threatened to interfere with the private affairs of the local bourgeoisie. Otherwise, urban leaders found, at least after bourgeois associations ceased to be a primary object of police surveillance, that their interests could usually be accommodated to those of the state in matters of policing. When, for example, in 1909 the Prussian state established royal police forces in the Ruhr, local elites welcomed the step, since they regarded royal Schutzmänner as better disciplined and more effective than municipal forces. Royal forces were also less of a burden on municipal budgets. Even city administrators did not object unduly to transfer of a responsibility typically viewed as burdensome, a source of discord and bitterness better left to state authorities. And, of course, insofar as socialists took up the issue of local accountability, this in itself was reason enough for royal officials and civic leaders to advocate greater centralization of Prussia's police.

In its oversight of the police, whether royal or municipal, Berlin paid particular attention to preservation of the prerogatives of the military. The state expected police recruitment to be coordinated with and subordinated to the manpower needs of the army. As long as the monarchy lasted, former noncommissioned officers continued to be favored as police recruits both because this served the staffing interests of the military and because such men had proven their loyalty to the existing order.[11] Despite significant changes in police organization and personnel policies in the late nineteenth and early twentieth centuries, state authorities persisted to 1914 and beyond in regarding the military model as of crucial importance for the police. The symbolic significance of conspicuous police adoption and retention of military forms and trappings, along with the preference for former military personnel, escaped no one's attention in military-conscious Prussia. The state did not intend that it should.

In terms of discipline and deportment, being more military and being more professional continued to be perceived by police officials as largely synonymous goals. They saw little need to choose between the two. To be sure, the need to cope with new and complex problems forced Prussia's urban police to go beyond military precedents and to develop their own procedures, especially in areas such as crime detection. During the last prewar decades, police officers increasingly prided themselves on the introduction of new equipment, new techniques, and new career specializations that were without military counterparts. They held conferences to discuss the finer points of police practice and to share their experiences. But at the same time they continued to assume that attitudes and discipline counted for more in an urban policeman than did specialized knowledge and skills. This assumption mirrored military claims that character counted for more than education in making a good soldier. For police officers, the armed forces remained unsurpassed as a behavioral model for their subordinates. The argument that a civilian force needed civilian norms made little headway. This persistence into the twentieth century of the military model for Prussia's urban police reflected both the exceptional prestige of the army and the government's preoccupation with internal enemies, against whom the military remained the ultimate bulwark.

Critics of the Prussian police regarded excessive police emulation of military deportment and attitudes as a key cause of tension and distrust between the police and much of the citizenry. State and local officials were not completely indifferent to such concerns, realizing that effective law enforcement required a large measure of public cooperation. They also realized that the political opposition was, over time, increasingly able to make effective use of police excesses and insensitivity for propaganda purposes. Opposition newspapers delighted in relating events that made the police appear brutal or ridiculous or both. They certainly did not lack for telling incidents to recount. And recount them they did at every opportunity, no matter how many libel suits the police filed in their efforts to discourage negative reporting.[12]

Police authorities issued repeated reminders, especially during the immediate prewar years, stressing that the police should act like approachable public servants, not like petty tyrants. And yet, pious pronouncements aside, the Prussian monarchy did not really want its policemen to become too approachable or too popular. The police were to be state servants before they were public servants. As David Arnold points out in his study of the police in Madras in British India, authorities deeply suspicious of the subordinate population have reason to welcome a substantial degree of tension between rank-and-file policemen and the general populace to maintain the social isolation of the police and to lessen the chances of their collusion with those to be policed.[13] Those who governed American cities, for example, were often able to make effective use of ethnic differences between policemen and suspect elements of the urban population.[14]

In Prussia, despite frequently cited instances of high-handed and one-sided police repression, all was not petty tyranny, militarized brutality, and bureaucratic tutelage. If many Prussians doubted that they had the best of police, they were certain that they did not have the worst. The French police, at least through the reign of Napoleon III, were widely regarded as oppressive and a model of what to avoid in police institutions. More important, from socialists to conservatives, Prussians viewed the Russian police with horror as the embodiment of brutal and benighted repression. That just beyond Prussia's frontiers were police who managed to make Prussia's patrolmen and their superiors look relatively benign and restrained by comparison, even from a social democratic perspective, would provide an important justification for working-class support of German national defense in 1914.

While Prussia's urban police forces grew dramatically, if unevenly, in size and resources in the decades between 1848 and 1914 and their powers and responsibilities remained broadly defined, they nevertheless operated under multiple limitations and restraints. They were incapable of doing all that their most hard-line advocates wished. Both municipalities and the state were often hard pressed to provide adequate financial resources to meet the manpower needs of labor-intensive policing. This was particularly true of new industrial settlements with rapidly growing proletarian populations, as in the case of many municipalities in the Düsseldorf administrative district.

Prussian authorities were likely to perceive the quality of manpower at their disposal as an even bigger problem than its quantity. Especially at the municipal level, police recruiters often were unable to employ and retain the kind of men they thought they wanted. In an effort to recruit more military men with long years of service for their police, cities were compelled to improve the terms of employment, offering, in the last prewar decades, higher wages, greater job security, at least a limited number of days off, and the prospect of paid vacations and a pension. The results were, however, often disappointing. The fact that before 1914 many cities, such as those of the Düsseldorf district, had to draw heavily upon a fluctuating pool of industrial workers to staff their police forces represented for defenders of an authoritarian order a worst-case situation.[15] Held in considerable contempt by their separately recruited superiors, rank-and-file municipal policemen were viewed as unfit to carry out any but the most routine assignments.

The Prussian police were not a power unto themselves and were subject, at least after the 1850s, to administrative and judicial bureaucracies that attempted to monitor their activities closely.[16] Although various interior ministers and other state authorities from time to time instructed the police to go to the outer limits of the law in counteracting political and social opposition to the existing order and often turned a blind eye to excessive police zeal, the police were substantially constrained by bureaucratic traditions espousing legality, rationality, and hierarchical order. Not above frequently bending the rules, especially where social democrats and social outcasts were concerned, Prussia's administrative bureaucracy was strongly influenced by the extended legal education that was the normal prerequisite for entry into the higher ranks of state service. Since rank-and-file policemen were held in such generally low regard, their superiors tried to keep them tied as

closely as possible to a few simple rules and procedures. The establishment of police schools during the last prewar years was first and
foremost an effort to ensure that policemen actually knew those basic
rules and did not inadvertently embarrass their superiors and the state
they served through their ignorance and caprice.

City councils, even though their influence over policing remained
sharply curtailed by the state bureaucracy, also articulated demands and
expectations that could not be completely ignored in the urban context.
Not only socialist and Center councilmen but liberals as well monitored
local police actions for failure to adhere to proper procedure. Strong
liberal concern for the protection of property and the preservation of
civic order did not totally eclipse the expectation that the police should
abide by the law and respect the established limits of state authority,
especially where private interests were concerned.

Where the police overstepped the bounds, victims had recourse to the
courts. Although enjoined to credit the testimony of policemen over
that of ordinary citizens, the courts on many occasions ruled in favor of
complainants. Unfortunately for the complainants, however, such rul-
ings often came too late to undo the damage police action had already
accomplished. Police disruption of picketing or other types of assembly,
for example, achieved its purpose even if the courts subsequently ruled
that the intervention had been inappropriate.

Concern about negative publicity resulting from irregular police
behavior increasingly caused officials to exercise restraint in their use of
the police. Particularly in politically tense times, they did not wish to
alienate more of the population than necessary. Unwilling to legitimate
the police by making them accountable to elected officeholders, the
administrators of the Prussian state instead strove for legitimacy by
attempting to project an image of bureaucratic, legalistic correctness
transcending class identification. The goal of correct and noninflamma-
tory police behavior frequently ran counter, however, to the authorities'
predisposition to believe that overreaction to an oppositional challenge
was better than inadequate or belated response. Better to err on the side
of too much rather than too little intervention and show of force. At
stake, they assumed, was not only speedy suppression of specific
incidents but also demonstration of the state's resolve to defend itself
with vigor under all circumstances.

In their interaction with various segments of the population, the
police had the advantage of being more familiar with many aspects of
everyday life than were most bureaucratic agencies. And the police were
often sympathetic to the plight of the poor and exploited, blaming on
many occasions rapacious or insensitive employers and landlords for

specific instances of unrest. Yet when unrest, whatever its cause, appeared even remotely to threaten the established order or the preservation of property, the police and their superiors saw little option but to act forcefully to reestablish outward tranquillity. In this respect Prussian police forces did not differ much from their counterparts in other capitalist societies, whether democratic or authoritarian. In such societies, private property had to be defended, not only against actual physical damage but also against significant disruption of its profitable utilization.

Among capitalist states, how urban police forces responded to social and economic conflict was influenced not only by directives emanating from national capitals but also by the nature of municipal franchises and the degree of local self-government permitted. In France at the end of the nineteenth century, for example, socialists dominated the city halls of several important municipalities, unthinkable in Prussia with its three-class system of voting and Berlin's careful vetting of mayoral candidates. Socialist mayors in republican France did their best to protect local workers against police repression, although their efforts were to be often frustrated by a strong, highly centralized bourgeois state that could intervene in local affairs through its prefects, its special police commissaires, its large gendarmerie, and its army.[17]

In England the tradition of local control over policing was far stronger than in France. That tradition, however, was increasingly challenged due to the upsurge in labor militancy beginning in 1910. Thereafter, where police were judged inadequate to the union challenge, the Home Office on its own initiative sent in soldiers and metropolitan policemen and supplied detailed instructions on policing to local authorities.[18]

In the United States, Democratic party machines mobilized the support of working-class and ethnic voters to gain control of urban governments. Given the decentralized nature of policing in the United States, American capitalists and those who shared their views might well worry that municipal police in cities governed by Democratic machines would fail to be vigorous enough in their defense of employer interests, especially in strike situations. One response was recourse to private policing such as that provided by the iron and steel police in Pennsylvania or by Pinkerton detectives. Another response was advocacy of more centralized control over policing, which led, for example, to the establishment of the Pennsylvania State Constabulary following the 1902 anthracite coal strike.[19]

In Prussia, not only the plutocratic municipal franchise but also vigilant state oversight of communal police administration represented vital reassurances for those most concerned about the growth of organized labor and the impact of possible future democratization of urban politics. Where such reassurances, strong as they were, seemed to state and local elites inadequate to meet the challenge of social and political change, royal Schutzmannschaften displaced municipal police forces. Prussian cities stood at the opposite end of the spectrum from nineteenth-century American municipalities with their open—although not unchallenged—interaction of policing and local partisan politics. Defenders of the established order in Prussia sought to maintain the fiction of nonpolitical policing, beyond special interest, and jealously guarded the police from democratic and socialist influences. Concessions on such issues remained few as long as the monarchy survived.

But while shielded to a high degree from local as well as national politics and strictly enjoined from above to take a hard line on issues deemed to relate to either the protection of property or to the survival of the state, the Prussian police were prepared to be increasingly flexible in regulating many aspects of everyday life, among them those relating to popular amusements. They refrained as much as possible from being enlisted by moral reformers in hopeless campaigns against such common indulgences as drinking and prostitution. Regarding prohibited pleasures, official inclination was to use the police for regulation rather than prohibition. Prussian police forces were aware of at least some of their limitations. Except in dealing with oppositional politics, they shied away from trying to enforce the unenforceable.

Prewar Prussian policemen on patrol were available to perform a multitude of overt and latent functions, but they served above all else as reminders of the pervasive and expanding authority of the state. Even when greatly outnumbered and surrounded by hostile assemblies, policemen by their mere presence brought to mind the extensive coercive forces that the state held ready for use if the orders of its individual uniformed representatives should be defied.

The services Prussia's policemen rendered and the protection and support they provided to various local groups and individuals helped justify the expense of enlarged and better financed police departments, but their primary obligation remained to the monarchy. As the agents of government most frequently encountered by urban residents (even more so in Prussia than in most societies), policemen played a significant role in shaping popular perceptions of the state. In particular, their wide-ranging activities reinforced a perception of many observers, both foreign and domestic, that the Prussian state was unnecessarily intrusive and overbearing. The police, by their manner and choice of symbols as much as by their acts, contributed to the reinforcement and perpetuation of long-established stereotypes about the character of the Prussian monarchy. And at the same time, the perceived authoritarian, militarized nature of the Prussian state provided a context in which the symbolic significance of the actions and deportment of its police forces often made them seem even more repressive than they actually were.

Appendix

TABLE A-1
Krefeld Police, 1853–1913

Year	Population	Full-time Policemen	Inhabitants per Policeman	Cost per Capita (M.)
1853	42,286	13	3,253	—
1854	44,090	13	3,391	—
1855	45,197	13	3,477	—
1856	46,958	16	2,935	—
1857	48,115	—	—	—
1858	49,349	—	—	—
1859	50,977	16	3,186	—
1860	52,442	—	—	—
1861	50,610	—	—	—
1862	51,415	—	—	—
1863	52,706	—	—	—
1864	53,455	16	3,341	—
1865	—	—	—	—
1866	53,562	—	—	—
1867	53,975	—	—	—
1868	53,363	—	—	—
1869	56,557	—	—	—
1870	57,772	17	3,398	—
1871	57,105	17	3,359	—
1872	58,505	20	2,925	—
1873	60,146	—	—	—
1874	62,783	26	2,415	—
1875	62,849	33[a]	1,904	1.63
1876	65,463	—	—	—
1877	67,857	40	1,696	1.78
1878	69,775	—	—	1.76
1879	72,566	—	—	1.74
1880	75,829	—	—	1.66
1881	77,158	53	1,456	1.87
1882	80,950	—	—	1.82
1883	84,887	—	—	1.92
1884	89,405	64	1,397	1.92
1885	90,295	68	1,328	2.04
1886	95,182	—	—	2.09

Table A–1, continued

Year	Population	Full-time Policemen	Inhabitants per Policeman	Cost per Capita (M.)
1887	100,375	71	1,141	2.11
1888	104,403	82	1,273	2.24
1889	106,626	90	1,185	2.27
1890	105,518	96	1,099	2.60
1891	105,714	96	1,101	2.66
1892	106,396	96	1,108	2.76
1893	107,184	98	1,094	2.73
1894	106,399	100	1,064	2.74
1895	107,245	99	1,083	2.77
1896	108,018	99	1,091	—
1897	107,963	105	1,028	3.12
1898	107,851	110	980	3.13
1899	108,290	111	975	3.22
1900	107,012	123	870	3.67
1901	109,764	125	878	3.66
1902	110,091	125	881	3.39[b]
1903	110,578	131	884	2.90[c]
1904	111,491	133	838	3.01
1905	110,472	143	772	3.24
1906	111,847	138	810	3.28
1907	127,502	151	844	3.14
1908	127,511	149	856	3.53
1909	128,732	149	864	3.62
1910	129,576	150	864	3.75
1911	130,409	145	899	3.85
1912	131,683	149	884	3.97
1913	133,062	152	875	4.21

Source: *Bericht über die Verwaltung und den Stand der Gemeinde-Angelegenheiten der Oberbürgermeisterei Crefeld* (Krefeld, 1855–1914).
[a]In 1875 the city's part-time night watchmen were replaced by full-time policemen for night duty.
[b]In 1902 fire-fighting costs were dropped from the police budget.
[c]In 1903 the cost of streetlighting was eliminated from the police budget.

TABLE A-2
Departures from Düsseldorf Police, 1877–1911

Cause	Day Force	Night Force
1877–81		
Death	6	2
Resignation	14	11
Dismissal	6	21
Retirement	2	1
TOTAL	28	35
1882–86		
Death	8	1
Resignation	9	3
Dismissal	1	1
Retirement	4	—
TOTAL	22	5
1887–91		
Death	11	2
Resignation	12	24
Dismissal	9	28
Retirement	2	1
TOTAL	34	55
1892–96		
Death	5	3
Resignation	11	37
Dismissal	1	8
Retirement	5	—
TOTAL	22	48

Cause	Integrated Day-Night Force
1897–1901	
Death	12
Resignation	109
Dismissal	8
Retirement	15
TOTAL	144
1902–6	
Death	18
Resignation	57
Dismissal	8
Retirement	8
TOTAL	91
1907–11	
Death	13
Resignation	29
Dismissal	20
Retirement	18
TOTAL	80
1912–13	
Death	8
Resignation	21
Dismissal	16
Retirement	10
TOTAL	55

Source: *Bericht über den Stand und die Verwaltung der Gemeinde-Angelegenheiten der Stadt Düsseldorf* (Düsseldorf, 1877–1911).

TABLE A–3
Penalties for Ordinance Violations (*Übertretungen*)
in Duisburg, 1864–1909

Year	Total Penalties[a]	Truancy	Disorderly Conduct	Failure to Register
1864	693.5	456.5	—	—
1865	619.2	409.8	—	—
1866	1006.7	687.7	—	—
1867	1466.8	815.3	—	—
1868	1323.0	525.0	—	—
1869	1580.7	722.5	—	—
1870	1113.1	598.6	—	—
1871	925.9	382.8	—	—
1872	1725.1	944.2	138.6	96.6
1873	1833.2	1063.0	—	—
1874	1905.5	1144.6	182.9	175.7
1875	1535.2	797.4	—	—
1876	1952.5	965.0	191.5	201.5
1877–78	1905.8	1041.9	180.7	96.9
1878–79	1305.5	699.8	179.4	74.2
1879–80	1195.7	605.3	147.5	70.5
1880–81	1175.1	553.6	191.4	70.3
1881–82	1134.7	571.9	138.9	65.4
1882–83	1115.6	614.8	118.0	66.8
1883–84	922.7	469.9	111.1	45.6
1884–85	965.3	516.0	75.1	48.9
1885–86	911.4	668.2	48.2	21.2
1886–87	920.7	583.4	53.9	32.1
1887–88	1005.2	631.9	70.1	35.7
1888–89	1122.1	603.0	85.2	42.0

Year	Total Penalties[a]	Truancy	Disorderly Conduct	Failure to Register
1889–90	781.5	346.7	78.8	46.5
1890–91	824.6	332.9	119.7	50.7
1891–92	1059.3	407.8	123.9	146.8
1892–93	958.1	374.5	109.3	83.6
1893–94	906.9	365.1	138.3	48.2
1894–95	1037.8	477.7	117.5	38.4
1895–96	1036.2	489.4	105.4	176.4
1896–97	1082.7	577.8	115.8	104.2
1897–98	1249.3	754.6	104.7	110.3
1898–99	1019.7	543.8	107.3	105.3
1899	1134.8	556.8	101.5	255.7
1900	1143.9	615.1	95.3	156.7
1901	1132.1	464.0	118.7	132.2
1902	1112.9	427.8	101.7	180.4
1903	923.6	282.5	117.0	127.7
1904	945.8	319.1	118.1	132.6
1905	1070.0	329.1	164.2	137.8
1906	1011.0	324.1	96.1	171.3
1907	1111.4	296.0	172.1	163.8
1908	1008.6	282.6	180.1	152.4
1909	981.6	247.9	166.8	153.7

Source: *Bericht über den Stand und die Verwaltung der Geminde-Angelegenheiten der Stadt Duisburg* (Duisburg, 1864–1909).

[a]Rates are per 10,000 population.

TABLE A-4
Reported Crimes (*Verbrechen* and *Vergehen*)
in Duisburg, 1864–1913

Year	Property Crimes[a]			Violent Crimes[b]		
	Total	Per 10,000 Population	Arrests	Total	Per 10,000 Population	Arrests
1864	117	54.9	68	10	4.7	9
1865	83	37.4	61	14	6.3	13
1866	107	46.7	84	13	5.7	12
1867	102	39.6	75	21	8.2	19
1868	106	41.4	79	15	5.8	14
1869	132	48.1	98	4	1.5	0
1870	167	58.2	140	21	7.3	18
1871	177	58.7	126	21	7.0	21
1872	229	71.3	112	45	14.0	41
1873	263	75.9	130	44	12.7	31
1874	251	69.7	194	39	10.8	38
1875	335	91.3	266	53	14.4	52
1876	351	95.2	221	84	22.8	78
1877–78	450	121.5	312	69	18.6	65
1878–79	308	81.0	243	73	19.2	64
1879–80	322	82.9	—	74	19.0	—
1880–81	364	89.8	—	53	13.1	—
1881–82	325	78.1	—	93	22.4	—
1882–83	365	84.6	—	114	26.4	—
1883–84	311	70.2	—	107	24.2	—
1884–85	333	73.4	—	169	37.3	—
1885–86	301	63.3	—	123	25.9	—
1886–87	346	71.8	—	138	28.6	—
1887–88	287	57.1	—	157	31.2	—
1888–89	314	59.2	—	137	25.8	—
1889–90	317	55.1	—	167	29.9	—
1890–91	368	63.3	—	171	29.4	—
1891–92	487	84.5	—	180	31.2	—

Table A–4, continued

Year	Property Crimes[a]			Violent Crimes[b]		
	Total	Per 10,000 Population	Arrests	Total	Per 10,000 Population	Arrests
1892–93	452	72.7	—	161	25.9	—
1893–94	489	76.9	—	180	28.3	—
1894–95	456	68.1	—	171	25.5	—
1895–96	387	55.1	—	152	21.6	—
1896–97	575	77.1	—	200	26.8	—
1897–98	633	81.0	—	192	24.6	—
1898–99	719	87.6	—	162	19.7	—
1899	792	91.1	—	200	23.0	—
1900	972	105.0	—	253	27.3	—
1901	1002	108.1	—	265	28.6	—
1902	1209	130.4	—	254	27.4	—
1903	1987	114.3	—	589	33.9	—
1904	2534	139.3	—	925	50.8	—
1905	2648	137.7	—	920	47.8	—
1906	3398	167.0	—	847	41.6	—
1907	4018	190.6	—	889	42.2	—
1908	3775	175.9	—	868	40.4	—
1909	4150	193.6	—	943	44.0	—
1910	4110	179.1	—	849	37.0	—
1911	4530	191.0	—	982	41.4	—
1912	4872	205.5	—	1341	56.5	—
1913	5122	209.0	—	1273	51.9	—

Source: *Bericht über den Stand und die Verwaltung der Gemeinde-Angelegenheiten der Stadt Duisburg* (Duisburg, 1864–1913).

[a]Property crime includes theft and attempts (excluding wood theft), burglary and attempts, arson, fraud, receiving stolen goods, and vandalism.

[b]Violent crime includes homicide, assault, robbery and attempts, and rape.

NOTES

PREFACE

1. For recent literature on innovations in policing in the nineteenth century and the debate surrounding the reasons for such innovations, see, especially, Victor Bailey, ed., *Policing and Punishment in Nineteenth-Century Britain* (New Brunswick, N.J., 1981); David H. Bayley, *Patterns of Policing: A Comparative International Analysis* (New Brunswick, N.J., 1985); John A. Davis, *Conflict and Control: Law and Order in Nineteenth-Century Italy* (Atlantic Highlands, N.J., 1988); Clive Emsley, *Policing and Its Context, 1750–1870* (London, 1983); V. A. C. Gatrell, "Crime, Authority, and the Policeman-State," in F. M. L. Thompson, ed., *The Cambridge Social History of Britain, 1750–1950*, vol. 3 (Cambridge, 1990), pp. 243–310; Ted Robert Gurr, Peter N. Grabosky, and Richard C. Hula, *The Politics of Crime and Conflict: A Comparative History of Four Cities* (Beverly Hills, 1977); Sidney L. Harring, *Policing a Class Society: The Experience of American Cities, 1865–1915* (New Brunswick, N.J., 1983); David R. Johnson, *Policing the Urban Underworld: The Impact of Crime on the Development of the American Police, 1800–1887* (Philadelphia, 1979); Stanley Palmer, *Police and Protest in England and Ireland, 1780–1850* (Cambridge, 1988); David Philips, *Crime and Authority in Victorian England: The Black Country, 1835–1860* (London, 1977); and Carolyn Steedman, *Policing the Victorian Community: The Formation of English Provincial Police Forces, 1856–1880* (London, 1984).

2. Wilbur R. Miller, *Cops and Bobbies: Police Authority in New York and London, 1830–1870* (Chicago, 1977).

3. Hsi-huey Liang, *The Berlin Police Force in the Weimar Republic* (Berkeley, 1970); Peter Leßmann, *Die preußische Schutzpolizei in der Weimarer Republik: Streifendienst und Straßenkampf* (Düsseldorf, 1989). See also Johannes Buder, *Die Reorganisation der preussischen Polizei, 1918–1923* (Frankfurt am Main, 1986).

4. Alf Lüdtke, *"Gemeinwohl," Polizei, und "Festungspraxis": Staatliche Gewaltsamkeit und innere Verwaltung in Preussen, 1815–1850* (Göttingen, 1982). Translated into English as *Police and State in Prussia, 1815–1850* (Cambridge, 1989).

5. Dieter Fricke, *Bismarcks Prätorianer: Die Berliner politische Polizei im Kampf gegen die deutsche Arbeiterbewegung (1871–1898)* (Berlin, 1962); Wolfram Siemann, *"Deutschlands Ruhe, Sicherheit, und Ordnung": Die Anfänge der politischen Polizei, 1806–1866* (Tübingen, 1985).

6. Albrecht Funk, *Polizei und Rechtsstaat: Die Entwicklung des staatlichen Gewaltmonopols in Preussen, 1848–1918* (Frankfurt am Main, 1986).

7. Ralph Jessen, *Polizei im Industrierevier: Modernisierung und Herrschaftspraxis im westfälischen Ruhrgebiet, 1848–1914* (Göttingen, 1991).

8. Elaine G. Spencer, *Management and Labor in Imperial Germany: Ruhr Industrialists as Employers, 1896–1914* (New Brunswick, N.J., 1984).

176 NOTES TO PAGES xiii–5

9. Friedrich-Wilhelm Henning, *Düsseldorf und seine Wirtschaft: Zur Geschichte einer Region*, vol. 2 (Düsseldorf, 1981), p. 387.

10. Giesbert Knopp, *Die Preussische Verwaltung des Regierungsbezirks Düsseldorf in den Jahren 1899–1919* (Cologne, 1974), p. 20.

11. James H. Jackson, Jr., "Migration in Duisburg, 1867–1890: Occupational and Familial Contexts," *Journal of Urban History* 8 (May 1982): 235–70; Wolfgang Köllmann, "Binnenwanderung und Bevölkerungsstrukturen der Ruhrgebietsgroßstädte im Jahre 1907," in Wolfgang Köllmann, *Bevölkerung in der industriellen Revolution: Studien zur Bevölkerungsgeschichte Deutschlands* (Göttingen, 1974), pp. 171–84.

12. Eric Monkkonen, "Municipal Reports as an Indicator Source: The Nineteenth-Century Police," *Historical Methods* 12 (Spring 1979): 57–65; Eric Monkkonen, *Police in Urban America, 1860–1920* (Cambridge, 1981).

CHAPTER I: PRUSSIANS AND RHINELANDERS TO 1848

1. On defining and extending police powers before the nineteenth century, see Marc Raeff, *The Well-ordered Police State: Social and Institutional Change through Law in the Germanies and Russia, 1600–1800* (New Haven, 1983); Georg-Christoph von Unruh, "Polizei, Polizeiwissenschaft, und Kameralistik," in Kurt G. A. Jeserich et al., eds., *Deutsche Verwaltungsgeschichte*, vol. 1 (Stuttgart, 1983), pp. 388–427.

2. C. A. B. Behrens, *Society, Government, and the Enlightenment: The Experience of Eighteenth-Century France and Prussia* (London, 1985), pp. 108, 228.

3. Compare Egon Bittner, *The Function of the Police in Modern Society: A Review of Background Factors, Current Practices, and Possible Role Models* (Washington, D.C., 1970), p. 15.

4. David H. Bayley, *Patterns of Policing: A Comparative International Analysis* (New Brunswick, N.J., 1985), p. 67; Bruce Lenman and Geoffrey Parker, "The State, the Community, and the Criminal Law in Early Modern Europe," in V. A. C. Gatrell, Bruce Lenman, and Geoffrey Parker, eds., *Crime and the Law: The Social History of Crime in Western Europe since 1500* (London, 1980), p. 39; Edgar Leoning, "Polizei," in J. Conrad et al., eds. *Handwörterbuch der Staatswissenschaften*, 2d ed. (Jena, 1901), p. 110.

5. Franz-Ludwig Knemeyer, "Polizei," in Otto Brunner, Werner Conze, and Reinhart Koselleck, eds., *Geschichtliche Grundbegriffe: Historisches Lexikon zur politisch-sozialen Sprache in Deutschland*, vol. 4 (Stuttgart, 1978), p. 887.

6. Walter Obenaus, *Die Entwicklung der preussischen Sicherheitspolizei bis zum Ende der Reaktionszeit* (Berlin, 1940), p. 39; Paul Schmidt, *Die ersten 50 Jahre der Königlichen Schutzmannschaft zu Berlin: Eine Geschichte des Korps für dessen Angehörige und Freunde* (Berlin, 1898), pp. 6–8.

7. Obenaus, *Die Entwicklung der preussischen Sicherheitspolizei*, pp. 37–38.

8. Compare Werner Danckert, *Unehrliche Leute: Die verfemten Berufe*, 2d ed. (Bern, 1979), pp. 46–47.

9. Obenaus, *Die Entwicklung der preussischen Sicherheitspolizei*, p. 31.

10. Unruh, "Polizei," pp. 388-427.

11. Albrecht Funk, *Polizei und Rechtsstaat: Die Entwicklung des staatlichen Gewaltmonopols in Preussen, 1848-1918* (Frankfurt am Main, 1986), p. 46.

12. Compare James F. Richardson, "Police in America: Functions and Control," in James A. Inciardi and Charles E. Faupel, eds., *History and Crime: Implications for Criminal Justice Policy* (Beverly Hills, 1980), pp. 214-15.

13. Obenaus, *Die Entwicklung der preussischen Sicherheitspolizei*, p. 68.

14. Hans-Gerhard Husung, *Protest und Repression im Vormärz: Norddeutschland zwischen Restauration und Revolution* (Göttingen, 1983), p. 224.

15. Funk, *Polizei und Rechtsstaat*, p. 59; Karl-Joseph Hummel, *München in der Revolution von 1848-1849* (Göttingen, 1987), p. 391; Alf Lüdtke, "Praxis und Funktion staatlicher Repression: Preussen, 1815-1850," *Geschichte und Gesellschaft* 3 (1978): 198. See also, Ralph Jessen, *Polizei im Industrierevier: Modernisierung und Herrschaftspraxis im westfälischen Ruhrgebiet, 1848-1914* (Göttingen, 1991), p. 353.

16. Joseph Hansen, ed., *Rheinische Briefe und Akten zur Geschichte der politische Bewegung, 1830-1850*, vol. 1, pt. 1 (Osnabrück, 1967, reprint of 1919 edition), pp. 81-82, 84-85, 240.

17. Funk, *Polizei und Rechtsstaat*, p. 45.

18. Ibid., p. 46.

19. Stanley Palmer, *Police and Protest in England and Ireland, 1780-1850* (Cambridge, 1988), table 4.2.

20. See, for example, Philip Thurmond Smith, *Policing Victorian London: Political Policing, Public Order, and the London Metropolitan Police* (Westport, Conn., 1985).

21. For the military presence in Paris, see Patricia O'Brien, "Urban Growth and Social Control: The Municipal Police of Paris in the First Half of the Nineteenth Century," *Proceedings of the Western Society for French History* 3 (1975): 314-22. For the domestic peacekeeping role of the Prussian military, see the various works of Alf Lüdtke, especially *"Gemeinwohl," Polizei, und "Festungspraxis": Staatliche Gewaltsamkeit und innere Verwaltung in Preussen, 1815-1850* (Göttingen, 1982).

22. Wilbur R. Miller, *Cops and Bobbies: Police Authority in New York and London, 1830-1870* (Chicago, 1977), p. 15.

23. On the transition from French to Prussian rule, see Jeffrey M. Diefendorf, *Businessmen and Politics in the Rhineland, 1789-1834* (Princeton, 1980); Rüdiger Schütz, "Zur Eingliederung der Rheinlande," in Peter Baumgart, ed., *Expansion und Integration: Zur Eingliederung neugewonnener Gebiete in den preussischen Staat* (Cologne, 1984), pp. 195-226.

24. Dirk Blasius, "Der Kampf um die Geschworenengerichte im Vormärz," in Hans-Ulrich Wehler, ed., *Sozialgeschichte Heute* (Göttingen, 1974), pp. 148-61; Friedrich-Wilhelm Henning, *Düsseldorf und seine Wirtschaft: Zur Geschichte einer Region*, vol. 1 (Düsseldorf, 1981), p. 350.

25. Reinhart Koselleck, *Preussen zwischen Reform und Revolution: Allgemeines Landrecht, Verwaltung, und soziale Bewegung von 1791 bis 1848* (Stuttgart, 1967), p. 461.

26. Lüdtke, *"Gemeinwohl," Polizei, und "Festungspraxis,"* p. 158.

27. Regierungspräsident, Trier, to Oberpräsident, Rheinprovinz, 24 September 1839, Landeshauptarchiv Koblenz (hereinafter referred to as Staatsarchiv Koblenz) 403/2435.

28. Hansen, *Rheinische Briefe und Akten,* vol. 2, pt. 1, p. 596.

29. Obenaus, *Die Entwicklung der preussischen Sicherheitspolizei,* p. 79.

30. Minister des Innern to Oberpräsident, Rheinprovinz, 8 May 1833, Staatsarchiv Koblenz 403/118. In addition to the three in the Rhine province, the other royal police administrators were located in Berlin, Königsberg, Breslau, Charlottenburg, Potsdam, Danzig, and Magdeburg. Funk, *Polizei und Rechtsstaat,* p. 52.

31. The police and the gendarmerie were not alone in lacking funds for expansion. During these same decades, a financially hard-pressed Prussian government—unwilling to appeal to representative institutions for support—likewise failed to provide resources permitting significant additions to either the administrative bureaucracy or the military. According to John R. Gillis, per capita expenditure for justice and administration declined during the *Vormärz.* John R. Gillis, *The Prussian Bureaucracy in Crisis, 1840–1860: Origins of an Administrative Ethos* (Stanford, 1971), p. 40. See also Hans Hattenbauer, *Geschichte des Beamtentums* (Cologne, 1980), p. 203; Hansjoachim Henning, *Die deutsche Beamtenschaften im 19. Jahrhundert* (Stuttgart, 1984), p. 32; Lüdtke, *"Gemeinwohl," Polizei, und "Festungspraxis,"* p. 332; Manfred Messerschmidt, "Die Armee in Staat und Gesellschaft—Die Bismarckzeit," in Michael Stürmer, ed., *Das kaiserliche Deutschland: Politik und Gesellschaft, 1870–1918* (Düsseldorf, 1970), p. 92.

32. Etat für die Polizeiverwaltung der Stadt Aachen 1832–34, Staatsarchiv Koblenz 403/97.

33. Minister des Innern und der Polizei to Oberpräsident, Rheinprovinz, 18 May 1839, Staatsarchiv Koblenz 403/118.

34. Wolfgang Schieder, "Kirche und Revolution: Aspekte der Trierer Wallfahrt 1844," *Archiv für Sozialgeschichte* 14 (1974): 421–31.

35. See, for example, Regierung Düsseldorf, Abteilung des Innern, to Oberpräsident, Rheinprovinz, 15 September and 30 December 1834, Staatsarchiv Koblenz 403/2612.

36. Compare, for example, the similarities of Polizeiverwaltung, Düsseldorf, 1 February 1807, and Regierung Düsseldorf to Oberpräsident, Rheinprovinz, 12 December 1827, both in Staatsarchiv Koblenz 403/2616.

37. Joseph Klersch, *Die Kölnische Fastnacht von ihren Anfängen bis zur Gegenwart* (Cologne, 1961), pp. 85–86, 112–17; Michael Müller, "Karneval als Politikum: Zum Verhältnis zwischen Preussen und dem Rheinland im 19. Jahrhundert," in Kurt Düwell and Wolfgang Köllmann, eds., *Rheinland-West-*

falen im Industriezeitalter, vol. 1 (Wuppertal, 1983), pp. 207–23. For similar developments, see Friedrich Schütz, "Das Verhältnis der Behörden zur Mainzer Fastnacht im Vormärz (1838–1846)," *Jahrbuch für Westdeutsche Landesgeschichte* 6 (1980): 291–318, and Jonathan Sperber, *Rhineland Radicals: The Democratic Movement and the Revolution of 1848–1849* (Princeton, 1991), pp. 98–101.

38. Regierung Düsseldorf, Abteilung des Innern, to Oberpräsident, Rheinprovinz, 4 April 1834, Staatsarchiv Koblenz 403/7063; Regierung Düsseldorf, Abteilung des Innern, to Landrat, Düsseldorf, 7 June 1834, Stadtarchiv Düsseldorf II/1433.

39. Hansen, *Rheinische Briefe und Akten,* vol. 2, pt. 1, pp. 73–89.

40. Hansen, *Rheinische Briefe und Akten,* vol. 1, p. 112; Minister des Innern to Oberpräsident, Rheinprovinz, 8 May 1833, Staatsarchiv Koblenz 403/118.

41. Hansen, *Rheinische Briefe und Akten,* vol. 1, pp. 116–17; Obenaus, *Die Entwicklung der preussischen Sicherheitspolizei,* pp. 107–8; Wolfram Siemann, *"Deutschlands Ruhe, Sicherheit, und Ordnung": Die Anfänge der politischen Polizei, 1806–1866* (Tübingen, 1985), pp. 176–80; Vierter Rheinische Landtag, Zwölfte Sitzung, 23 November 1833, Staatsarchiv Koblenz 403/118.

42. Hansen, *Rheinische Briefe und Akten,* vol. 1, p. 198.

43. Ibid., p. 40.

44. Ibid., p. 75.

45. Ibid., p. 51.

46. Wolfgang Köllmann, "Pauperismus in Rheinland-Westfalen im Vormärz," in Kurt Düwell and Wolfgang Köllmann, eds., *Rheinland-Westfalen im Industriezeitalter,* vol. 1 (Wuppertal, 1983), p. 150.

47. Steve Hochstadt, "Migration and Industrialization in Germany, 1815–1977," *Social Science History* 5 (Fall 1981): 448; Wolfgang Zorn, "Die wirtschaftliche Struktur der Rheinprovinz um 1820," *Vierteljahrschrift für Sozial- und Wirtschaftsgeschichte* 54 (October 1967): 293.

48. Dieter Dowe, "Legale Interessenvertretung und Streik: Der Arbeitskampf in den Tuchfabriken des Kreises Lennep (Bergisches Land) 1850," in Klaus Tenfelde and Heinrich Volkmann, eds., *Streik: Zur Geschichte des Arbeitskampfes in Deutschland während der Industrialisierung* (Munich, 1981), p. 32.

49. Heinrich Silbergleit, *Preussens Städte: Denkschrift zum 100 jährigen Jubiläum der Städteordnung von 19. November 1808* (Berlin, 1908), pp. 2–3.

50. Eberhard Illner, *Bürgerliche Organisierung in Elberfeld, 1775–1850* (Neustadt an der Aisch, 1982), pp. 22, 29.

51. Illner, *Bürgerliche Organisierung,* pp. 63, 79; Friedrich Engels, "Briefe aus dem Wuppertal," in Karl Marx and Friedrich Engels, *Werke,* vol. 1 (Berlin, 1964), p. 417.

52. Illner, *Bürgerliche Organisierung,* pp. 65–67.

53. Hansen, *Rheinische Briefe und Akten,* vol. 2, pt. 1, pp. 238–40; Landrat, Elberfeld, to Regierung Düsseldorf, 29 April 1847, Nordrhein-Westfälisches Hauptstaatsarchiv, Düsseldorf (hereinafter cited as Staatsarchiv Düsseldorf), Regierung Düsseldorf 215.

54. See, for example, Hansen, *Rheinische Briefe und Akten*, vol. 1, p. 671.

55. Heinrich Rösen, "Der Aufstand der Krefelder 'Seidenfabrikarbeiter' 1828 und die Bildung einer 'Sicherheitswache': Eine Dokumentation," *Die Heimat: Zeitschrift für niederrheinische Heimatpflege* 36 (1965): 32–61. Compare Lüdtke, "Praxis und Funktion," *Geschichte und Gesellschaft* 3 (1978): 205, for similar comments about policemen in the county of Lennep (Bergisches Land) in 1835.

56. Landrat, Krefeld, to Regierung Düsseldorf, 23 November 1839, Staatsarchiv Düsseldorf, Regierung Düsseldorf 8695.

57. Polizeiverwaltungskosten, 1853, 1854, 1855, Stadtarchiv Krefeld 4/940.

58. Meeting, Stadtrat, Elberfeld, 23 July 1844, Staatsarchiv Düsseldorf, Regierung Düsseldorf 217a. On the early development of urban policing in the Wuppertal, see Rolf Becker, "Gründerzeit im Wuppertal—dargestellt am Verhältnis von Polizei und Alltag in Elberfeld und Barmen 1806–1870," in Karl-Hermann Beeck and Rolf Becker, eds., *Gründerzeit: Versuch einer Grenzbestimmung im Wuppertal* (Cologne, 1984), pp. 64–108.

59. Oberbürgermeister, Elberfeld, to Landrat, 24 July 1844, Staatsarchiv Düsseldorf, Regierung Düsseldorf 217a.

60. Lüdtke, *"Gemeinwohl," Polizei, und "Festungspraxis,"* p. 149; Regierung Düsseldorf, Abteilung des Innern, to Landrat, Düsseldorf, 13 February 1836, Stadtarchiv Düsseldorf II/1335.

61. See, for example, Oberbürgermeister, Elberfeld, to Landrat, 10 October 1844, Staatsarchiv Düsseldorf, Regierung Düsseldorf 217a.

62. *Allgemeine Dienst-Instruktion für die Polizei-Sergeanten der Oberbürgermeisterei Elberfeld* (Elberfeld, 1847), Stadtarchiv Duisburg 306/92.

63. Rösen, "Der Aufstand der Krefelder 'Seidenfabrikarbeiter,' " p. 58.

64. Gendarmen, Regierungsbezirk Düsseldorf, 5 February 1829, Staatsarchiv Koblenz 403/2197.

65. Regierung Düsseldorf, Abteilung des Innern, to Oberpräsident, Rheinprovinz, 16 January 1832, Staatsarchiv Koblenz 403/97.

66. Hugo Weidenhaupt, "Von der französischen zur preussischen Zeit (1806–1856)," in Hugo Weidenhaupt, ed., *Düsseldorf: Geschichte von den Ursprüngen bis ins 20. Jahrhundert*, vol. 2 (Düsseldorf, 1988), p. 363.

67. Police budget, Oberbürgermeisterei Düsseldorf, 1848, Staatsarchiv Düsseldorf, Regierung Düsseldorf, Präs. Büro 915.

68. Friedrich Lenger, *Zwischen Kleinbürgertum und Proletariat: Studien zur Sozialgeschichte der Düsseldorfer Handwerker, 1816–1878* (Göttingen, 1986), p. 41.

69. Carl-Ludwig Holtfrerich, *Quantitative Wirtschaftsgeschichte des Ruhrkohlenbergbaus im 19. Jahrhundert: Eine Führungssektoranalyse* (Dortmund, 1973), p. 56.

70. Illner, *Bürgerliche Organisierung*, p. 29; Köllmann, *Sozialgeschichte der Stadt Barmen im 19. Jahrhundert* (Tübingen, 1960), p. 138.

71. Polizeiinspektor Walther, Krefeld, to Landrat, Krefeld, 10 July 1847; Regierung Düsseldorf, Abteilung des Innern, to Landrat, Krefeld, 16 July 1847;

Regierung Düsseldorf, Abteilung des Innern, to Oberpräsident, Rheinprovinz, 27 July 1847; all in Staatsarchiv Koblenz 403/163.

72. Bürgermeister, Essen, to Landrat, Duisburg, 5 March 1841: Landrat, Duisburg, to Regierung Düsseldorf, 28 September 1842; both in Staatsarchiv Düsseldorf, Regierung Düsseldorf 206.

73. Regierung Düsseldorf, Abteilung des Innern, to Landräte, 6 September 1847, Staatsarchiv Düsseldorf, Regierung Düsseldorf 86.

74. *Regelment für die städtische Nachtwache zu Elberfeld* (Elberfeld, 1847), p. 4, Staatsarchiv Düsseldorf, Regierung Düsseldorf 213.

75. Nachweise des Personals der Nachtsicherheitswache, Mülheim/Ruhr, 8 January 1828, Staatsarchiv Düsseldorf, Regierung Düsseldorf 206.

76. Projekt und Kostenanschlag zur einer Nachtwache für den Stadtbezirk von Barmen, 10 April 1844; Landrat, Elberfeld, to Bürgermeister, Barmen, 7 June 1845; both in Staatsarchiv Düsseldorf, Regierung Düsseldorf 213.

77. *Regelment für die städtische Nachtwache zu Elberfeld* (Elberfeld, 1847), Staatsarchiv Düsseldorf, Regierung Düsseldorf 213.

78. Gesetz über die Aufnahme neu anziehender Personen, 31 December 1842, Stadtarchiv Krefeld 4/958; James Harvey Jackson, Jr., "Migration and Urbanization in the Ruhr Valley, 1850–1900" (Ph.D. diss., University of Minnesota, 1980), pp. 202–3.

79. Regierung Düsseldorf to Landräte, Bürgermeister, and Steuereinnehmer, 14 February 1834, Stadtarchiv Düsseldorf II/1495.

80. Compare Gustav Zimmermann, *Wesen, Geschichte, Literatur, characteristische Tätigkeiten und Organisation der modernen Polizei: Ein Leitfaden für Polizisten und Juristen* (Hanover, 1852), pp. 203–10.

81. *Allgemeine Dienst-Instruktion für die Polizei-Sergeanten der Oberbürgermeisterei Elberfeld* (Elberfeld, 1847), pp. 9–10, Stadtarchiv Duisburg 306/92.

82. Regierung Düsseldorf, Abteilung des Innern, to Oberpräsident, Rheinprovinz, 6 October 1844, Staatsarchiv Koblenz 403/6807.

83. Friedrich Wilhelm IV to Staats- und Kabinets-Minister von Bodelschwingh, 31 October 1845, Staatsarchiv Koblenz 403/6807.

84. Regierungspräsident, Düsseldorf, to Oberpräsident, Rheinprovinz, 15 August 1839, Staatsarchiv Koblenz 403/2435.

85. Gendarmen, Regierungsbezirk Düsseldorf, 5 October 1823 and 8 September 1849, both in Staatsarchiv Koblenz 403/2197.

86. Rösen, "Der Aufstand der Krefelder 'Seidenfabrikarbeiter,' " pp. 32–61.

87. Ibid., p. 53.

88. Regierungsprasident, Düsseldorf, to Oberpräsident, Rheinprovinz, 4 September 1830, Staatsarchiv Koblenz 403/2275.

89. Michael Müller, "Die preussische Rheinprovinz unter dem Einfluss von Julirevolution und Hambacher Fest, 1830–1834," *Jahrbuch für Westdeutsche Landesgeschichte* 6 (1980): 280.

90. Denunciation, Gendarme Lestmann, 27 May 1845, Staatsarchiv Düsseldorf, Regierung Düsseldorf 204.

91. Bürgermeister, Essen, to Regierung Düsseldorf, 22 May 1845, Staats-archiv Düsseldorf, Regierung Düsseldorf 204.

92. Letter signed by forty Essen citizens to Regierung Düsseldorf, 28 May 1845, Staatsarchiv Düsseldorf, Regierung Düsseldorf 204.

93. Hansen, *Rheinische Briefe und Akten,* vol. 2, pt. 1, p. 20; Vernehmungs-protokoll des Polizeiinspektors Leonard Walther, 22 July 1846; Generalprocura-tor, Cologne, to Regierung Düsseldorf, 6 November 1846; both in Staatsarchiv Düsseldorf, Regierung Düsseldorf 8695.

CHAPTER II: REVOLUTION AND REACTION, 1848–1858

1. Gutachten in der disziplinar Untersuchungssache gegen den Polizei-agenten Scheffler, Elberfeld, 16 July 1849, Staatsarchiv Düsseldorf, Regierung Düsseldorf 220.

2. Wolfram Siemann, *"Deutschlands Ruhe, Sicherheit, und Ordnung":* Die Anfänge der politischen Polizei, 1806–1866 (Tübingen, 1985), p. 342.

3. See, for example, Report, Bürgermeister, Essen, 16 May 1848, Staats-archiv Düsseldorf, Regierung Düsseldorf 8806; Oberpräsident, Rheinprovinz, to Regierungspräsident, Düsseldorf, 30 May 1849, Staatsarchiv Düsseldorf, Regierung Düsseldorf 8984; Regierung Düsseldorf, Abteilung des Innern, to Landrat, Krefeld, 19 October 1848, Stadtarchiv Krefeld 4/989.

4. Proposal to pension Polizeiinspektor Peter Joseph Holthausen, 10 July 1850, Staatsarchiv Düsseldorf, Regierung Düsseldorf 8703.

5. Minister des Innern to Regierung Düsseldorf, 24 August 1848, Staats-archiv Düsseldorf, Regierung Düsseldorf 8702; Polizeiinspektor Zeller to Regie-rung Düsseldorf, 18 November 1848, Staatsarchiv Düsseldorf, Regierung Düs-seldorf, Präs. Büro 740; Regierungspräsident, Düsseldorf, to Polizeiinspektor Zeller, 24 November 1848, Staatsarchiv Düsseldorf, Regierung Düsseldorf 201.

6. Christoph Klessmann, "Zur Sozialgeschichte der Reichsverfassungs-kampagne von 1849," *Historische Zeitschrift* 218 (1974): 303.

7. Joseph Hansen, ed., *Rheinische Briefe und Akten zur Geschichte der politische Bewegung, 1830–1850,* vol. 2, pt. 1 (Bonn, 1942), p. 689.

8. Eberhard Illner, *Bürgerliche Organisierung in Elberfeld, 1775–1850* (Neu-stadt an der Aisch, 1982), p. 177; Klessmann, "Zur Sozialgeschichte der Reichsverfassungskampagne," pp. 297–99; Jonathan Sperber, *Rhineland Radicals: The Democratic Movement and the Revolution of 1848–1849* (Princeton, 1991), pp. 349–86.

9. Hansen, *Rheinische Briefe und Akten,* vol. 2, pt. 1, p. 716; Regierungs-präsident, Düsseldorf, to Oberpräsident, Rheinprovinz, 24 March 1848, Staats-archiv Koblenz 403/2275; Statuten der Duisburger Bürgerwehr, 2 April 1848, Stadtarchiv Duisburg 306/350.

10. Klaus Goebel and Manfred Wichelhaus, eds., *Aufstand der Bürger: Revolution 1849 im westdeutschen Industriezentrum* (Wuppertal, 1974), pp. 223–34,

241. For the imposition of similar sanctions on French municipalities, see Roger Price, "Techniques of Repression: The Control of Popular Protest in Mid-Nineteenth-Century France," *Historical Journal* 25 (1982): 886.

11. In the case of the demolition of the iron foundry, local notables were apparently not totally displeased to see the new competitor eliminated. See Manfred Gailus, *Strasse und Brot: Sozialer Protest in den deutschen Staaten unter besonderer Berücksichtigung Preussens, 1847–1849* (Göttingen, 1990), pp. 161–62; Sperber, *Rhineland Radicals*, pp. 65–69.

12. Hansen, *Rheinische Briefe und Akten*, vol. 2, pt. 1, pp. 669–70; Illner, *Bürgerliche Organisierung*, pp. 148, 175–76.

13. Generalkommando des VII. Armee Corps to Oberpräsident, Rhein-provinz, 24 November 1849, Staatsarchiv Düsseldorf, Regierung Düsseldorf 99.

14. Friedrich Lenger, *Zwischen Kleinbürgertum und Proletariat: Studien zur Sozialgeschichte der Düsseldorfer Handwerker, 1816–1878* (Göttingen, 1986), pp. 154, 160, 167, 189; Hugo Weidenhaupt, "Von der französischen zur preussischen Zeit (1806–1856)," in Hugo Weidenhaupt, ed., *Düsseldorf: Geschichte von den Ursprüngen bis ins 20. Jahrhundert*, vol. 2 (Düsseldorf, 1988), pp. 426–35. Report, Regierung Düsseldorf, 22 November 1848; Proclamation, General-Lieutenant und Commandeur der 14. Division von Drigalski to Regierungspräsident, Düsseldorf, 22 November 1848, both in Staatsarchiv Düsseldorf, Regierung Düsseldorf 813.

15. Illner, *Bürgerliche Organisierung*, p. 176; Report, Polizeiinspektor Zeller, Düsseldorf, 5 October 1848; Landratsamt Elberfeld to Regierung, Düsseldorf, 24 May 1850; both in Staatsarchiv Düsseldorf, Regierung Düsseldorf 99.

16. Goebel and Wichelhaus, *Aufstand der Bürger*, pp. 233–34.

17. Paul Schmidt, *Die ersten 50 Jahre der Königlichen Schutzmannschaft zu Berlin: Eine Geschichte des Korps für dessen Angehörige und Freunde* (Berlin, 1898), pp. 19–31; Frank J. Thomason, "The Prussian Police State in Berlin, 1848–1871" (Ph.D. diss., Johns Hopkins, 1978), pp. 95, 114–16.

18. Thomason, "The Police State in Berlin," pp. 117–19, 259–67.

19. *Stenographische Berichte über die Verhandlungen des Preussischen Hauses der Abgeordneten*, 9 February 1850, p. 2470.

20. Albrecht Funk, *Polizei und Rechtsstaat: Die Entwicklung des staatlichen Gewaltmonopols in Preussen, 1848–1918* (Frankfurt am Main, 1986), p. 64.

21. On the significance of this initiative for American cities and the resistance it encountered, see Eric H. Monkkonen, *Police in Urban America, 1860–1920* (Cambridge, 1981), pp. 53–55.

22. Clive Emsley, *Policing and Its Context, 1750–1870* (London, 1983), pp. 96–97.

23. V. A. C. Gatrell, "The Decline of Theft and Violence in Victorian and Edwardian England," in V. A. C. Gatrell, Bruce Lenman, and Geoffrey Parker, eds., *Crime and the Law: The Social History of Crime in Western Europe since 1500* (London, 1980), p. 275; Stanley Palmer, *Police and Protest in England*

and Ireland, 1780–1850 (Cambridge, 1988) p. 511; David Philips, *Crime and Authority in Victorian England: The Black Country, 1835–1860* (London, 1977), p. 70.

24. *Stenographische Berichte über die Verhandlungen des Preussischen Hauses der Abgeordneten, Anlagen,* 1859, p. 288.

25. Ibid., p. 293.

26. Ibid.

27. Minister des Innern to Oberregierungsrat von Pankeren, 26 May 1849, Staatsarchiv Düsseldorf, Regierung Düsseldorf 8805.

28. Verhandelt, Elberfeld, 4 July 1849; Disziplinaruntersuchung den Polizeisergeanten Samuel Scheffler, 31 January 1850; both in Staatsarchiv Düsseldorf, Regierung Düsseldorf 220. Goebel and Wichelhaus, *Aufstand der Bürger,* pp. 105–6.

29. Polizeiinspektor Walther to Oberbürgermeister, Krefeld, 21 March 1851; Oberbürgermeister, Krefeld, to Polizeiinspektor Walther and Polizeikommissare Heligus and Klinge, 22 March 1851; Regierung Düsseldorf, Abteilung des Innern, 7 April 1851; all in Staatsarchiv Düsseldorf, Regierung Düsseldorf 8695.

30. Bericht der Commission über den Antrag des Polizeiinspektors Walther, 16 April 1851, Staatsarchiv Düsseldorf, Regierung Düsseldorf 8695.

31. Minister des Innern to Oberbürgermeister, Krefeld, 25 February 1853, Stadtarchiv Krefeld 4/940.

32. "Eduard Viedebantt," *Die Heimat: Mitteilungen der Vereine für Heimatkunde in Krefeld und Verdingen* 6 (1927): 82–83.

33. Gesetz über die Polizeiverwaltung, 11 March 1850, Stadtarchiv Wuppertal O I 156.

34. Funk, *Polizei und Rechtsstaat,* p. 57.

35. Minister des Innern to Polizeipräsident Hinckeldey, 5 December 1851; Minister des Innern to Regierungspräsidenten, 11 February 1854; both in Staatsarchiv Koblenz 403/6593. Minister des Innern to Regierungspräsident, Düsseldorf, 13 March 1853 and 19 September 1854, both in Staatsarchiv Düsseldorf, Regierung Düsseldorf 8612. On Hinckeldey's flamboyant career, see Berthold Schulze, "Polizeipräsident Karl von Hinckeldey," *Jahrbuch für Geschichte Mittel- und Ostdeutschlands* 4 (1955): 81–108, and Heinrich von Sybel, "Karl Ludwig von Hinckeldey, 1852–1856," *Historische Zeitschrift* 189 (1959): 108–23.

36. Siemann, *"Deutschlands Ruhe, Sicherheit und Ordnung,"* pp. 390–97.

37. Regierungspräsident, Düsseldorf, to Minister des Innern 26 November 1848, Staatsarchiv Koblenz 403/2550.

38. Polizeiinspektor Falderen to Regierung Düsseldorf, Abteilung des Innern, 8 May and 14 September 1849, both in Staatsarchiv Düsseldorf, Regierung Düsseldorf 8702.

39. Polizeiinspektor Falderen to Regierung Düsseldorf, Abteilung des Innern, 21 June, 30 July, and 14 December 1849, all in Staatsarchiv Düsseldorf,

Regierung Düsseldorf 8702; Falderen to Minister des Innern, 3 January 1850, Staatsarchiv Düsseldorf, Regierung Düsseldorf 8703.

40. *Kölnische Zeitung* (13 December 1860), clipping in Staatsarchiv Düsseldorf, Regierung Düsseldorf 8708.

41. Regierung Düsseldorf, Abteilung des Innern, to Oberbürgermeister, Düsseldorf, 11 January 1850, Stadtarchiv Düsseldorf II/780; Regierungspräsident, Düsseldorf, to Oberpräsident, Rheinprovinz, 1 December 1851, Staatsarchiv Koblenz 403/163.

42. Staatsprokurator to Regierung Düsseldorf, 28 January 1855, Staatsarchiv Düsseldorf, Regierung Düsseldorf 8707. Compare the fate of another royal appointee, Polizeiinspektor Perizonius in Barmen. So unpopular that he was snubbed when he sought to join local bourgeois social clubs, his stay in the city was marred by rumors of moral and financial improprieties. In 1856 Berlin arranged for his transfer to Königsberg. Minister des Innern to Regierungspräsident, Düsseldorf, 13 February 1854; Polizeidirectorium, Elberfeld-Barmen, to Regierungspräsident, Düsseldorf, 25 February 1856; Oberpräsident, Rheinprovinz, to Regierungspräsident, Düsseldorf, 29 July 1856; all in Staatsarchiv Düsseldorf, Regierung Düsseldorf, Präs. Büro 742. Minister des Innern to Oberpräsident, Rheinprovinz, 9 July 1856, Staatsarchiv Koblenz 403/6606.

43. Bürgermeister and Gemeindeverordnete, Düsseldorf, to Minister des Innern, 29 April 1851, Staatsarchiv Düsseldorf, Regierung Düsseldorf 8704; Bürgermeister, Elberfeld, to Regierungspräsident, Düsseldorf, 1 February 1852, Staatsarchiv Koblenz 403/6606; Beigeordneter, Düsseldorf, to Regierung Düsseldorf, Abteilung des Innern, 5 September 1852, Staatsarchiv Düsseldorf, Regierung Düsseldorf 8705; Oberbürgermeister, Beigeordnete, and Stadtverordnete, Düsseldorf, to Minister des Innern, 10 February 1859, Staatsarchiv Koblenz 403/6587.

44. Bürgermeister, Elberfeld, to Regierungspräsident, Düsseldorf, 12 November 1851, Staatsarchiv Düsseldorf, Regierung Düsseldorf, Präs. Büro 742.

45. Nachweisungen der von der Gemeinde Elberfeld getragenen Polizeiverwaltungskosten, 1853–1855, Stadtarchiv Wuppertal O I 123.

46. Funk, *Polizei und Rechtsstaat*, p. 110; Minister des Innern to Oberpräsident, Rheinprovinz, 7 October 1859, Staatsarchiv Düsseldorf, Regierung Düsseldorf 8708; *Bergische Zeitung* (19 July 1862) and *Elberfelder Zeitung* (26 July 1862), both clippings in Stadtarchiv Wuppertal O I 123.

47. *Stenographische Berichte über die Verhandlungen des Preussischen Hauses der Abgeordneten*, 20 January 1868, p. 992.

48. Sitzung, Stadtverordnetenversammlung, Krefeld, 28 April 1864; Finanz Minister and Minister des Innern to Generalstaatskasse, 9 November 1864; both in Staatsarchiv Düsseldorf, Regierung Düsseldorf 8697.

49. Nachweisung über die Zahl der executiven Polizeibeamten in den Städten Düsseldorf, Barmen, Elberfeld, und Remscheid, Staatsarchiv Koblenz 403/6595.

50. Polizeidirection, Elberfeld-Barmen, to Regierung Düsseldorf, Abteilung des Innern, 3 January 1859, Staatsarchiv Düsseldorf, Regierung Düsseldorf 8612.

51. *Bericht über die Verwaltung und den Stand der Gemeinde-Angelegenheiten der Stadt Elberfeld* (Elberfeld, 1859), p. 13.

52. Reinhard Spree, *Wachstumstrends und Konjunkturzyklen in der deutschen Wirtschaft von 1820 bis 1913* (Göttingen, 1978), pp. 186, 188.

53. Carl-Ludwig Holtfrerich, *Quantitative Wirtschaftsgeschichte des Ruhrkohlenbergbaus im 19. Jahrhundert* (Dortmund, 1973), p. 22.

54. Ibid., p. 54.

55. *Bericht über den Stand und die Verwaltung der Gemeinde-Angelegenheiten der Stadt Düsseldorf* (Düsseldorf, 1852–59).

56. *Crefelder Kreis- und Intelligenzblatt* (4 November 1855), clipping in Stadtarchiv Düsseldorf II/787.

57. Friedrich-Wilhelm Henning, *Düsseldorf und seine Wirtschaft: Zur Geschichte einer Region*, vol. 1 (Düsseldorf, 1981), p. 366.

58. Petitions, Polizeisergeanten, Krefeld, to Oberbürgermeister, 19 April and 10 October 1849, 14 April and 26 November 1850, 29 May 1852, 25 January and 23 November 1853, 1 August 1856, and 14 June 1858; all in Stadtarchiv Krefeld 4/936.

59. Entwurf, Etat pro 1851, Düsseldorf, Staatsarchiv Düsseldorf, Regierung Düsseldorf 8703.

60. See, for example, petition, Polizeidiener, Langenberg, to Bürgermeister, 12 April 1858, Staatsarchiv Düsseldorf, Regierung Düsseldorf 217b.

61. See the petitions from Krefeld policemen listed in note 58.

62. Polizeiinspektor, Krefeld, to Oberbürgermeister, 3 November 1859, Stadtarchiv Krefeld 4/936.

63. See petitions from Polizeikommissare in Stadtarchiv Krefeld 4/936 and in Staatsarchiv Düsseldorf, Regierung Düsseldorf, Präs. Büro 915.

64. Polizeiinspektor Falderen to Minister des Innern, 26 August 1854, Staatsarchiv Düsseldorf, Regierung Düsseldorf, Präs. Büro 915.

65. Polizeidirektor Raffel, Düsseldorf, to Regierung Düsseldorf, Abteilung des Innern, 27 March 1855, Staatsarchiv Düsseldorf, Regierung Düsseldorf 8707.

66. *Instruktion für die Polizeiverwaltung der Oberbürgermeisterei Düsseldorf* (Düsseldorf, 1860), p. 6.

67. Entwurf, Gehalts- und Dienstordnung für die Polizeiverwaltung zu Krefeld, 14 June 1852; Polizeiinspektor Junkermann, Krefeld, to Regierung Düsseldorf, Abteilung des Innern, 3 July 1852; both in Staatsarchiv Düsseldorf, Regierung Düsseldorf 8696.

68. See, for example, Polizeikommissare Helgius and Klinge, Krefeld, to Oberbürgermeister, 28 August 1851, Stadtarchiv Krefeld 4/936; *Bericht über die Verwaltung und den Stand der Gemeinde-Angelegenheiten der Stadt Elberfeld* (Elberfeld, 1864), pp. 18–19.

69. Oberpräsident, Rheinprovinz, to Regierungspräsident, Düsseldorf, 12 February 1855, Staatsarchiv Düsseldorf, Regierung Düsseldorf, Präs. Büro 742.

70. Regierung Düsseldorf, Abteilung des Innern, to Oberbürgermeister, Krefeld, 16 November 1856, Stadtarchiv Krefeld 4/948; Extrabeilage zum Amtsblatt, 1867, pp. 1–3, Stadtarchiv Düsseldorf II/1335.

71. Compare the very similar expectations for preemptive police action in postrevolutionary provincial France as described in Robert Liebman, "Repressive Strategies and Working-Class Protest: Lyon, 1848–1852," *Social Science History* 4 (February 1980): 33–55.

72. Denkschrift über die gesetzliche Bestimmungen welche die politische Vereine und deren Versammlungen betreffen, Staatsarchiv Düsseldorf, Regierung Düsseldorf 30421.

73. Illner, *Bürgerliche Organisierung*, p. 115; Peter Hüttenberger, *Die Industrie- und Verwaltungsstadt (20. Jahrhundert)*, vol. 3 of Weidenhaupt, *Düsseldorf*, p. 90.

74. Eugene N. Anderson, *The Social and Political Conflict in Prussia, 1858–1864* (Lincoln, Nebr., 1954), p. 64.

75. Regierungspräsident, Düsseldorf, to Landräte, 17 December 1850, Stadtarchiv Krefeld 4/989.

76. *Polizeiverordnung betreffend das Meldewesen* (Düsseldorf, 1860), Staatsarchiv Düsseldorf, Regierung Düsseldorf 8708.

77. Regierungspräsident, Düsseldorf, to Landratsamt Krefeld, 12 February 1850, Stadtarchiv Krefeld 4/956.

78. Minister des Innern to Regierungspräsident, Düsseldorf, 18 August 1851, Stadtarchiv Krefeld 4/989. Polizeidirektor, Düsseldorf, to Regierung Düsseldorf, Abteilung des Innern, 2 October 1851; Minister des Innern to Regierung Düsseldorf, 20 September 1851 and 11 July 1852; both in Staatsarchiv Düsseldorf 149.

79. Minister des Innern to Regierung Düsseldorf, 15 October 1852 and 18 May 1861, both in Staatsarchiv Düsseldorf, Regierung Düsseldorf 149.

80. Minister des Innern to Regierungspräsidenten, 6 November 1851, Stadtarchiv Krefeld 4/989.

81. Minister des Innern to Regierungspräsident, Düsseldorf, 30 September 1852, Staatsarchiv Düsseldorf, Regierung Düsseldorf, Präs. Büro 742.

82. See, for example, Oberpräsident, Rheinprovinz, to Regierungspräsident, 14 May 1850, Staatsarchiv Düsseldorf, Regierung Düsseldorf 8805.

83. See, for instance, Regierung Düsseldorf, Abteilung des Innern, 5 September 1851, Stadtarchiv Krefeld 4/974. Compare Jonathan Sperber, *Popular Catholicism in Nineteenth-Century Germany* (Princeton, 1984), p. 54.

84. Verhandelt, Krefeld, 28 March 1851, Stadtarchiv Krefeld 4/989.

85. Polizeiinspektor, Düsseldorf, to Regierung Düsseldorf, Abteilung des Innern, 22 June 1850, Stadtarchiv Düsseldorf II/1433; Regierung Düsseldorf, Abteilung des Innern, to Oberpräsident, Rheinprovinz, 26 October 1851,

Staatsarchiv Koblenz 403/7063; Regierung Düsseldorf, Abteilung des Innern, 24 November 1852, Stadtarchiv Krefeld 4/974.

86. Minister des Innern to Prince-Regent, 16 December 1858; Minister des Innern to Oberpräsident, Rheinprovinz, 18 February 1859; both in Staatsarchiv Koblenz 403/7063.

87. See, for example, *Stenographische Berichte über die Verhandlungen des Preussischen Hauses der Abgeordneten*, debates from 9–12 April 1858; Funk, *Polizei und Rechtsstaat*, pp. 96–99.

88. Funk, *Polizei und Rechtsstaat*, pp. 101–2.

89. Jahresbericht der Polizeiinspektor, Krefeld, 2 January 1860, Stadtarchiv Krefeld 4/936.

90. *Bericht über die Verwaltung und den Stand der Gemeinde-Angelegenheiten der Oberbürgermeisterei Crefeld* (Krefeld, 1862).

91. *Niederrheinische Volks-Zeitung* (13 March 1861), clipping in Staatsarchiv Düsseldorf, Regierung Düsseldorf 8998.

92. Landrat Devens, *Statistik des Kreises Essen für die Jahre 1859–1861* (Essen, 1863), p. 308.

93. *Bericht über die Verwaltung und den Stand der Gemeinde-Angelegenheiten der Oberbürgermeisterei Crefeld* (Krefeld, 1870), p. 3, and (1879–80), p. 8.

CHAPTER III: POLICE FOR INDUSTRIALIZING CITIES, 1850–1878

1. See, for example, Polizeiinspektor, Düsseldorf, to Regierung Düsseldorf, Abteilung des Innern, 24 January 1851, Staatsarchiv Düsseldorf, Regierung Düsseldorf 8704; Commission report, Krefeld, 23 June 1852, Staatsarchiv Düsseldorf, Regierung Düsseldorf 8696.

2. Polizeiinspektor, Elberfeld, to Oberbürgermeister, Elberfeld, 4 February 1850, Stadtarchiv Wuppertal O I 137.

3. Polizeiinspektor, Krefeld, to Oberbürgermeister, Krefeld, 20 February 1877, Stadtarchiv Krefeld 4/936.

4. *Verwaltungsbericht für das Jahr 1857* (Barmen, 1858), p. 27. See also Polizeiinspektor, Krefeld, to Regierung Düsseldorf, Abteilung des Innern, 3 May 1852, Staatsarchiv Düsseldorf, Regierung Düsseldorf 8696.

5. Albrecht Funk, *Polizei und Rechtsstaat: Die Entwicklung des staatlichen Gewaltmonopols in Preussen, 1848–1918* (Frankfurt am Main, 1986), pp. 84–89; Oberstaatsanwalt to Regierung Düsseldorf, Abteilung des Innern, 2 August 1878, Stadtarchiv Krefeld 4/938.

6. Polizeiinspektor, Düsseldorf, to Regierung Düsseldorf, Abteilung des Innern, 24 January 1851, Staatsarchiv Düsseldorf, Regierung Düsseldorf 8704.

7. Oberbürgermeister, Düsseldorf, to Regierung Düsseldorf, Abteilung des Innern, 12 February and 16 July 1860, Staatsarchiv Düsseldorf, Regierung Düsseldorf 8708.

8. Oberbürgermeister, Düsseldorf, to Regierung Düsseldorf, Abteilung des Innern, 16 July 1860, Staatsarchiv Düsseldorf, Regierung Düsseldorf 8708.

9. Polizeiinspektor, Krefeld, to Regierung Düsseldorf, Abteilung des Innern, 6 May 1852, Staatsarchiv Düsseldorf, Regierung Düsseldorf 8696.

10. *Stenographische Berichte über die Verhandlungen des Preussischen Hauses der Abgeordneten,* 27 January 1874, p. 838.

11. Ibid., 4 December 1866, pp. 868, 870.

12. Polizeiinspektor, Düsseldorf, to Oberbürgermeister, Düsseldorf, 18 November 1878, Stadtarchiv Düsseldorf III/4350.

13. Regelment für die städtische Brand- und Sicherheitswache, 1853; Verzeichnis der Nachtwächter der städtische Brand- und Sicherheitswache, 1858; Regelment für die städtische Feuer- und Sicherheitswache, 1860; all in Stadtarchiv Düsseldorf II/1336. Even though city policy called for preferential hiring of those with military experience, in 1853 nine out of twenty of Düsseldorf's night watchmen were without military training. Verzeichnis der Mannschaften welche zu der neu eingerichteten Brand- und Sicherheitswache ernannt worden sind, 1853, Stadtarchiv Düsseldorf II/1336.

14. See, for instance, Landrat, Elberfeld, to Regierung Düsseldorf, 19 June 1850, Staatsarchiv Düsseldorf, Regierung Düsseldorf 8805.

15. Verein gegen Seidendiebstahl to Oberbürgermeister, Krefeld, 15 June 1864, Stadtarchiv Krefeld 4/936.

16. Regierungsrat Illing to Regierungspräsident, Düsseldorf, 21 December 1864, Staatsarchiv Düsseldorf, Regierung Düsseldorf 8698; Sitzungsprotokoll der Stadtverordneten, Essen, 26 January 1866, Stadtarchiv Essen XIII/48.

17. Carolyn Steedman, *Policing the Victorian Community: The Formation of English Provincial Police Forces, 1856–1880* (London, 1984), pp. 45–46.

18. Regierung Düsseldorf, Abteilung des Innern, to Oberpräsident, Rheinprovinz, 10 September 1862, Staatsarchiv Koblenz 403/6760.

19. Polizeiinspektor Falderen to Regierung Düsseldorf, Abteilung des Innern, 24 January 1851, Staatsarchiv Düsseldorf, Regierung Düsseldorf 8704.

20. Minister des Innern to Oberpräsident, Rheinprovinz, 26 August 1862, Staatsarchiv Koblenz 403/6760.

21. Minister des Innern to Regierung Düsseldorf, 19 January 1865, Staatsarchiv Düsseldorf, Regierung Düsseldorf 8698.

22. *Bericht über die Verwaltung und den Stand der Gemeinde-Angelegenheiten der Stadt Elberfeld* (Elberfeld, 1866), p. 25; Oberbürgermeister, Barmen, to Minister des Innern, 1 May 1873, Staatsarchiv Düsseldorf, Regierung Düsseldorf 215.

23. Oberbürgermeister, Barmen, to Regierung Düsseldorf, Abteilung des Innern, 23 May 1874, Staatsarchiv Düsseldorf, Regierung Düsseldorf 30218; Minister des Innern to Regierung Düsseldorf, 14 June 1879, Staatsarchiv Düsseldorf, Regierung Düsseldorf 215.

24. Zeitungsberichte der Königlichen Regierung zu Düsseldorf, 1859–1867, Staatsarchiv Koblenz 403/177. On the prevalence of wood theft, see also

Dirk Blasius, *Kriminalität und Alltag: Zur Konfliktgeschichte des Alltagslebens im 19. Jahrhundert* (Göttingen, 1978), pp. 16, 21.

25. Zeitungsberichte der Königlichen Regierung zu Düsseldorf, 1859–1867, Staatsarchiv Koblenz 403/177.

26. Polizeianzeige, 1859–1868, Stadtarchiv Essen XIII/1.

27. Landrat, Essen, to Regierung Düsseldorf, Abteilung des Innern, 16 December 1864, Staatsarchiv Düsseldorf, Regierung Düsseldorf 8698; Regierungsrat Illing to Regierungspräsident, Düsseldorf, 20 December 1864, Staatsarchiv Düsseldorf, Regierung Düsseldorf 8698.

28. Polizeianzeige, 1859–1868, Stadtarchiv Essen XIII/1.

29. Bürgermeister, Essen, to Landrat, Essen, 12 May 1868, Staatsarchiv Koblenz 403/6607.

30. Landrat, Essen, to Regierung Düsseldorf, 9 February 1869, Staatsarchiv Koblenz 403/6607.

31. Regierung Düsseldorf, Abteilung des Innern, to Landrat, Essen, 18 November 1868, Staatsarchiv Koblenz 403/6607; Regierung Düsseldorf, Abteilung des Innern, to Landrat, Essen, 1 March 1869; Bürgermeister, Essen, to Landrat, Essen, 22 September 1872; both in Stadtarchiv Essen XIII/48.

32. Funk, *Polizei und Rechtsstaat,* p. 215.

33. *Stenographische Berichte über die Verhandlungen des Preussischen Hauses der Abgeordneten,* 14 December 1878, p. 393.

34. Ibid., 17 December 1878, p. 408.

35. Annemarie Lange, *Berlin zur Zeit Bebels und Bismarcks: Zwischen Reichsgründung und Jahrhundertwende* (Berlin, 1972), pp. 134–37; Lothar Machtan and Rene Ott, " 'Batzbier!' Überlegungen zur sozialen Protestbewegung in den Jahren nach der Reichsgründung am Beispiel der süddeutsche Bierkravalle vom Frühjahr 1873," in Heinrich Volkmann and Jürgen Bergmann, eds., *Sozialer Protest: Studien zu traditioneller Resistenz und kollektiver Gewalt in Deutschland von Vormärz bis zur Reichsgründung* (Opladen, 1984), pp. 128–66.

36. John D. Hunley, "The Working Classes, Religion, and Social Democracy in the Düsseldorf Area, 1867–1878," *Societas* 4 (1974): 142.

37. Bürgermeister, Essen, to Landrat, Essen, 22 September 1872, Stadtarchiv Essen XIII/48.

38. Oberbürgermeister, Barmen, to Regierung Düsseldorf, Abteilung des Innern, 12 December 1875, Staatsarchiv Düsseldorf, Regierung Düsseldorf 30218.

39. *Bericht über den Stand und die Verwaltung der Gemeinde-Angelegenheiten der Stadt Düsseldorf* (Düsseldorf, 1878), p. 84.

40. *Bericht über die Verwaltung und den Stand der Gemeinde-Angelegenheiten der Stadt Elberfeld* (Elberfeld, 1882), p. 35.

41. See, for example, Oberbürgermeister, Düsseldorf, to Regierung Düsseldorf, Abteilung des Innern, 17 July 1874, Staatsarchiv Düsseldorf, Regierung Düsseldorf 177; Oberbürgermeister, Düsseldorf, to Regierung Düsseldorf, Abteilung des Innern, 19 October 1874, Staatsarchiv Düsseldorf, Regierung Düsseldorf 30218.

42. Beigeordneter, Düsseldorf, to Regierung Düsseldorf, Abteilung des Innern, 31 January 1879, Staatsarchiv Düsseldorf, Regierung Düsseldorf 178; *Bericht über die Verwaltung und den Stand der Gemeinde-Angelegenheiten der Stadt Elberfeld* (Elberfeld, 1884), p. 40.

43. *Bericht über den Stand und die Verwaltung der Gemeinde-Angelegenheiten der Stadt Duisburg* (Duisburg, 1870–1884).

44. Petition, Krefeld Polizeisergeanten to Oberbürgermeister, Krefeld, 15 October 1873, Stadtarchiv Krefeld 4/936.

45. See, for example, numerous petitions, 1865–1877, in Stadtarchiv Essen XIII/48; Petition, Polizeisergeanten, Krefeld, Stadtarchiv Krefeld 4/936.

46. Gerhard Bry, *Wages in Germany, 1871–1945* (Princeton, 1960), p. 325.

47. Carl-Ludwig Holtfrerich, *Quantitative Wirtschaftsgeschichte des Ruhrkohlenbergbaus im 19. Jahrhundert: Eine Führungssektoranalyse* (Dortmund, 1973), p. 23.

48. *Bericht über den Stand und die Verwaltung der Gemeinde-Angelegenheiten der Stadt Düsseldorf* (Düsseldorf, 1868, 1874).

49. *Bericht über die Verwaltung und den Stand der Gemeinde-Angelegenheiten der Oberbürgermeisterei Crefeld* (Krefeld, 1872), p. 7, and (1875), p. 5; Stadtverordnetenversammlung, Krefeld, 20 October 1870, Stadtarchiv Krefeld 4/936.

50. Oberbürgermeister, Barmen, to Regierung Düsseldorf, Abteilung des Innern, 12 December 1875, Staatsarchiv Düsseldorf, Regierung Düsseldorf 30218.

51. Regulativ für die Besoldung der Beamten der Stadt Düsseldorf, 12 March 1877, Stadtarchiv Düsseldorf II/1335.

52. Holtfrerich, *Quantitative Wirtschaftsgeschichte*, p. 55.

53. Petition, Essen Polizeisergeanten, 6 December 1871, Stadtarchiv Essen XIII/48.

54. Regulativ für die Besoldung der Beamten der Stadt Düsseldorf, 12 March 1877, Stadtarchiv Düsseldorf II/1335.

55. Henning, *Düsseldorf und seine Wirtschaft*, vol. 1, p. 541.

56. Polizeiinspektor, Krefeld, to Oberbürgermeister, Krefeld, 20 February 1877, Stadtarchiv Krefeld 4/936; Nachweisung über die Zahl der Polizeibeamten in den einen eigenen Stadtkreis bildenden Städten, 1888–89, Staatsarchiv Düsseldorf, Regierung Düsseldorf 8611.

57. *Bericht über die Verwaltung und den Stand der Gemeinde-Angelegenheiten der Oberbürgermeisterei Crefeld* (Krefeld, 1876), p. 5.

58. Oberbürgermeister, Essen, Zeitungsbericht, 30 September 1876, Staatsarchiv Düsseldorf, Regierung Düsseldorf 8698.

59. *Stenographische Berichte über die Verhandlungen des Preussischen Hauses der Abgeordneten*, 7 December 1868, p. 528; *Bericht über den Stand und die Verwaltung der Gemeinde-Angelegenheiten der Stadt Duisburg* (Duisburg, 1868), p. 34.

60. *Armeeverordnungsblatt*, 1875, p. 157, Stadtarchiv Düsseldorf II/1335.

61. Oberbürgermeister, Elberfeld, to Regierung Düsseldorf, Abteilung des Innern, 17 December 1868, Staatsarchiv Düsseldorf, Regierung Düsseldorf

8614; Meeting, Elberfeld Stadtverordneten, 26 October 1875, Staatsarchiv Düsseldorf, Regierung Düsseldorf 30218; Meeting, Barmen Stadtverordneten, 2 November 1875, Staatsarchiv Düsseldorf, Regierung Düsseldorf 8645.

62. Nachweisung der städtischen Polizeiexekutivbeamten in Essen, 1873, Stadtarchiv Essen XIII/48.

63. Petition, Polizeibeamten, Krefeld, to Oberbürgermeister, Krefeld, 14 November 1875, Stadtarchiv Krefeld 4/936.

64. Oberbürgermeister, Barmen, to Regierung Düsseldorf, Abteilung des Innern, 12 December 1875, Staatsarchiv Düsseldorf, Regierung Düsseldorf 30218.

65. Dienst der hiesigen Polizeisergeanten, 5 September 1872, Stadtarchiv Essen XIII/48.

66. *Dienstinstruktion für die Polizeiverwaltung der Bürgermeisterei Duisburg* (Duisburg, 1873), p. 7.

CHAPTER IV: POLICING URBAN LIFE, 1850–1878

1. "Eine brennende Localfrage," *Düsseldorfer Zeitung* (16 November 1879), clipping in Staatsarchiv Düsseldorf, Regierung Düsseldorf 178.

2. See, for example, *Düsseldorfer Zeitung* (22 May 1875), clipping in Staatsarchiv Düsseldorf, Regierung Düsseldorf 30218.

3. Compare David R. Johnson, *Policing the Urban Underworld: The Impact of Crime on the Development of the American Police, 1800–1887* (Philadelphia, 1979), pp. 13, 19, 124–26.

4. Polizeiinspektor Falderen to Regierung Düsseldorf, Abteilung des Innern, 24 April 1849, 27 November 1851, and 9 November 1854, all in Staatsarchiv Düsseldorf, Regierung Düsseldorf 175. Compare Jeffrey S. Adler, "Vagging the Demons and Scoundrels: Vagrancy and the Growth of St. Louis, 1830–1861," *Journal of Urban History* 13 (November 1986): 3–30.

5. Polizeiinspektor Walther to Oberbürgermeister, Krefeld, 2 October 1850, Stadtarchiv Krefeld 4/954.

6. See, for example, Regierungspräsident, Düsseldorf, to Landratsamt, Krefeld, 12 February 1850, Stadtarchiv Krefeld 4/956.

7. *Bericht über den Stand und die Verwaltung der Gemeinde-Angelegenheiten der Stadt Duisburg* (Duisburg, 1864), p. 10.

8. Polizeiinspektor, Elberfeld, to Regierung Düsseldorf, 30 June 1873, Staatsarchiv Düsseldorf, Regierung Düsseldorf 8904.

9. *Bericht über den Stand und die Verwaltung der Gemeinde-Angelegenheiten der Stadt Duisburg* (Duisburg, 1876), p. 77.

10. *Bericht über den Stand und die Verwaltung der Gemeinde-Angelegenheiten der Stadt Düsseldorf* (Düsseldorf, 1884), p. 117.

11. See, for instance, *Bericht über den Stand und die Verwaltung der Gemeinde-Angelegenheiten der Stadt Duisburg* (Duisburg, 1879), p. 104.

12. *Bericht über den Stand und die Verwaltung der Gemeinde-Angelegenheiten der Stadt Düsseldorf* (Düsseldorf, 1877–83).

13. *Bericht über die Verwaltung und den Stand der Gemeinde-Angelegenheiten der Oberbürgermeisterei Crefeld* (Krefeld, 1880), p. 8.

14. Gesetz über die Polizeiverwaltung, 11 March 1850, Stadtarchiv Wuppertal O I 156.

15. *Bericht über den Stand und die Verwaltung der Gemeinde-Angelegenheiten der Stadt Düsseldorf* (Düsseldorf, 1876), p. 66.

16. Ralph Jessen, *Polizei im Industrierevier: Modernisierung und Herrschaftspraxis im westfälischen Ruhrgebiet, 1848–1914* (Göttingen, 1991), pp. 213–82.

17. See, for instance, Landrat, Essen, to Regierung Düsseldorf, 17 October 1868, Staatsarchiv Koblenz 403/6607.

18. *Bericht über den Stand und die Verwaltung der Gemeinde-Angelegenheiten der Stadt Duisburg* (Duisburg, 1866), p. 22.

19. *Bericht über den Stand und die Verwaltung der Gemeinde-Angelegenheiten der Stadt Düsseldorf* (Düsseldorf, 1879), p. 92.

20. *Bericht über den Stand und die Verwaltung der Gemeinde-Angelegenheiten der Stadt Duisburg* (Duisburg, 1872), pp. 40–41.

21. Compare James Harvey Jackson, Jr., "Migration and Urbanization in the Ruhr Valley, 1850–1900" (Ph.D. diss., University of Minnesota, 1980), p. 108; Howard Zehr, "The Modernization of Crime in Germany and France, 1830–1913," *Journal of Social History* (Summer 1975): 117–41.

22. Pastor H. Stursberg, *Die Zunahme der Vergehen und Verbrechen und ihre Ursachen* (Düsseldorf, 1879), Stadtarchiv Krefeld 4/961.

23. Compare the similar views contained in Zeitungsberichte der Königlichen Regierung zu Düsseldorf, 1868–1877, Staatsarchiv Koblenz 403/17962.

24. Nachweisung der in der Oberbürgermeisterei Düsseldorf vom 15. Februar bis ultimo August 1860 vorgekommenen Diebstähle, Staatsarchiv Düsseldorf, Regierung Düsseldorf 8708.

25. Compare Landrat Devens, *Statistik des Kreises Essen für die Jahre 1859–1861* (Essen, 1863), p. 296.

26. Regierungspräsident, Düsseldorf, Zeitungsbericht, 29 January 1877, Staatsarchiv Koblenz 403/17962.

27. Oberbürgermeister, Düsseldorf, to Regierung Düsseldorf, Abteilung des Innern, 16 July and 6 September 1860, Staatsarchiv Düsseldorf 8708.

28. Minister des Innern to Regierung Merseburg, 22 November 1877; Landratsvertreter, Mülheim/Ruhr, to Regierung Düsseldorf, Abteilung des Innern, 17 February 1879; both in Staatsarchiv Düsseldorf, Regierung Düsseldorf 8813.

29. On alcohol consumption in nineteenth-century Germany, see James S. Roberts, *Drink, Temperance, and the Working Class in Nineteenth-Century Germany* (Boston, 1984); Irmgard Vogt, "Einige Fragen zum Alkoholkonsum der Arbeiter: Kommentar zu J. S. Roberts," *Geschichte und Gesellschaft* 8 (1982): 134–40.

30. Polizeidirektor Hirsch, Wochenbericht, 31 July 1853, Staatsarchiv Koblenz 403/6595.

31. Täglicher Anzeiger für Berg und Mark (28 May 1856), clipping in Staatsarchiv Düsseldorf, Regierung Düsseldorf 8998.

32. Polizeidirektor Hirsch to Regierung Düsseldorf, 16 March 1856, Staatsarchiv Koblenz 403/7062.

33. List, Düsseldorf, 6 October 1854; Polizeiverordnung, Düsseldorf, 16 March 1857; both in Stadtarchiv Düsseldorf II/1361.

34. List, Essen, February 1861, Staatsarchiv Düsseldorf, Regierung Düsseldorf 8998.

35. See, for example, the letter of complaint from Essen printed in the Berliner Börsen Zeitung (5 February 1859), clipping in Staatsarchiv Düsseldorf, Regierung Düsseldorf 8998; Regierungsrat Illing, Report of interview with Polizeikommissar Dähne, Essen, 20 December 1864, Staatsarchiv Düsseldorf, Regierung Düsseldorf 8698.

36. Bürgermeister, Essen, to Minister des Innern, 19 October 1871, Staatsarchiv Düsseldorf, Regierung Düsseldorf 8998.

37. Roberts, Drink, Temperance, and the Working Class, p. 50.

38. Minister des Innern to Regierung Düsseldorf, 30 March 1879, Stadtarchiv Düsseldorf III/5752.

39. See, for example, Regierung Düsseldorf to Oberbürgermeister, Elberfeld, 5 August 1882, Stadtarchiv Wuppertal O I 46.

40. Bericht über die Verwaltung und den Stand der Gemeinde-Angelegenheiten der Oberbürgermeisterei Crefeld (Krefeld, 1879), p. 6.

41. Bericht über den Stand und die Verwaltung der Gemeinde-Angelegenheiten der Stadt Düsseldorf (Düsseldorf, 1879), p. 86. See also Bericht über den Stand und die Verwaltung der Gemeinde-Angelegenheiten der Stadt Duisburg (Duisburg, 1879), p. 104.

42. Polizeiverordnung, Düsseldorf, 18 January 1879, Stadtarchiv Düsseldorf III/5752; Regierung Düsseldorf, Abteilung des Innern, to Landräte and Oberbürgermeister, 25 January 1879, Stadtarchiv Krefeld 4/974.

43. Oberbürgermeister, Elberfeld, to Regierung Düsseldorf, Abteilung des Innern, 13 December 1878, Staatsarchiv Düsseldorf, Regierung Düsseldorf 8956.

44. See, for instance, Dietrich Milles, ". . . aber es kam kein Mensch nach den Gruben, um anzufahren": Arbeitskämpfe der Ruhrbergarbeiter, 1867-1878 (Frankfurt am Main, 1983), p. 288.

45. Oberbürgermeister, Düsseldorf, to Regierung Düsseldorf, Abteilung des Innern, 9 April 1880, Staatsarchiv Düsseldorf, Regierung Düsseldorf 8939.

46. On shifts in official policy, see Zur Prostitutionsfrage: Aus den Verhandlungen der 56. Generalversammlung der Rheinisch-Westfälische Gefängnisgesellschaft am 9. Oktober 1884 in Düsseldorf (Düsseldorf, 1884); Richard Evans, "Prostitution, State, and Society in Imperial Germany," Past and Present 70 (February 1976): 106-29.

47. Report, Polizeiinspektor Frankfurth, 15 October 1880, Staatsarchiv Düsseldorf, Regierung Düsseldorf 8939. See also Polizeiinspektor, Düsseldorf, to Regierung Düsseldorf, Abteilung des Innern, 9 November 1854, Staatsarchiv Düsseldorf, Regierung Düsseldorf 8706.

48. See, for example, *Germania* (13 March 1877), clipping in Staatsarchiv Düsseldorf, Regierung Düsseldorf 177; Regierung Düsseldorf, Abteilung des Innern, to Oberbürgermeister, Elberfeld, 5 August 1882, Stadtarchiv Wuppertal O I 46.

49. Compare Robert Liebman and Michael Polen, "Perspectives on Policing in Nineteenth-Century America," *Social Science History* 2 (1978): 356.

50. Wolfgang Köllmann, ed. *Wuppertaler Färbergesellen-Innung und Färbergesellen-Streiks, 1848–1857: Akten zur Frühgeschichte der Arbeiterbewegung in Deutschland* (Wiesbaden, 1962), p. 16. Compare Dieter Dowe, "Legale Interessenvertretung und Streik: Der Arbeitskampf in den Tuchfabriken des Kreises Lennep (Bergisches Land) 1850," in Klaus Tenfelde and Heinrich Volkmann, eds., *Streik: Zur Geschichte des Arbeitskampfes in Deutschland während der Industrialisierung* (Munich, 1981), p. 45.

51. Köllmann, *Wuppertaler Färbergesellen*, pp. 19–20.

52. Ibid., pp. 16–17.

53. Polizeidirektor Hirsch to Regierungspräsident, Düsseldorf, 18 September 1855, in Köllmann, *Wuppertaler Färbergesellen*, p. 66.

54. Polizeidirektor Hirsch to Regierungspräsident, Düsseldorf, 15 September 1855, in Köllmann, *Wuppertaler Färbergesellen*, p. 54.

55. Regierungspräsident, Düsseldorf, to Minister des Innern, 18 September 1855, in Köllmann, *Wuppertaler Färbergesellen*, pp. 58–59.

56. On the extensive latitude of the Prussian military for deciding on their own initiative when to intervene in civil disturbances, see Instruktion über den Waffengebrauch des Militärs und über die Mitwirkung desselben zur Unterdrückung innerer Unruhen, und Erläuterungen zu dem Gesetze über den Belagerungszustand vom 4 Juni 1851 (Berlin, 1891), Stadtarchiv Essen XIII/11.

57. Mary Nolan, *Social Democracy and Society: Working-Class Radicalism in Düsseldorf, 1890–1920* (Cambridge, 1981), p. 5.

58. Regierungsrat Rust to Oberpräsident, Rheinprovinz, 10 April 1869, Staatsarchiv Koblenz 403/6607.

59. John Breuilly, "Civil Society and the Labour Movement, Class Relations and the Law: A Comparison between Germany and England," in Jürgen Kocka, ed., *Arbeiter und Bürger im 19. Jahrhundert: Varianten ihres Verhältnisses im europäischen Vergleich* (Munich, 1986), pp. 287–318.

60. Milles, ". . . aber es kam kein Mensch," pp. 114–16.

61. Ibid., p. 247; Klaus Tenfelde, *Sozialgeschichte der Bergarbeiterschaft an der Ruhr im 19. Jahrhundert*, 2d ed. (Bonn, 1981), p. 473.

62. Regierungspräsident, Düsseldorf, to Minister des Innern, 27 July 1878, Staatsarchiv Koblenz 403/6825.

CHAPTER V: THE EMPIRE AND ITS INTERNAL ENEMIES, 1871–1890

1. Jonathan Sperber, *Popular Catholicism in Nineteenth-Century Germany* (Princeton, 1984), pp. 44–45.

2. Margaret Lavinia Anderson, "The Kulturkampf and the Course of German History," *Central European History* 19 (March 1986): 82–115.

3. Dietrich Milles, ". . . *aber es kam kein Mensch nach den Gruben, um anzufahren*": *Arbeitskämpfe der Ruhrbergarbeiter, 1867–1878* (Frankfurt am Main, 1983), pp. 284–86.

4. Friedrich Lenger, *Zwischen Kleinbürgertum und Proletariat: Studien zur Sozialgeschichte der Düsseldorfer Handwerker, 1816–1878* (Göttingen, 1986), p. 224; Norbert Schlossmacher, *Düsseldorf im Bismarckreich: Politik und Wahlen, Parteien und Vereine* (Düsseldorf, 1985), pp. 43–48; Sperber, *Popular Catholicism,* pp. 211–14; Klaus Tenfelde, *Sozialgeschichte der Bergarbeiterschaft an der Ruhr im 19. Jahrhundert,* 2d ed. (Bonn, 1981), p. 495.

5. See, for example, Schlossmacher, *Düsseldorf im Bismarckreich,* p. 37.

6. Oberbürgermeister, Düsseldorf, to Regierung Düsseldorf, Abteilung des Innern, 9 April 1875, Staatsarchiv Düsseldorf, Regierung Düsseldorf 8801.

7. Regierung Düsseldorf, Abteilung des Innern, to Landräte, 5 June 1876, Stadtarchiv Düsseldorf III/5752.

8. Sperber, *Popular Catholicism,* pp. 225–26; Schlossmacher, *Düsseldorf im Bismarckzeit,* p. 111. Regierung Düsseldorf, Abteilung des Innern, to Oberbürgermeister, Düsseldorf, 18 July 1874, Stadtarchiv Düsseldorf II/1433.

9. Regierung Düsseldorf, Abteilung des Innern, to Landräte and Oberbürgermeister, 31 December 1874, Staatsarchiv Düsseldorf, Regierung Düsseldorf 8800. See also Margaret Lavinia Anderson and Kenneth Barkin, "The Myth of the Puttkamer Purge and the Reality of the Kulturkampf: Some Reflections on the Historiography of Imperial Germany," *Journal of Modern History* 54 (December 1982): 647–86; Ronald J. Ross, "Enforcing the Kulturkampf in the Bismarckian State and the Limits of Coercion in Imperial Germany," *Journal of Modern History* 56 (September 1984): 456–82; Sperber, *Popular Catholicism,* p. 241.

10. Verzeichnis der Nachtwachen der städtischen Brand- und Sicherheitswache, 1858, Stadtarchiv Düsseldorf II/1336.

11. See the biographies accompanying proposals for decorations in Staatsarchiv Düsseldorf, Regierung Düsseldorf 8618. See also Stadtarchiv Düsseldorf III/4393.

12. Schlossmacher, *Düsseldorf im Bismarckzeit,* p. 222; Pastor H. Stursberg, *Die Zunahme der Vergehen und Verbrechen und ihre Ursachen* (Düsseldorf, 1879), Stadtarchiv Krefeld 4/961.

13. Regierung Düsseldorf, Abteilung des Innern, to Landräte, 5 January 1875, Stadtarchiv Essen XIII/68; Regierung Düsseldorf, Abteilung des Innern, to Oberbürgermeister, Düsseldorf, 11 April 1883, Stadtarchiv Krefeld 4/977.

14. Report, Polizeikommissar, Krefeld, 11 October 1869; Petition with 176 signatures to Oberbürgermeister, Krefeld, 4 November 1869; both in Stadtarchiv Krefeld 4/977.

15. *Crefelder Zeitung* (18 February 1908), clipping in Stadtarchiv Krefeld 4/977.

16. *Düsseldorfer Zeitung* (31 August 1885); *Düsseldorfer Anzeiger* (8 September 1885); both clippings in Stadtarchiv Düsseldorf III/4636. *Düsseldorfer Volkszeitung* (29 July 1887), clipping in Staatsarchiv Düsseldorf, Regierung Düsseldorf 8729. See also Verzeichnis denjenigen Personen welche wegen Sonntagsentheiligung bestraft worden, 19 July 1890, Stadtarchiv Essen XIII/68.

17. Regierung Düsseldorf to Landräte, 14 June 1886, Staatsarchiv Düsseldorf, Regierung Düsseldorf 30428.

18. Oberbürgermeister, Elberfeld, to Regierungspräsident, Düsseldorf, 29 May 1890; Polizeiverwaltung, Barmen, to Regierungspräsident, Düsseldorf, 11 June 1890; Report, Polizeikommissar Schulze, Barmen, 11 June 1890; all in Staatsarchiv Düsseldorf, Regierung Düsseldorf 8816a.

19. Regierung Düsseldorf, Abteilung des Innern, to Landräte, 29 August 1874, Staatsarchiv Düsseldorf, Regierung Düsseldorf 30428.

20. Peter Hüttenberger, *Die Industrie- und Verwaltungsstadt (20. Jahrhundert)*, vol. 3 of Hugo Weidenhaupt, ed., *Düsseldorf: Geschichte von den Ursprüngen bis ins 20. Jahrhundert* (Düsseldorf, 1989), pp. 30–38; Schlossmacher, *Düsseldorf im Bismarckzeit*, p. 136.

21. Wolfgang Köllmann, *Sozialgeschichte der Stadt Barmen im 19. Jahrhundert* (Tübingen, 1960), pp. 257–58.

22. Andrew R. Carlson, "Anarchism and Individual Terror in the German Empire, 1870–1890," in Wolfgang Mommsen and Gerhard Hirschfeld, eds., *Social Protest, Violence, and Terror in Nineteenth- and Twentieth-Century Europe* (New York, 1982), pp. 175–200.

23. Günther Bergmann, *Das Sozialistengesetz im rechtsrheinischen Industriegebiet: Ein Beitrag zur Auseinandersetzung zwischen Staat und Sozialdemokratie im Wuppertal und im Bergischen Land 1878–1890* (Hanover, 1970), p. 32; Tenfelde, *Sozialgeschichte der Bergarbeiterschaft*, p. 572.

24. John Dillard Hunley, "The Working Classes, Religion, and Social Democracy in the Düsseldorf Area, 1867–1878," *Societas* 4 (1974): 131–49; Sperber, *Popular Catholicism*, pp. 178–79.

25. Tenfelde, *Sozialgeschichte der Bergarbeiterschaft*, pp. 464–70.

26. Zeitungsbericht, Regierung Düsseldorf, 3 February 1882, Staatsarchiv Koblenz 403/9047.

27. Horst Lademacher, "Wirtschaft, Arbeiterschaft, und Arbeiterorganisationen in der Rheinprovinz am Vorabend des Sozialistengesetzes 1878," *Archiv für Sozialgeschichte* 15 (1975): 120, 125.

28. For an overview of the enforcement of the antisocialist law in the Wuppertal, see Bergmann, *Das Sozialistengesetz im rechtsrheinischen Industriegebiet*.

29. For the concern of the Berlin police president about reported inadequacies in the antisocialist efforts in the Wuppertal, see Polizeipräsident, Berlin, to Regierungspräsident, Düsseldorf, 25 August 1881, Staatsarchiv Düsseldorf, Landgericht Elberfeld 5/465.

30. Bergmann, *Das Sozialistengesetz im rechtsrheinischen Industriegebiet*, p. 100.

31. Erster Staatsanwalt, Elberfeld, to Regierungspräsident, Düsseldorf, 9 January 1886; Oberbürgermeister, Barmen, to Regierung Düsseldorf, Abteilung des Innern, 17 February 1886; both in Staatsarchiv Düsseldorf, Regierung Düsseldorf 8736.

32. Bergmann, *Das Sozialistengesetz im rechtsrheinischen Industriegebiet*, p. 56.

33. Polizeiinspektor Daum, Elberfeld, to Erster Staatsanwalt, Elberfeld, 6 January 1882, Staatsarchiv Düsseldorf, Landgericht Elberfeld 5/465.

34. Joachim Wagner, *Politischer Terrorismus und Strafrecht im Deutsche Kaiserreich von 1871* (Heidelberg, 1981), pp. 12–14.

35. Report, Polizeikommissar Wilsing, Barmen, 9 February 1884; Report, Polizeikommissar Gottschalk, Elberfeld, 10 September 1884; both in Staatsarchiv Düsseldorf, Regierung Düsseldorf, Präs. Büro 747.

36. Report, Kriminalkommissar, political police, 27 October 1883, Staatsarchiv Düsseldorf, Regierung Düsseldorf, Präs. Büro 747; Erster Staatsanwalt, Elberfeld, to Regierungspräsident, 3 February 1884, Staatsarchiv Koblenz 403/6830.

37. Erster Staatsanwalt, Elberfeld, to Regierungspräsident, 3 February 1884, Staatsarchiv Koblenz 403/6830.

38. Regierungspräsident, Düsseldorf, to Vicepräsident, Ministerium des Innern, 9 March 1884, Staatsarchiv Koblenz 403/6830.

39. Regierungspräsident, Düsseldorf, to Vicepräsident, Ministerium des Innern, 9 March 1884, Staatsarchiv Koblenz 403/6830; Bergmann, *Das Sozialistengesetz im rechtsrheinischen Industriegebiet*, p. 42.

40. Regierungspräsident, Düsseldorf, to Vicepräsident, Ministerium des Innern, 9 March 1884, Staatsarchiv Koblenz 403/6830.

41. Oberbürgermeister, Elberfeld, to ministers of war and interior, 14 December 1886, Staatsarchiv Koblenz 403/6609.

42. Minister des Innern to Regierungspräsident, Düsseldorf, 22 June 1884 and 11 August 1890, both in Staatsarchiv Düsseldorf, Regierung Düsseldorf, Präs. Büro 747; Oberpräsident, Rheinprovinz, to Regierungspräsident, Düsseldorf, Staatsarchiv Düsseldorf, Regierung Düsseldorf 8710.

43. Regierung Düsseldorf, Abteilung des Innern, to Oberbürgermeister, Elberfeld, 17 August 1882, Stadtarchiv Wuppertal O I 46.

44. Report, Landrat, Essen, 19 October 1886, Staatsarchiv Düsseldorf, Landgericht Elberfeld 5/391.

45. Regierung Düsseldorf, Abteilung des Innern, to Oberbürgermeister, Elberfeld, 9 March 1887, Stadtarchiv Wuppertal O I 46; Polizeikommissar

Kammhoff to Staatsanwaltschaft, 24 July 1888, Staatsarchiv Düsseldorf, Landgericht Elberfeld 5/462.

46. *Elberfelder Zeitung* (13 August 1886), clipping in Staatsarchiv Düsseldorf, Landgericht Elberfeld 5/391.

47. See, for example, reports on Polizeikommissar Otto Kammhoff, Staatsarchiv Düsseldorf, Regierung Düsseldorf 15993.

48. Verhandelt, Polizeisergeant Heinrich Hinze, 16 August 1882, Staatsarchiv Düsseldorf, Landgericht Elberfeld 5/467.

49. *Bergisch-Märkische Morgen-Zeitung* (3 September 1882), clipping in Stadtarchiv Wuppertal O I 46; Oberbürgermeister, Elberfeld, to Regierung Düsseldorf, Abteilung des Innern, 5 September 1882, Staatsarchiv Düsseldorf, Regierung Düsseldorf 8688.

50. *Barmer Zeitung* (26 October 1888); Oberbürgermeister, Barmen, to Regierungspräsident, Düsseldorf, 25 January 1889; both in Staatsarchiv Düsseldorf, Regierung Düsseldorf 8645.

51. Oberbürgermeister, Duisburg, to Regierungspräsident, Düsseldorf, 6 July 1889, Staatsarchiv Düsseldorf, Regierung Düsseldorf 8626.

52. On employer reaction to the 1889 coal strike, see Maura Kealey, "Kampfstrategien der Unternehmerschaft im Ruhrbergbau seit dem Bergarbeiterstreik von 1889," in Hans Mommsen and Ulrich Borsdorf, eds., *Glück auf, Kameraden! Die Bergarbeiter und ihre Organisationen in Deutschland* (Cologne, 1979), pp. 175–97.

53. Wolfgang Köllmann, ed., *Der Bergarbeiterstreik von 1889 und die Gründung des "Alten Verbandes" in ausgewählten Dokumenten der Zeit* (Bochum, 1969), p. 13.

54. Wilhelm Diest, "Der Armee in Staat und Gesellschaft 1890–1914," in Michael Stürmer, ed., *Das kaiserliche Deutschland* (Düsseldorf, 1970), p. 319; Gustav Seeber and Walter Wittwer, "Friedrich Hammachers Aufzeichnungen über den Bergarbeiterstreik von 1889," *Jahrbuch für Geschichte* 16 (1977): 445, 449. The Ruhr, incidentally, did finally receive a military garrison in 1899, with one being established in Mülheim. To the west, Krefeld was provided with a garrison in 1906. *Bericht über die Verwaltung und den Stand der Gemeinde-Angelegenheiten der Oberbürgermeisterei Crefeld* (Krefeld, 1906), p. 6.

55. Albrecht Funk, *Polizei und Rechtsstaat: Die Entwicklung des staatlichen Gewaltmonopols in Preussen, 1848–1918* (Frankfurt am Main, 1986), pp. 228–35.

56. Telegram, William II to Oberpräsident, Rheinprovinz, 12 May 1889, in Köllmann, ed., *Der Bergarbeiterstreik von 1889,* p. 83; Klaus Saul, "Zwischen Repression und Integration: Staat, Gewerkschaften, und Arbeitskampf im kaiserlichen Deutschland 1884 bis 1914," in Klaus Tenfelde and Heinrich Volkmann, eds., *Streik: Zur Geschichte des Arbeitskampfes in Deutschland während der Industrialisierung* (Munich, 1981), pp. 216–17; Walter Wittwer, "Zur Taktik der herrschenden Klasse gegenüber dem Bergarbeiterstreik von 1889," in Horst Bartel, ed., *Evolution und Revolution in der Weltgeschichte: Festschrift für Ernst Engelberg,* vol. 2 (Berlin, 1976), pp. 547–48.

57. Wittwer, "Zur Taktik der herrschenden Klasse," p. 555.

58. Minister des Innern to Oberpräsident, Rheinprovinz, 20 June 1890, Staatsarchiv Düsseldorf, Regierung Düsseldorf 8611; Minister des Innern to Regierungspräsident, Düsseldorf, 18 July 1890, Stadtarchiv Duisburg 306/349.

CHAPTER VI: BIG-CITY POLICE, 1890–1914

1. Gerhard Bry, *Wages in Germany, 1871–1945* (Princeton, 1960), pp. 474–80; Reinhard Spree, *Wachstumstrends und Konjunkturzyklen in der deutschen Wirtschaft von 1820 bis 1913* (Göttingen, 1978), pp. 101–12.

2. Jürgen Reulecke, *Geschichte der Urbanisierung in Deutschland* (Frankfurt am Main, 1985), pp. 203–4.

3. See, for example, Minister des Innern to Regierungspräsident, Düsseldorf, 12 August 1898, Stadtarchiv Wuppertal O I 47; Landrat, Solingen, to Regierungspräsident, Düsseldorf, 9 January 1907, Staatsarchiv Düsseldorf, Regierung Düsseldorf 15953.

4. *Bericht über den Stand und die Verwaltung der Gemeinde-Angelegenheiten der Stadt Düsseldorf* (Düsseldorf, 1914), p. 13.

5. On the growth of municipal services, see, for example, Brian Ladd, *Urban Planning and Civic Order in Germany, 1860–1914* (Cambridge, Mass., 1990).

6. Heinrich Silbergleit, *Preussens Städte: Denkschrift zum 100 jährigen Jubiläum der Städteordnung von 19. November 1808* (Berlin, 1908), p. 485.

7. Hugo Weidenhaupt, "Von der französischen zur preussischen Zeit (1806–1856)," in Hugo Weidenhaupt, ed., *Düsseldorf: Geschichte von den Ursprüngen bis ins 20. Jahrhundert*, vol. 2 (Düsseldorf, 1988), p. 354.

8. Bernd Balkenhol, *Armut und Arbeitslosigkeit in der Industrialisierung dargestellt am Beispiel Düsseldorfs, 1850–1900* (Düsseldorf, 1976), p. 87.

9. Polizeiinspektor, Elberfeld, to Oberbürgermeister, Elberfeld, 7 April 1891, Stadtarchiv Wuppertal O I 46.

10. Verzeichnis der im Stadtkriese Düsseldorf angestellten Schutzleute, 1883, Staatsarchiv Düsseldorf, Regierung Düsseldorf 8728.

11. Oberbürgermeister, Düsseldorf, to Regierung Düsseldorf, Abteilung des Innern, 5 September 1883; Nachweisung derjenigen Personen, welche sich zur Anstellung als Schutzleute im Stadtkreise Düsseldorf gemeldet haben, 1883; both in Staatsarchiv Düsseldorf, Regierung Düsseldorf 8728.

12. Oberbürgermeister, Krefeld, to Regierung Düsseldorf, Abteilung des Innern, 26 March 1887, Staatsarchiv Düsseldorf, Regierung Düsseldorf 8620.

13. Oberbürgermeister, Krefeld, to Regierung Düsseldorf, Abteilung des Innern, 8 December 1883, Staatsarchiv Düsseldorf, Regierung Düsseldorf 8620.

14. Reports from individual cities, April 1891, Staatsarchiv Düsseldorf, Regierung Düsseldorf 8611.

15. Report, Polizeiinspektor Blase, Düsseldorf, 18 January 1911, Stadtarchiv Düsseldorf III/4537.

16. Polizeiverwaltung, Düsseldorf, to Regierungspräsident, Düsseldorf, 18 September 1898, Staatsarchiv Düsseldorf, Regierung Düsseldorf 3027.

17. Nachweisung über die Militärdienstzeit der Polizeisergeanten, Düsseldorf, 26 October 1904, Stadtarchiv Düsseldorf III/4393.

18. Urlaubsliste, Düsseldorf, 1900, Stadtarchiv Düsseldorf III/4397.

19. Reports from individual cities, 1913, Staatsarchiv Düsseldorf, Regierung Düsseldorf 30268.

20. By 1911, however, the director of the police school in Düsseldorf noted that such positions were becoming overfilled and as a consequence more holders of the Zivilversorgungsschein were seeking employment as policemen. Conference on police schools, Koblenz, 23 October 1911, Staatsarchiv Koblenz 403/13491.

21. On shortages of militarily qualified recruits for the Schutzmannschaft, see Albrecht Funk, *Polizei und Rechtsstaat: Die Entwicklung des staatlichen Gewaltmonopols in Preussen, 1848–1918* (Frankfurt am Main, 1986), pp. 290–91; Paul Schmidt, *Die ersten 50 Jahre der Königlichen Schutzmannschaft zu Berlin: Eine Geschichte des Korps für dessen Angehörige und Freunde* (Berlin, 1898), pp. 102, 120, 127, 145. See also Ausserordentliche Beilage zum Amtsblatt, 1882, Stadtarchiv Düsseldorf II/1335; Minister des Innern to Regierungspräsident, Düsseldorf, 8 November 1909, Staatsarchiv Düsseldorf, Regierung Düsseldorf 30326.

22. Report, Polizeiinspektor Blase, Düsseldorf, Stadtarchiv Düsseldorf III/4537.

23. Nachweisung über die Militärdienstzeit der Polizeisergeanten Düsseldorf, 26 October 1904, Stadtarchiv Düsseldorf III/4393.

24. Register of communal police prepared to transfer to state service, Essen, 1908, Stadtarchiv Essen XIII/21.

25. Raymond B. Fosdick, *European Police Systems* (Montclair, N.J., 1969, reprint of 1915 edition), p. 211.

26. Register of communal police prepared to transfer to state service, Essen, 1908, Stadtarchiv Essen XIII/21.

27. Nachweisung, Essen, 1908, Stadtarchiv Essen XIII/55.

28. Ibid.

29. Register of communal police prepared to transfer to state service, Essen, 1908, Stadtarchiv Essen XIII/21.

30. See, for example, Urlaubsliste, Düsseldorf, 1900, Stadtarchiv Düsseldorf III/4397.

31. Gesuch der Polizeiwachtmeister der Stadt Elberfeld um Versetzung in der Klasse der Subalternbeamten, 25 March 1908, Stadtarchiv Wuppertal O I 48. Polizeiwachtmeister Lenge to Polizeiverwaltung, 16 August 1912; Polizeiverwaltung, Krefeld, to Polizeiverwaltung, Düsseldorf, 30 September 1912; Polizeiverwaltung, Krefeld, to Polizeiverwaltung, Düsseldorf, 24 October 1912; all in Stadtarchiv Düsseldorf III/4394.

32. Oberbürgermeister, Elberfeld, to Polizeiverwaltung, Meiderich, 13 July 1903, Stadtarchiv Wuppertal O I 48.

33. Kommissare, Düsseldorf, 1893–1912, Staatsarchiv Düsseldorf, Regierung Düsseldorf 30356.

34. Fosdick, *European Police Systems*, p. 159.

35. Nachweisung, Essen, 1908, Stadtarchiv Essen XIII/55. See also *Düsseldorfer Neueste Nachrichten* (22 December 1907), clipping in Stadtarchiv Düsseldorf III/4394.

36. Hansjoachim Henning, *Das Westdeutsche Bürgertum in der Epoche der Hochindustrialisierung 1860–1914: Soziales Verhalten und Soziale Strukturen*, pt. 1, *Das Bildungsbürgertum in der preussischen Westprovinzen* (Wiesbaden, 1972), pp. 188–94.

37. Nachweisung, Essen, 1908, Stadtarchiv Essen XIII/55.

38. Regierung Düsseldorf, Abteilung des Innern, 19 July 1883, Staatsarchiv Düsseldorf, Regierung Düsseldorf 8998. *General Anzeiger* (11 December 1906), clipping in Stadtarchiv Düsseldorf III/4393; Report, Oberbürgermeister, Düsseldorf, 25 April 1914, Stadtarchiv Düsseldorf III/4394.

39. For recruitment of noncommissioned officers as communal Polizeikommissare throughout Prussia, see Franz Laufer, *Die preussische Kommunalpolizei: Vorschläge zu ihrer zeitgemässigen Umgestaltung* (Schwelm, 1903), p. 15.

40. Kommissare, Düsseldorf, 1893–1912, Staatsarchiv Düsseldorf, Regierung Düsseldorf 30356; *Düsseldorfer Neueste Nachrichten* (25 December 1907), clipping in Stadtarchiv Düsseldorf III/4394.

41. Urlaubsliste, Düsseldorf, 1900, Stadtarchiv Düsseldorf III/4397; Register of communal policemen prepared to transfer to state service, 1908, Stadtarchiv Essen XIII/21.

42. Compare Laufer, *Die preussische Kommunalpolizei*, p. 19.

43. Polizeisergeanten, Essen, to Oberbürgermeister, Essen, 10 April 1885, Stadtarchiv Essen XIII/11.

44. Verzeichnis der in Stadtbezirk Düsseldorf definitiv angestellten Schutzleute, 1897, Stadtarchiv Düsseldorf III/4393.

45. Oberbürgermeister, Barmen, to Regierungspräsident, Düsseldorf, 14 May 1900, Staatsarchiv Düsseldorf, Regierung Düsseldorf 8738; Report, Oberbürgermeister, Krefeld, 9 September 1905, Stadtarchiv Krefeld 4/948.

46. Zusammenstellung wie in den verschiedenen Städten die Polizeisergeanten zum Tages- und Nachtdienst verwendet werden, 5 January 1907, Stadtarchiv Duisburg 306/123.

47. Petition, Polizeisergeanten der Nachtdienst, to Oberbürgermeister, Krefeld, 20 November 1903, Stadtarchiv Krefeld 4/949.

48. Oberbürgermeister, Düsseldorf, to Regierung Düsseldorf, Abteilung des Innern, 25 April 1883, Staatsarchiv Düsseldorf, Regierung Düsseldorf 8728; Polizeiinspektor Terpe, Duisburg, to Oberbürgermeister, Duisburg, 28 February 1907, Stadtarchiv Duisburg 306/123.

49. Schmidt, *Die ersten 50 Jahre der Königlichen Schutzmannschaft*, p. 129; Polizeiverwaltung, Düsseldorf, to Polizeiverwaltung, Elberfeld, 3 January 1900, Stadtarchiv Düsseldorf III/4396; Polizeiinspektor Terpe, Duisburg, 22 April

1907, Stadtarchiv Duisburg 306/123; *Bericht über die Verwaltung und den Stand der Gemeinde-Angelegenheiten der Stadt Elberfeld* (Elberfeld, 1910), p. 321.

50. *Niederrheinische Volkstribune* (5 January 1906), clipping in Staatsarchiv Düsseldorf, Regierung Düsseldorf 30284.

51. Rechtsanwalt Wahl, Barmen, to Oberpräsident, Rheinprovinz, 13 December 1907; Regierungspräsident, Düsseldorf, to Oberpräsident, Rheinprovinz, 31 December 1907; both in Staatsarchiv Koblenz 403/13498.

52. See, for instance, Dienstanweisung für die Kriminalabteilung der Polizeiverwaltung, Duisburg, Verwaltungsstelle Duisburg-Ruhrort, 13 October 1905, Stadtarchiv Duisburg 306/126.

53. Polizeiinspektor Lemke, *Zusammenstellung der in der preussischen Städte über je 10000 Einwohner angestellten Polizei-Exekutivbeamten* (Osnabrück, 1901); *Bericht über die Verwaltung und den Stand der Gemeinde-Angelegenheiten der Stadt Elberfeld* (Elberfeld, 1910), pp. 278, 322.

54. Erster Staatsanwalt, Elberfeld, to Landgerichtspräsident, Elberfeld, 10 February 1906; Landrichter to Landgerichtspräsident, Elberfeld, 14 February 1906; Regierungspräsident, Düsseldorf, to Bürgermeister, Barmen, 18 August 1906; all in Staatsarchiv Düsseldorf, Regierung Düsseldorf, Präs. Büro 747.

55. Polizeipräsident, Essen, to Regierungspräsident, Düsseldorf, 26 May 1911, Staatsarchiv Düsseldorf, Regierung Düsseldorf 30341.

56. *Bericht über den Stand und die Verwaltung der Gemeinde-Angelegenheiten der Stadt Duisburg* (Duisburg, 1911), p. 81.

57. *Bericht über die Verwaltung und den Stand der Gemeinde-Angelegenheiten der Stadt Elberfeld* (1910), p. 322.

58. Beigeordneter, Elberfeld, to Regierungspräsident, 12 January 1903, Staatsarchiv Düsseldorf, Regierung Düsseldorf 30389.

59. Nachweis über den Zahl und die Verhältnisse der Gemeindepolizei-Exekutivbeamten, 1898, Staatsarchiv Düsseldorf, Regierung Düsseldorf 8612; *Die Verwaltung der Stadt Essen im XIX. Jahrhundert mit besonderer Berücksichtigung der letzten fünfzehn Jahre* (Essen, 1902), p. 47; Report, Essen, 1902, Staatsarchiv Düsseldorf, Regierung Düsseldorf 30270.

60. Oberbürgermeister, Essen, to Oberbürgermeister, Krefeld, 1 April 1897, Stadtarchiv Krefeld 4/949.

61. Bry, *Wages in Germany*, pp. 325–26; Carl-Ludwig Holtfrerich, *Quantitative Wirtschaftsgeschichte des Ruhrkohlenbergbaus im 19. Jahrhundert: Eine Führungssektoranalyse* (Dortmund, 1973), pp. 23–24; Peter Hüttenberger, *Die Industrie- und Verwaltungsstadt (20. Jahrhundert)*, vol. 3 of Weidenhaupt, *Düsseldorf*, p. 123.

62. Report, Elberfeld, 1913, Staatsarchiv Düsseldorf, Regierung Düsseldorf 30268.

63. Holtfrerich, *Quantitative Wirtschaftsgeschichte des Ruhrkohlenbergbaus*, pp. 55–56; Wolfgang Köllmann, *Sozialgeschichte der Stadt Barmen im 19. Jahrhundert* (Tübingen, 1960), p. 145; Report, Barmen, 23 April 1891, Staatsarchiv Düsseldorf, Regierung Düsseldorf 8611; Report, Barmen, 1913, Staatsarchiv Düsseldorf, Regierung Düsseldorf 30268.

64. Henning, *Das Westdeutsche Bürgertum*, pt. 1, p. 247.
65. Auszug aus dem *Polizei-Nachrichtenblatt* (19 May 1911), Stadtarchiv Wuppertal O I 49; *Die Polizei*, no. 26 (1912), Stadtarchiv Düsseldorf III/4394.
66. Minister des Innern to Regierungspräsidenten, 6 March 1901 and 16 May 1903, both in Staatsarchiv Koblenz 403/6591. While individual policemen were forbidden to profit from the preparation of news reports, city administrations might order preferential provision of police news for the benefit of favored newspapers. See, for example, Oberbürgermeister, Elberfeld, to Polizeibezirke, 24 October 1902, Stadtarchiv Wuppertal O I 47.
67. Verfügung vom 22. November 1901 betreffend die Annahme von Geschenken für Amtsverrichtungen seitens der Verwaltungsbeamten, Stadtarchiv Duisburg 306/144; *Volkszeitung* (1 February 1912), clipping in Staatsarchiv Düsseldorf, Regierung Düsseldorf 46073; Minister des Innern to Regierungspräsidenten, 11 February 1914, Staatsarchiv Koblenz 403/13491.
68. See, for example, Köllmann, *Sozialgeschichte der Stadt Barmen*, pp. 133–34.
69. Die Postenstehenden Polizeisergeanten, Elberfeld, to Oberbürgermeister, Elberfeld, 16 January 1893, Stadtarchiv Wuppertal O I 46; Polizeisergeanten, Elberfeld, to Oberbürgermeister, 11 March 1903, Stadtarchiv Wuppertal O I 47.
70. Einführung einer neuen Diensteinteilung für die Polizeisergeanten, 9 September 1905, Stadtarchiv Krefeld 4/948. See also Polizeiinspektor Koehl, Duisburg-Ruhrort, 2 April 1907, Stadtarchiv Duisburg 306/123.
71. See, for instance, Polizeisergeanten, Elberfeld, to Oberbürgermeister, Elberfeld, 11 March 1903; Polizeiwachtmeister, Elberfeld, to Oberbürgermeister, Elberfeld, 17 March 1906; both in Stadtarchiv Wuppertal O I 47.
72. Auszug aus dem *Polizei-Nachrichtenblatt* (31 January 1913), Stadtarchiv Wuppertal O I 51.
73. Polizeiverwaltung, Essen, 30 January 1896, Stadtarchiv Essen XIII/11. See also Polizeipräsident, Essen, to Regierungspräsident, Düsseldorf, 28 September 1910, Staatsarchiv Düsseldorf, Regierung Düsseldorf 30328.
74. Dienstinstruktion für die Nachtdienst-Polizeibeamten der Stadt Düsseldorf, 12 June 1892, Stadtarchiv Essen XIII/11.
75. Dienstinstruktion für die Nachtdienst-Polizeibeamten der Stadt Düsseldorf, 12 June 1892, Stadtarchiv Essen XIII/11; Oberbürgermeister, Düsseldorf, to Beigeordnete, Bureau- und Dienststellenvorsteher, 27 February 1913, Stadtarchiv Düsseldorf III/4329; Polizeipräsident, Essen, to Regierungspräsident, Düsseldorf, 27 November 1913, Staatsarchiv Düsseldorf, Regierung Düsseldorf 16038.
76. Oberbürgermeister, Barmen, to Regierungspräsident, Düsseldorf, 24 December 1900; Oberbürgermeister, Düsseldorf, 11 January 1901; both in Staatsarchiv Düsseldorf, Regierung Düsseldorf 30210.
77. On the training of Kommissare, see Kommissare, Düsseldorf, 1893–1912, Staatsarchiv Düsseldorf, Regierung Düsseldorf 30356.

78. See, for example, Oberbürgermeister, Duisburg, to Regierungspräsident, Düsseldorf, 4 June 1892, Staatsarchiv Düsseldorf, Regierung Düsseldorf 8626; Oberbürgermeister, Duisburg, to Regierungspräsident, Düsseldorf, 19 September 1898, Staatsarchiv Düsseldorf, Regierung Düsseldorf 30271; Regierungspräsident, Düsseldorf, to Vorsitzender des Kuratoriums der Polizeischule in Düsseldorf, 8 November 1907, Stadtarchiv Düsseldorf III/4394; Polizeiverwaltung, Düsseldorf, 10 June 1910, Stadtarchiv Düsseldorf III/4329.

79. Regierungspräsident, Düsseldorf, to Landräte and Oberbürgermeister, 13 December 1900, Staatsarchiv Düsseldorf, Regierung Düsseldorf 30210.

80. Frank J. Thomason, "The Prussian Police State in Berlin, 1848–1871" (Ph.D. diss., Johns Hopkins, 1978), p. 299.

81. Laufer, *Die preussische Kommunalpolizei*, p. 19.

82. Conference proceedings, 23 October 1911, Staatsarchiv Koblenz 403/13491.

83. Ibid.

84. Anordnung, Regierungspräsident, Düsseldorf, 10 June 1906, Stadtarchiv Düsseldorf III/4393.

85. Conference proceedings, 23 October 1911, Staatsarchiv Koblenz 403/13491.

86. *General-Anzeiger* (10 July 1911), clipping in Stadtarchiv Wuppertal O I 68; *Kölnische Zeitung* (15 July 1911), clipping in Staatsarchiv Koblenz 403/13498.

87. Report, Bürgermeister, Wesel, 14 June 1911; Bürgermeister, Wesel, to Landrat, Wesel, 11 and 25 July 1911; all in Staatsarchiv Koblenz 403/13498.

88. Landrat, Wesel, to Regierungspräsident, Düsseldorf, 27 July 1911, Staatsarchiv Koblenz 403/13498.

89. See, for example, Beschwerde, Polizeisergeant Kunkel, Elberfeld, 15 October 1903, Staatsarchiv Düsseldorf, Regierung Düsseldorf 30389; Polizeiverwaltung, Duisburg, to Regierungspräsident, Düsseldorf, 26 August 1910, Staatsarchiv Düsseldorf, Regierung Düsseldorf 30308.

90. Polizeiverwaltung, Düsseldorf, to Polizeikommissare and Wachtmeister, 22 February 1911, Stadtarchiv Düsseldorf III/4394.

91. Polizeiwachtmeister, Elberfeld, to Minister des Innern, 25 March 1908, Stadtarchiv Wuppertal O I 48.

92. Reports, Polizeiinspektor Blase, Düsseldorf, 20 March and 15 November 1911; *Volkszeitung* (4 October 1911); all in Stadtarchiv Düsseldorf III/4394.

93. See the complaints of the Minister des Innern to Regierungspräsident, Düsseldorf, 14 January 1901, Staatsarchiv Düsseldorf, Regierung Düsseldorf 8612.

94. Personalakten des Polizeisergeanten Aloysius Brun, Elberfeld, Staatsarchiv Düsseldorf, Regierung Düsseldorf 30389.

95. Zusammenstellung derjenigen Fälle, in welchen Polizeibeamte in den Jahren 1892 und 1893 gerichtlich bestraft worden sind; Regierungspräsident,

Düsseldorf, to Landräte and Oberbürgermeister, 4 December 1893; both in Staatsarchiv Düsseldorf, Regierung Düsseldorf 30273.

96. Nachweisung derjenigen Beamten die durch Erlass des Herrn Minister des Innern wegen Bestrafungen von der Übernahme in den Staatsdienst ausgeschlossen werden sollen, 1908, Stadtarchiv Essen XIII/55.

97. *Polizei Post* (1 March 1912), clipping in Stadtarchiv Wuppertal O I 49.

98. Polizeiverwaltung, Duisburg, to Regierungspräsident, Düsseldorf, 8 December 1911; Polizeiverwaltung, Elberfeld, to Regierungspräsident, Düsseldorf, 11 December 1911; Polizeiverwaltung, Düsseldorf, to Regierungspräsident, Düsseldorf, 28 December 1911; all in Staatsarchiv Düsseldorf, Regierung Düsseldorf 30277.

99. Gesuch der Polizeisergeanten betreffend Bekanntgabe der über dieselben verhängten Disziplinarstrafen im Polizei-Nachrichtenblatt, Elberfeld, 16 March 1911, Stadtarchiv Wuppertal O I 49.

100. Polizei-Exekutivbeamten, Beschwerde, Duisburg, 1913, Stadtarchiv Duisburg 306/77.

101. Amtsgericht, Duisburg-Ruhrort, to Oberbürgermeister, Duisburg, 29 March 1913, Stadtarchiv Duisburg 306/77.

102. *Bürger Zeitung* (5 January 1901), clipping in Stadtarchiv Düsseldorf III/4399.

103. Regierungspräsident, Düsseldorf, to Landräte and Oberbürgermeister, 6 September 1913, Stadtarchiv Duisburg 306/77.

104. Polizeiverwaltung, Düsseldorf, 7 July 1910, Stadtarchiv Düsseldorf III/4394.

105. Vereinigung der Polizeioberbeamten des westlichen Industriegebiets to Regierungspräsident, Münster, 22 January 1901, Staatsarchiv Düsseldorf, Regierung Düsseldorf 8612; Regierungspräsident, Arnsberg, to Minister des Innern, 25 December 1907, Staatsarchiv Koblenz 403/6592; Minister des Innern to Oberpräsident, Rheinprovinz, 7 March 1908, Staatsarchiv Düsseldorf, Regierung Düsseldorf 30278.

106. Regierungspräsident, Arnsberg, to Minister des Innern, 3 August 1912, Staatsarchiv Düsseldorf, Regierung Düsseldorf 30278.

107. Oberbürgermeister, Essen, to Regierungspräsident, Düsseldorf, 30 August 1912; Oberbürgermeister, Solingen, to Regierungspräsident, Düsseldorf, 16 July 1913; both in Staatsarchiv Düsseldorf, Regierung Düsseldorf 30278. Regierungspräsident, Düsseldorf, to Minister des Innern, 15 November 1912, Staatsarchiv Koblenz 403/13491.

108. Report, Polizeiinspektor Blase, 12 March 1908, Stadtarchiv Düsseldorf III/4394.

CHAPTER VII: POLICE AND DAILY LIFE, 1890–1914

1. *Täglicher Anzeiger für Berg und Mark* (14 December 1909), clipping in Staatsarchiv Düsseldorf, Regierung Düsseldorf 30393.

2. *Bericht über den Stand und die Verwaltung der Gemeinde-Angelegenheiten der Stadt Duisburg* (Duisburg, 1901), p. 167; *Bericht über die Verwaltung und den Stand der Gemeinde-Angelegenheiten der Oberbürgermeisterei Crefeld* (Krefeld, 1908), p. 21; Erhard Lucas, *Zwei Formen von Radikalismus in der deutschen Arbeiterbewegung* (Frankfurt am Main, 1976), p. 48. In his study of the American urban police, Eric Monkkonen ascribed great importance to the development of alternatives to using jails as shelters for the homeless. Monkkonen saw this change as symptomatic of a significant shift in police function from class control to crime control. See Eric Monkkonen, *Police in Urban America, 1860–1920* (Cambridge, 1981), pp. 106–8. Such a shift was, however, less apparent in the Düsseldorf district prior to the First World War. Compare Barbara Weinberger and Herbert Reinke, "A Diminishing Function? A Comparative Historical Account of Policing the City," *Police and Society* 1 (1991): 213–23.

3. *Bericht über den Stand und die Verwaltung der Gemeinde-Angelegenheiten der Stadt Duisburg* (Duisburg, 1907), pp. 385–86; Polizeiverwaltung, Krefeld, to Regierungspräsident, Düsseldorf, 2 April 1912, Staatsarchiv Düsseldorf, Regierung Düsseldorf 30290.

4. Polizeiverwaltung, Barmen, to Regierungspräsident, Düsseldorf, 12 September 1896; Oberbürgermeister, Elberfeld, to Regierungspräsident, Düsseldorf, 17 September 1896; both in Staatsarchiv Düsseldorf, Regierung Düsseldorf 30463.

5. Herbert Reinke, "Die Polizei und die 'Reinhaltung der Gegend': Prostitution und Sittenpolizei im Wuppertal im 19. und im frühen 20. Jahrhundert," in Jürgen Reulecke and Adelheid Gräfin zu Castell Rüdenhausen, eds., *Stadt und Gesundheit: Zum Wandel von "Volksgesundheit" und kommunaler Gesundheitspolitik im 19. und frühen 20. Jahrhundert* (Stuttgart, 1991), pp. 131–32.

6. *Bericht über den Stand und die Verwaltung der Gemeinde-Angelegenheiten der Stadt Duisburg* (Duisburg, 1894), p. 115.

7. *Bericht über den Stand und die Verwaltung der Gemeinde-Angelegenheiten der Stadt Düsseldorf* (Düsseldorf, 1903), pp. 28–29, and (1910), p. 17.

8. Lucas, *Zwei Formen von Radikalismus*, p. 54; Franz Brüggemeier and Lutz Niethammer, "Schlafgänger, Schnapskasinos, und schwerindustrielle Kolonie: Aspekte der Arbeiterwohnungsfrage im Ruhrgebiet vor dem Ersten Weltkrieg," in Jürgen Reulecke and Wolfhard Weber, eds., *Fabrik, Familie, Feierabend: Beiträge zur Sozialgeschichte des Alltags im Industriezeitalter* (Wuppertal, 1978), p. 157; Brüggemeier, *Leben vor Ort: Ruhrbergleute und Ruhrbergbau, 1889–1919* (Munich, 1983), pp. 71–72.

9. *Bericht über die Verwaltung und den Stand der Gemeinde-Angelegenheiten der Stadt Elberfeld* (Elberfeld, 1910), p. 329; *Täglicher Anzeiger für Berg und Mark* (9 March 1909), clipping in Staatsarchiv Düsseldorf, Regierung Düsseldorf 30393.

10. Minister des Innern to Regierungspräsident, Düsseldorf, 14 May 1900, Stadtarchiv Krefeld 4/958; Minister des Innern to Regierungspräsident, 26 September 1902, Staatsarchiv Düsseldorf, Regierung Düsseldorf 30469.

11. Oberbürgermeister, Düsseldorf, to Regierungspräsident, Düsseldorf, 18 April 1913; Polizeipräsident, Essen, to Regierungspräsident, Düsseldorf, 14 June 1913; both in Staatsarchiv Düsseldorf, Regierung Düsseldorf 30469.

12. See, for example, Polizeiverwaltung, Düsseldorf, to Regierungspräsident, Düsseldorf, 19 June 1912, Staatsarchiv Düsseldorf, Regierung Düsseldorf 46073; Polizeiverwaltung, Krefeld, to Regierungspräsident, Düsseldorf, 11 April 1913, Staatsarchiv Düsseldorf, Regierung Düsseldorf 30290.

13. Report, Polizeiverwaltung, Elberfeld, 9 October 1906, Stadtarchiv Wuppertal O I 47.

14. Bericht über den Stand und die Verwaltung der Gemeinde-Angelegenheiten der Stadt Düsseldorf (Düsseldorf, 1908), p. 20.

15. Regierungspräsident, Düsseldorf, to Minister des Innern, 29 December 1910, Staatsarchiv Koblenz 403/13537.

16. Recent research lends support to this view. See Eric A. Johnson, "The Roots of Crime in Imperial Germany," Central European History 15 (December 1982): 351–76; Eric A. Johnson and Vincent McHale, "Socioeconomic Aspects of the Delinquency Rate in Imperial Germany," Journal of Social History 13 (Spring 1980): 384–402.

17. Presentation by District Polizeikommissar Krohn to conference, Essen, 22 February 1906, Staatsarchiv Düsseldorf, Regierung Düsseldorf 15995.

18. Giesbert Knopp, Die Preussische Verwaltung des Regierungsbezirks Düsseldorf in den Jahren 1899–1919 (Cologne, 1974), p. 23.

19. James Harvey Jackson, "Migration and Urbanization in the Ruhr Valley, 1850–1900" (Ph.D. diss., University of Minnesota, 1980), p. 114.

20. Lucas, Zwei Formen von Radikalismus, p. 110.

21. Klaus Tenfelde, "Die 'Krawalle von Herne' im Jahre 1899," Internationale wissenschaftliche Korrespondenz zur Geschichte der deutschen Arbeiterbewegung 15 (March 1979): 71–104.

22. District Polizeikommissar Koch, Düsseldorf, to Regierungspräsident, Düsseldorf, 12 February 1904, Staatsarchiv Düsseldorf, Regierung Düsseldorf 30417.

23. See, for example, Düsseldorfer Neueste Nachrichten (25 April 1900), clipping in Stadtarchiv Düsseldorf III/4396; Wuppertaler Volksblatt (24 November 1904) and General Anzeiger für Elberfeld und Barmen (27 November 1904), both clippings in Stadtarchiv Wuppertal O I 117; Regierungspräsident, Düsseldorf, to Oberpräsident, Rheinprovinz, 15 November 1910 and 5 September 1912, both in Staatsarchiv Koblenz 403/13498.

24. Bericht über den Stand und die Verwaltung der Gemeinde-Angelegenheiten der Stadt Duisburg (Duisburg, 1880–1910).

25. Nachweisung derjenigen Verletzungen, welche Polizeibeamte bei Ausübung des Dienstes davongetragen haben, 6 August 1900; Düsseldorfer Neueste Nachrichten (12 August 1900); both in Stadtarchiv Düsseldorf III/4398.

26. Ausschnitt aus dem Amtsblatt (12 May 1894), Stadtarchiv Düsseldorf III/5518.

27. Report, Polizeiverwaltung, Krefeld, 15 December 1900; Bürgermeister, Meiderich, to Regierungspräsident, Düsseldorf, 17 June 1904, both in Staatsarchiv Düsseldorf, Regierung Düsseldorf 30417.

28. District Polizeikommissar, Düsseldorf, to Regierungspräsident, Düsseldorf, 12 February 1904, Staatsarchiv Düsseldorf, Regierung Düsseldorf 30417.

29. Nachweisung der wegen der Polizeiverordnungen vom 11. Mai 1872 und 8. Mai 1894 in den Jahren 1898, 1899, und 1900 vorgekommenen Bestrafungen betreffend Tragen von Waffen, Staatsarchiv Düsseldorf, Regierung Düsseldorf 30417.

30. Minister des Innern to Oberpräsident, Rheinprovinz, 9 April 1904, Staatsarchiv Düsseldorf, Regierung Düsseldorf 30417.

31. *Bericht über den Stand und die Verwaltung der Gemeinde-Angelegenheiten der Stadt Duisburg* (Duisburg, 1898), p. 118.

32. Roger Lane, *Policing the City: Boston, 1822–1885* (New York, 1971), p. 203; Wilbur R. Miller, *Cops and Bobbies: Police Authority in New York and London, 1830–1870* (Chicago, 1977), p. 51.

33. Regierungspräsident, Düsseldorf, to Oberbürgermeister, Essen, 4 May 1896, Stadtarchiv Essen XIII/11; Beigeordneter, Elberfeld, to Regierungspräsident, Düsseldorf, 8 and 18 May 1903, both in Staatsarchiv Düsseldorf, Regierung Düsseldorf 30389.

34. Landrat, Essen, to Regierungspräsident, Düsseldorf, 26 January 1905, Staatsarchiv Düsseldorf, Regierung Düsseldorf 15927.

35. Minister des Innern to Regierungspräsident, Düsseldorf, 21 October 1910, Staatsarchiv Düsseldorf, Regierung Düsseldorf 15964.

36. Polizeipräsident, Essen, to Regierungspräsident, Düsseldorf, 25 October, 24 and 29 December 1910, and 2 June 1914; all in Staatsarchiv Düsseldorf, Regierung Düsseldorf 15964.

37. Presentation, Polizeiinspektor Adolph, Elberfeld, for conference, 16 April 1913, Staatsarchiv Düsseldorf, Regierung Düsseldorf 30278.

38. Polizeiverwaltung, Düsseldorf, to Regierungspräsident, Düsseldorf, 25 August 1903, Staatsarchiv Düsseldorf, Regierung Düsseldorf 30267; *Bericht über den Stand und die Verwaltung der Gemeinde-Angelegenheiten der Stadt Duisburg* (Duisburg, 1905), pp. 371–72.

39. *Bericht über den Stand und die Verwaltung der Gemeinde-Angelegenheiten der Stadt Duisburg* (Duisburg, 1898), p. 118; Report, Polizeiverwaltung, Essen, 25 May 1898, Stadtarchiv Essen XIII/11.

40. See, for example, Freiherr von Gamp-Massaunen in *Stenographische Berichte über die Verhandlungen des deutschen Reichstags,* vol. 234 (Berlin, 1909), p. 6778; *Rheinisch-Westfälischer Anzeiger* (26 May 1910), clipping Stadtarchiv Essen XIII/8.

41. Regierungspräsident, Düsseldorf, to Polizeiverwaltung, Düsseldorf, 5 June 1907, Stadtarchiv Düsseldorf III/4394; Regierungspräsident, Düsseldorf, to Landräte and Polizeiverwaltungen, 5 March 1908, Stadtarchiv Essen XIII/5.

42. Regierungspräsident, Düsseldorf, to Oberbürgermeister, Düsseldorf, 18 November 1900, Stadtarchiv Düsseldorf III/4393.

43. Regierungspräsident, Düsseldorf, to Oberbürgermeister and Landräte, 18 January 1899, Stadtarchiv Wuppertal O I 156.

44. Minister des Innern to Polizeipräsident (Essen), Landräte, and Polizeiverwaltungen, 4 February 1911, Stadtarchiv Duisburg 306/332. See also Beigeordneter, Elberfeld, to Regierungspräsident, Düsseldorf, 29 March 1893, Staatsarchiv Düsseldorf, Regierung Düsseldorf 8905; Rainer Hehemann, *Die "Bekämpfung des Zigeunerunwesens" im Wilhelminischen Deutschland und in der Weimarer Republik, 1871–1933* (Frankfurt am Main, 1987), pp. 245–71.

45. Polizeiverwaltung, Krefeld, to Regierungspräsident, Düsseldorf, 30 November 1899; Polizeiverwaltung, Düsseldorf, to Regierungspräsident, Düsseldorf, 1 December 1899; both in Staatsarchiv Düsseldorf, Regierung Düsseldorf 8905. Compare Franz Laufer, *Die preussische Kommunalpolizei: Vorschläge zu ihrer zeitgemässigen Umgestaltung* (Schwelm, 1903), p. 7.

46. Minister des Innern to Oberpräsidenten, 20 March 1912, Staatsarchiv Koblenz 403/6801; Polizeiverordnung betreffend das bandenmässige Umherziehen der Zigeuner, 7 May 1912, Stadtarchiv Duisburg 306/332.

47. Report, Polizeiverwaltung, Düsseldorf, 10 January 1899; *Düsseldorfer Zeitung* (9 December 1901); both in Stadtarchiv Düsseldorf III/5521.

48. *Düsseldorfer General-Anzeiger* (12 January 1907); *Allgemeiner Beobachter* (14 January 1907); Beigeordneter Wülffing, Düsseldorf, to Regierungspräsident, Düsseldorf, 23 January 1907; all in Staatsarchiv Düsseldorf, Regierung Düsseldorf 46069.

49. Wolfgang Köllmann, *Sozialgeschichte der Stadt Barmen im 19. Jahrhundert* (Tübingen, 1960), pp. 133–34.

50. *Kölnische Zeitung* (11 May 1911), clipping in Staatsarchiv Koblenz 403/13432; Wolfram Fischer, *Herz des Reviers* (Essen, 1965), pp. 291–92; Erhard Lucas, *Zwei Formen von Radikalismus*, pp. 104–5; Brüggemeier, *Leben vor Ort*, p. 148.

51. Peter Hüttenberger, *Die Industrie- und Verwaltungsstadt (20. Jahrhundert)*, vol. 3 of Hugo Weidenhaupt, ed., *Düsseldorf: Geschichte von den Ursprüngen bis ins 20. Jahrhundert* (Düsseldorf, 1989), p. 210.

52. Ibid., pp. 208–13.

53. *Die Verwaltung der Stadt Elberfeld in den Zeitabschnitte 1900 bis 1910* (Elberfeld, 1915), p. 328.

54. Regierungspräsident, Düsseldorf, to Oberpräsident, Rheinprovinz, 29 November 1909, Staatsarchiv Koblenz 403/13432; Brüggemeier, *Leben vor Ort*, pp. 149–51.

55. Polizeiverwaltung, Krefeld, to Regierungspräsident, Düsseldorf, 22 November 1895; Polizeiverwaltung, Barmen, to Regierungspräsident, Düsseldorf, 10 January 1896; Oberbürgermeister, Düsseldorf, to Regierungspräsident, Düsseldorf, 14 January 1896; Polizeiverwaltung, Essen, to Regierungspräsident, Düsseldorf, 17 January 1896; Oberbürgermeister, Duisburg, to Regierungspräsident, Düsseldorf, 21 January 1896; all in Staatsarchiv Düsseldorf, Regierung Düsseldorf 8999.

56. Polizeiverwaltung, Barmen, to Regierungspräsident, Düsseldorf, 4 April 1906, Staatsarchiv Düsseldorf, Regierung Düsseldorf 8999.

57. Polizeiverwaltung, Krefeld, to Regierungspräsident, Düsseldorf, 24 March 1906; Polizeiverwaltung, Düsseldorf, to Regierungspräsident, Düsseldorf, 3 April 1906; Polizeiverwaltung, Düsseldorf, to Regierungspräsident, Düsseldorf, 3 June 1909; Polizeiverwaltung, Barmen, to Regierungspräsident, Düsseldorf, 5 June 1909; all in Staatsarchiv Düsseldorf, Regierung Düsseldorf 8999.

58. Minister des Innern to Regierungspräsident, Düsseldorf, 28 June 1911; Regierungspräsident, Düsseldorf, to Minister des Innern, 30 October 1911; both in Staatsarchiv Düsseldorf, Regierung Düsseldorf 30458. Lynn Abrams, "Prostitutes in Imperial Germany, 1870–1918: Working Girls or Social Outcasts?" in Richard Evans, ed., *The German Underworld: Deviants and Outcasts in German History* (London, 1988), p. 203.

59. Dr. Olshaufen, "Die Frühpolizeistunde im Deutschen Reich," *Jahrbuch für Gesetzgebung, Verwaltung, und Volkswirtschaft im Deutschen Reich* 29 (1905): 845–82.

60. *Täglicher Anzeiger* (26 March and 1 May 1887), both clippings in Stadtarchiv Düsseldorf III/4636; Verfügung, Polizeiverwaltung, Elberfeld, 26 September 1905, Stadtarchiv Wuppertal O I 47; Polizeiverwaltung, Düsseldorf, to Regierungspräsident, Düsseldorf, 1 March 1913, Staatsarchiv Düsseldorf, Regierung Düsseldorf 46073.

61. Gary D. Stark, "Cinema, Society, and the State: Policing the Film Industry in Imperial Germany," in Gary D. Stark and Bede Karl Lackner, eds., *Essays on Culture and Society in Modern Germany* (College Station, Tex., 1982), pp. 122–66. See also Lynn Abrams, "From Control to Commercialization: The Triumph of Mass Entertainment in Germany, 1900–1925?" *German History* 8 (October 1990): 278–93; Derek S. Linton, *"Who Has the Youth, Has the Future": The Campaign to Save Young Workers in Imperial Germany* (Cambridge, 1991), pp. 61–62.

62. Regierungspräsident, Düsseldorf, to Oberpräsident, Rheinprovinz, 19 January 1892, Staatsarchiv Koblenz 403/7061; Polizeiverwaltung, Barmen, to Kreisarzt, 29 July 1914, Staatsarchiv Düsseldorf, Regierung Düsseldorf 46075. See, however, Oberbürgermeister, Barmen, to Regierungspräsident, Düsseldorf, 12 December 1908, Staatsarchiv Düsseldorf, Regierung Düsseldorf 30463 for a more cautious evaluation of the appropriateness of using the police to try to protect youthful morals, in this case against exposure to trashy literature.

63. Brüggemeier and Niethammer, "Schlafgänger, Schnapskasinos, und schwerindustrielle Kolonie," in Reulecke and Weber, eds., *Fabrik, Familie, Feierabend*, p. 165.

64. Vermerk, Regierung Düsseldorf, 17 June 1908, Staatsarchiv Düsseldorf, Regierung Düsseldorf 30466.

65. Abrams, "Prostitutes in Imperial Germany," pp. 198–99.

66. Oberbürgermeister, Barmen, to Regierungspräsident, 14 May 1900, Staatsarchiv Düsseldorf, Regierung Düsseldorf 8738.

67. Polizeiverwaltung, Krefeld, to Regierungspräsident, Düsseldorf, 2 February 1894, Staatsarchiv Düsseldorf, Regierung Düsseldorf 8935; Report,

Regierungspräsident, Düsseldorf, 31 January 1895, Staatsarchiv Düsseldorf, Regierung Düsseldorf 30458; Polizeiverwaltung, Krefeld, to Regierungspräsident, Düsseldorf, 5 July 1913, Staatsarchiv Düsseldorf, Regierung Düsseldorf 30290. Compare Richard J. Evans, "Prostitution, State, and Society in Imperial Germany," *Past and Present* 70 (February 1976): 106–29.

68. *Düsseldorfer Neueste Nachrichten* (8 May 1906); Polizeiverwaltung, Düsseldorf, to Regierungspräsident, Düsseldorf, 31 May 1906; both in Staatsarchiv Düsseldorf, Regierung Düsseldorf 46069. Polizeiverwaltung, Düsseldorf, to Regierungspräsident, Düsseldorf, 20 December 1907, Staatsarchiv Düsseldorf, Regierung Düsseldorf 46070.

69. Regina Schulte, *Sperrbezirke: Tugendhaftigkeit und Prostitution in der bürgerlichen Welt* (Frankfurt am Main, 1979), p. 182.

70. Street celebrations of carnival continued to be banned, however, in Barmen, Duisburg, Elberfeld, and Essen, as well as in smaller towns with largely proletarian populations. Regierungspräsident, Düsseldorf, to Oberpräsident, Rheinprovinz, 29 December 1904, Staatsarchiv Koblenz 403/7061.

71. See, for example, Oberpräsident, Rheinprovinz, to Regierungspräsident, Düsseldorf, 30 September 1899, Stadtarchiv Krefeld 4/974.

CHAPTER VIII: POLICE AND ORGANIZED WORKERS, 1890–1914

1. Polizeiverwaltung, Düsseldorf, to Regierungspräsident, Düsseldorf, 27 July 1905, Staatsarchiv Düsseldorf, Regierung Düsseldorf 30411.

2. Minister des Innern to Regierungspräsidenten, 2 August 1898, Staatsarchiv Koblenz 403/6590; Charles Tilly, Louise Tilly, and Richard Tilly, *The Rebellious Century, 1830–1930* (London, 1975), p. 226.

3. Minister des Innern to Regierungspräsident, Düsseldorf, 10 November 1893, Staatsarchiv Düsseldorf, Regierung Düsseldorf 9061; Regierungspräsident, Düsseldorf, to Oberbürgermeister, Duisburg, 19 November 1894, Stadtarchiv Duisburg 306/186; Giesbert Knopp, *Die Preussische Verwaltung des Regierungsbezirks Düsseldorf in den Jahren 1899–1919* (Cologne, 1974), pp. 117–19.

4. Klaus Saul, *Staat, Industrie, Arbeiterbewegung im Kaiserreich: Zur Innen- und Aussenpolitik des Wilhelminischen Deutschland* (Düsseldorf, 1974), p. 10.

5. Bewilligung von Geldmitteln für Zwecke der politischen Polizei, 1895–1901, Staatsarchiv Düsseldorf, Regierung Düsseldorf 15989.

6. Minister des Innern to Oberpräsident, Rheinprovinz, 25 December 1895, Staatsarchiv Düsseldorf, Regierung Düsseldorf 9061.

7. Dienstanweisung für die königliche Polizei-Bezirkskommissare im niederrheinisch-westfälischen Industriegebiet, 1896, Stadtarchiv Duisburg 306/11.

8. Oberbürgermeister, Düsseldorf, to Regierungspräsident, Düsseldorf, Staatsarchiv Düsseldorf, Regierung Düsseldorf 9061; District Polizeikommissar

Koch, Düsseldorf, to Regierungspräsident, Düsseldorf, 19 January 1901, Staatsarchiv Düsseldorf, Regierung Düsseldorf 15991.

9. Polizeiverwaltung, Elberfeld, to Oberbürgermeister, Elberfeld, 15 May 1905, Stadtarchiv Duisburg 306/11.

10. Polizeiverwaltung, Barmen, to District Polizeikommissar Koch, Düsseldorf, 6 June 1904, Staatsarchiv Düsseldorf, Regierung Düsseldorf 15991; Oberbürgermeister, Solingen, to Oberbürgermeister, Duisburg, 10 May 1905, Stadtarchiv Duisburg 306/11.

11. Polizeiverwaltung, Elberfeld, to Oberbürgermeister, Duisburg, 15 May 1905, Stadtarchiv Duisburg 306/11.

12. Regierungspräsident, Düsseldorf, to Oberbürgermeister and Landräte, 9 June 1909, Stadtarchiv Essen XIII/5; Regierungspräsident, Düsseldorf, to Landräte, Oberbürgermeister, and Polizeipräsident (Essen), 5 July 1909, Stadtarchiv Duisburg 306/349; Minister des Innern to Regierungspräsident, Düsseldorf, 17 September 1911, Stadtarchiv Wuppertal O I 79.

13. Regierungspräsident, Düsseldorf to Landräte and Oberbürgermeister, 6 December 1891, Stadtarchiv Düsseldorf III/5518; Alex Hall, *Scandal, Sensation, and Social Democracy: The SPD Press and Wilhelmine Germany, 1890–1914* (Cambridge, 1977), p. 228.

14. Wolfgang Köllmann, *Sozialgeschichte der Stadt Barmen im 19. Jahrhundert* (Tübingen, 1960), p. 259.

15. Richard J. Evans, " 'Red Wednesday' in Hamburg: Social Democrats, Police, and Lumpenproletariat in the Suffrage Disturbances of 17 January 1906," *Social History* 4 (January 1979): 1–31.

16. Mary Nolan, *Social Democracy and Society: Working-Class Radicalism in Düsseldorf, 1890–1920* (Cambridge, 1981), pp. 192–93.

17. Knopp, *Die Preussische Verwaltung des Regierungsbezirks Düsseldorf*, pp. 115–16.

18. Franz-Josef Brüggemeier, *Leben vor Ort: Ruhrbergleute und Ruhrbergbau, 1889–1919* (Munich, 1983), p. 282; Erhard Lucas, *Zwei Formen von Radikalismus in der deutschen Arbeiterbewegung* (Frankfurt am Main, 1976), p. 93.

19. Franz-Josef Brüggemeier and Lutz Niethammer, "Schlafgänger, Schnapskasinos, und schwerindustrielle Kolonie: Aspekte der Arbeiterwohnungsfrage im Ruhrgebiet vor dem Ersten Weltkrieg," in J. Reulecke and W. Weber, eds., *Fabrik, Familie, Feierabend* (Wuppertal, 1978), p. 163.

20. Presentation by District Polizeikommissar Hansch to conference, Essen, 3 December 1904, Staatsarchiv Düsseldorf, Regierung Düsseldorf 15995.

21. District Polizeikommissar Hansch to Regierungspräsident, Düsseldorf, 21 October 1899, Staatsarchiv Düsseldorf, Regierung Düsseldorf 30466.

22. Register of communal police prepared to transfer to state service, Essen, 1908, Stadtarchiv Essen XIII/21.

23. See, for example, presentation by District Polizeikommissar Hansch to conference, Essen, 3 December 1904, Staatsarchiv Düsseldorf, Regierung Düsseldorf 15995; Polizeipräsident, Essen, to Regierungspräsident, Düsseldorf, 15 November 1909, Staatsarchiv Düsseldorf, Regierung Düsseldorf 30326.

24. Minister des Innern to Oberpräsident, Rheinprovinz, 13 July 1909, Staatsarchiv Düsseldorf, Regierung Düsseldorf 15991; Christoph Klessmann, *Polnische Bergarbeiter im Ruhrgebiet 1870–1945: Soziale Integration und nationale Subkultur einer Minderheit in der deutschen Industriegesellschaft* (Göttingen, 1978), p. 19.

25. Gerd Fesser, "Von der 'Zuchthausvorlage' zum Reichsvereinsgesetz: Staatsorgane, bürgerliche Parteien, und Vereinsgesetzgebung im Deutschen Reich, 1899–1906," *Jahrbuch für Geschichte* 28 (1983): 107–32; Albrecht Funk, *Polizei und Rechtsstaat: Die Entwicklung des staatlichen Gewaltmonopols in Preussen, 1848–1918* (Frankfurt am Main, 1986), p. 172.

26. Hans-Ulrich Wehler, "Die Polen im Ruhrgebiet bis 1918," in Hans-Ulrich Wehler, *Krisenherde des Kaiserreiches, 1871–1918* (Göttingen, 1970), p. 236.

27. For government efforts to prevent the participation of youth in opposition politics, see Alex Hall, "Youth in Rebellion: The Beginnings of the Socialist Youth Movement, 1904–1914," in Richard J. Evans, ed., *Society and Politics in Wilhelmine Germany* (London, 1978): 241–66; Derek S. Linton, *"Who Has the Youth, Has the Future": The Campaign to Save Young Workers in Imperial Germany* (Cambridge, 1991), pp. 122–25; Nolan, *Social Democracy and Society,* pp. 218–19.

28. Linton, *"Who Has the Youth,"* pp. 135–37.

29. District Polizeikommissar, Elberfeld, to Regierungspräsident, Düsseldorf, 15 March 1908, Staatsarchiv Düsseldorf, Regierung Düsseldorf 30422.

30. Polizeiverwaltung, Krefeld, to Regierungspräsident, Düsseldorf, 25 February 1909; Polizeiverwaltung, Düsseldorf, to Regierungspräsident, Düsseldorf, 2 March 1909; Polizeiverwaltung, Duisburg, to Regierungspräsident, Düsseldorf, 11 March 1909; all in Staatsarchiv Düsseldorf, Regierung Düsseldorf 30422.

31. Polizeiverwaltung, Elberfeld, to Regierungspräsident, Düsseldorf, 4 March 1909, Staatsarchiv Düsseldorf, Regierung Düsseldorf 30422.

32. For an example of direct worker appeals to a police officer assigned to their surveillance and his sympathetic portrayal of their cause, see District Polizeikommissar, Essen, to Regierungspräsident, Düsseldorf, 24 January 1904, Staatsarchiv Düsseldorf, Regierung Düsseldorf 15915. See also the Regierungspräsident's censure of the Kommissar for his receptivity to the workers' point of view. Regierungspräsident, Düsseldorf, to District Polizeikommissar, Essen, 18 February 1904, Staatsarchiv Düsseldorf, Regierung Düsseldorf 15915.

33. Klaus Tenfelde and Heinrich Volkmann, eds., *Streik: Zur Geschichte des Arbeitskampfes in Deutschland während der Industrialisierung* (Munich, 1981), p. 21.

34. On the composition of the district's local councils, see Helmuth Croon, *Die gesellschaftlichen Auswirkungen des Gemeindewahlrechtes in den Gemeinden und Kreisen des Rheinlandes und Westfalens im 19. Jahrhundert* (Cologne, 1960).

35. See, for example, Düsseldorfer Eisen- und Draht-Industrie to Oberbürgermeister, Düsseldorf, 22 May 1896; Polizeiverwaltung, Oberhausen, to

Oberbürgermeister, Düsseldorf, 21 July 1896; Düsseldorfer Eisen-und Draht-Industrie to Polizeiverwaltung, Düsseldorf, 14 April 1899; all in Stadtarchiv Düsseldorf III/4493; Lucas, *Zwei Formen von Radikalismus*, p. 113.

36. Generaldirektor Paul Reusch to Hauptverwaltung, Gutehoffnungs-hütte, 13 May 1907, Historisches Archiv der Gutehoffnungshütte 30103/0.

37. Polizeipräsident, Essen, to Regierungspräsident, Düsseldorf, 13 December 1909, Staatsarchiv Düsseldorf, Regierung Düsseldorf 30326.

38. See, for example, Zeche Helene und Amalie to Polizeikommissar Kappelrele, Essen-West, 23 March 1912; Zeche Helene und Amalie to Polizei-kommissar Petersen, Altenessen, 23 March 1912; Zeche Helene und Amalie to Kriminalkommissar Stromberg, Altenessen, 26 March 1912; all in Bergbau Archiv 20/312.

39. Minister des Innern to Regierungspräsident, Düsseldorf, 10 May and 6 July 1912, both in Staatsarchiv Düsseldorf, Regierung Düsseldorf 15944; *Rheinisch-Westfälische Zeitung* (18 September 1912), clipping in Bergbau Archiv 20/312.

40. Minister für Handel und Gewerbe to Regierungspräsidenten, 6 October 1899, Staatsarchiv Düsseldorf, Regierung Düsseldorf 15919.

41. See, for example, the police reports collected in Historisches Archiv der Gutehoffnungshütte 300 143/0. See also Nolan, *Social Democracy and Society*, pp. 62–63.

42. *Arbeiterzeitung* (18 March 1912), clipping in Staatsarchiv Düsseldorf, Regierung Düsseldorf, Präs. Büro 751; *Arbeiterzeitung* (26 February 1914), clipping in Staatsarchiv Düsseldorf, Regierung Düsseldorf 16039.

43. Report, Polizeiassessor Hansch, Essen, 21 March 1912, Staatsarchiv Düsseldorf, Regierung Düsseldorf, Präs. Büro 751.

44. Regierungspräsident, Düsseldorf, to Vorsitzende, Steigerverband, 23 March 1912, Staatsarchiv Düsseldorf, Regierung Düsseldorf, Präs. Büro 751.

45. Minister des Innern to Regierungspräsident, Düsseldorf, 16 April 1912, Staatsarchiv Düsseldorf, Regierung Düsseldorf, Präs. Büro 751.

46. Polizeipräsident, Essen, to Bergassessor Krawehl, Essen, 6 January 1911, Bergbau Archiv 20/312; Regierungspräsident, Düsseldorf, to Oberbür-germeister, Duisburg, 10 January 1911, Stadtarchiv Duisburg 306/201; *Deutsche Bergwerks-Zeitung* (14 March 1912).

47. Landrat, Ruhrort, to Regierungspräsident, Düsseldorf, 9 October 1905, Staatsarchiv Düsseldorf, Regierung Düsseldorf 15928; Regierungspräsi-dent, Düsseldorf, to Oberpräsident, Rheinprovinz, 29 October 1905, Staatsar-chiv Koblenz 403/7029.

48. Landrat, Mülheim an der Ruhr, to Regierungspräsident, Düsseldorf, 27 July 1895; Landrat, Ruhrort, to Regierungspräsident, Düsseldorf, 27 September 1895; both in Staatsarchiv Düsseldorf, Regierung Düsseldorf 30273. Otto Krawehl to Polizeipräsident, Essen, 12 January 1911, Bergbau Archiv 20/312; Niederschrift über die Besprechung am 1. Juni 1912 über die beim letzten Bergarbeiterstreik gemachten Erfahrungen, Staatsarchiv Koblenz 403/13534.

49. Otto Krawehl to Polizeikommissar, Essen-West, 9 March 1912, Bergbau Archiv 20/312; Conference, Zeche Sterkrade, 12 March 1912, Historisches Archiv der Gutehoffnungshütte 301054.

50. Saul, *Staat, Industrie, Arbeiterbewegung im Kaiserreich,* pp. 226–37.

51. See, for instance, *Rheinische Zeitung* (16 November 1900), clipping in Staatsarchiv Koblenz 403/7028; Regierungspräsident, Düsseldorf, to Minister des Innern, 22 February 1900, Staatsarchiv Düsseldorf, Regierung Düsseldorf 30410; Niederschrift über die Besprechung am 1. Juni 1912 über die beim letzten Bergarbeiterstreik gemachten Erfahrungen, Staatsarchiv Koblenz 403/13534; Polizeiverwaltung, Krefeld, Betr. Verhalten der Polizeibeamten bei Streiks, 3 April 1913, Staatsarchiv Düsseldorf, Regierung Düsseldorf 30290.

52. Regierungspräsident, Düsseldorf, to Minister des Innern, 22 February 1900; Minister des Innern to Regierungspräsident, Düsseldorf, 6 March 1900; both in Staatsarchiv Düsseldorf, Regierung Düsseldorf 30410. See also Saul, *Staat, Industrie, Arbeiterbewegung,* pp. 216–20.

53. Sidney L. Harring, *Policing a Class Society: The Experience of American Cities, 1865–1915* (New Brunswick, N.J., 1983), p. 133; Jane Morgan, *Conflict and Order: The Police and Labour Disputes in England and Wales, 1900–1939* (Oxford, 1987), p. 152.

54. Landrat, Ruhrort, to Regierungspräsident, Düsseldorf, 20 January 1905, Staatsarchiv Düsseldorf, Regierung Düsseldorf, Präs. Büro 841; Regierungspräsident, Düsseldorf, to Oberbürgermeister, Duisburg, 10 January 1911, Stadtarchiv Duisburg 306/201; Donald Rosenberg, "The Ruhr Coal Strike and the Prussian Mining Law of 1905: A Social and Political Conflict of Working Class Aspirations and Industrial Authoritarianism" (Ph.D. diss., University of California, Los Angeles, 1971), p. 76.

55. Erich Hoffmann, *Dr. Francis Kruse: Königlich Preussischer Regierungspräsident: Ein Lebensbild* (Leipzig, 1937), pp. 80–81.

56. Regierungspräsident, Düsseldorf, to Oberbürgermeister, Duisburg, 10 January 1911, Stadtarchiv Duisburg 306/201.

57. Knopp, *Die Preussische Verwaltung des Regierungsbezirks Düsseldorf,* p. 142; Niederschrift über die Besprechung am 1. Juni 1912 im Königlichen Landratsamt in Essen über die beim letzten Bergarbeiterstreik gemachten Erfahrungen, Staatsarchiv Koblenz 403/13534.

58. Hoffmann, *Dr. Francis Kruse,* pp. 79–81; Niederschrift über die Besprechung am 1. Juni 1912 über die beim letzten Bergarbeiterstreik gemachten Erfahrungen, Staatsarchiv Koblenz 403/13534.

59. Dieter Dreetz, "Der Erlass des preussischen Kriegsministers vom 8. Februar 1912 über die Verwendung der Armee zur Bekämpfung innerer Unruhen," *Militärgeschichte* 14 (1975): 561–71.

60. Regierungspräsident, Düsseldorf, to Landräte, 6 May 1912, Stadtarchiv Duisburg 306/357. Compare Oberbürgermeister, Duisburg, to Regierungspräsident, Düsseldorf, 26 June 1907, Staatsarchiv Düsseldorf, Regierung Düsseldorf 15919.

61. See, for example, Minister des Innern to Regierungspräsident, Düsseldorf, 4 February 1900, Staatsarchiv Düsseldorf, Regierung Düsseldorf 30410; Oberbürgermeister, Elberfeld, to Regierungspräsident, Düsseldorf, 7 May 1900, Staatsarchiv Düsseldorf, Regierung Düsseldorf 8738; Arbeitgeberverein der Holzindustrie to Oberbürgermeister, Düsseldorf, Staatsarchiv Düsseldorf, Regierung Düsseldorf 30411; Grafenberger Walzwerk GmbH to Polizeikommissariat, Düsseldorf, 30 December 1905, Stadtarchiv Düsseldorf III/4521.

62. Polizeiverwaltung, Düsseldorf, to Regierungspräsident, Düsseldorf, 8 February 1900, Staatsarchiv Düsseldorf, Regierung Düsseldorf 30410; District Polizeikommissar, Essen, to Regierungspräsident, Düsseldorf, 1 February 1904, Staatsarchiv Düsseldorf, Regierung Düsseldorf 15915; Polizeiverwaltung, Düsseldorf, to Regierungspräsident, Düsseldorf, 27 July 1905, Staatsarchiv Düsseldorf, Regierung Düsseldorf 30411.

63. Minister des Innern to Regierungspräsident, Düsseldorf, 4 and 7 February 1900; Polizeiverwaltung, Düsseldorf, to Regierungspräsident, Düsseldorf, 8 February 1900; Report, Polizeiinspektor Setzermann, Düsseldorf, 10 February 1900; all in Staatsarchiv Düsseldorf, Regierung Düsseldorf 30410.

64. Regierungspräsident, Düsseldorf, to Minister des Innern, 22 February 1900; Minister des Innern to Regierungspräsident, Düsseldorf, 6 March 1900; both in Staatsarchiv Düsseldorf, Regierung Düsseldorf 30410.

CHAPTER IX: ON THE EVE OF WAR AND BEYOND

1. Oberpräsident, Rheinprovinz, to Regierungspräsident, Düsseldorf, 25 May 1892; Oberbürgermeister, Elberfeld, to Regierungspräsident, Düsseldorf, 3 December 1892; both in Staatsarchiv Düsseldorf, Regierung Düsseldorf 8710. Also Regierung Düsseldorf, Betrifft Einrichtung einer Königlichen Polizeiverwaltung in Elberfeld-Barmen, 19 July 1892, Staatsarchiv Koblenz 403/6608.

2. See, for example, *Westdeutsche Zeitung* (9 April 1908), clipping in Stadtarchiv Essen XIII/21.

3. Regierungspräsident, Düsseldorf, to Oberpräsident, Rheinprovinz, 10 December 1905; Regierungspräsident, Düsseldorf, to Minister des Innern, 9 August 1910; both in Staatsarchiv Koblenz 403/13500.

4. Oberbürgermeister, Essen, to Regierungspräsident, Düsseldorf, 2 November 1905, Staatsarchiv Koblenz 403/13500.

5. Oberbürgermeister, Essen, to Regierungspräsident, Düsseldorf, 2 November 1905; Regierungspräsident, Düsseldorf, to Oberpräsident, Rheinprovinz, 10 December 1905; both in Staatsarchiv Koblenz 403/13500.

6. Polizeipräsident, Essen, to Regierungspräsident, Düsseldorf, 10 August and 14 December 1910, Staatsarchiv Düsseldorf, Regierung Düsseldorf 30328; Niederschrift über die Besprechung am 1. Juni 1912 im Königlichen Landratsamt in Essen über die beim letzten Bergarbeiterstreik gemachten Erfahrungen, Staatsarchiv Koblenz 403/13534.

7. Max Roetger (chairman of executive committee of Krupp steelworks and former Essen Landrat) to Minister des Innern, 11 June 1908, Staatsarchiv Koblenz 403/13500. See also Franz Laufer, *Die preussische Kommunalpolizei: Vorschläge zu ihrer zeitgemässen Umgestaltung* (Schwelm, 1903), pp. 15–18.

8. Oberbürgermeister, Essen, to Regierungspräsident, Düsseldorf, 2 November 1905; Bericht über die Besprechung im Kreishause zu Dortmund am 22 Mai 1906; both in Staatsarchiv Koblenz 403/13500.

9. Max Roetger to Minister des Innern, 11 June 1908, Staatsarchiv Koblenz 403/13500.

10. On the character of the district's Landräte, see Lysbeth Muncy, "The Prussian Landräte in the Last Years of the Monarchy: A Case Study of Pomerania and the Rhineland in 1890–1918," *Central European History* 6 (December 1973): 299–338.

11. Giesbert Knopp, *Die Preussische Verwaltung des Regierungsbezirks Düsseldorf in den Jahren 1899–1919* (Cologne, 1974), pp. 82–84.

12. Erich Hoffmann, *Dr. Francis Kruse: Königlich Preussischer Regierungspräsident: Ein Lebensbild* (Leipzig, 1937), pp. 73–74.

13. Regierungspräsident, Düsseldorf, to Minister des Innern, 9 August 1910, Staatsarchiv Koblenz 403/13500.

14. Regierungspräsident, Düsseldorf, to Oberpräsident, Rheinprovinz, 10 December 1905, Staatsarchiv Koblenz 403/13500. See also Franz-Josef Brüggemeier and Lutz Niethammer, "Schlafgänger, Schnapskasinos, und schwerindustrielle Kolonie: Aspekte der Arbeiterwohnungsfrage im Ruhrgebiet vor dem Ersten Weltkrieg," in J. Reulecke and W. Weber, eds., *Fabrik, Familie, Feierabend* (Wuppertal, 1978), p. 148.

15. Oberbürgermeister, Essen, to Regierungspräsident, Düsseldorf, 2 November 1905, Staatsarchiv Koblenz 403/13500.

16. Helmuth Croon, "Das Vordringen der politischen Parteien im Bereich der kommunalen Selbstverwaltung," in Helmuth Croon, Wolfgang Hofmann, and Georg Christoph von Unruh, eds., *Kommunale Selbstverwaltung im Zeitalter der Industrialisierung* (Stuttgart, 1971), pp. 15–58.

17. Wilhelm Henning, *Geschichte der Stadtverordnetenversammlung von Essen, 1890–1914* (Essen, 1965), p. 150, and tables 1, 2, and 3 in appendix.

18. Wolfgang Köllmann, *Sozialgeschichte der Stadt Barmen im 19. Jahrhundert* (Tübingen, 1960), pp. 264, 269.

19. *Täglicher Anzeiger* (27 April 1912), clipping in Stadtarchiv Wuppertal O I 49.

20. *Grenzen der Zuständigkeit der Stadtverordnetenversammlung gegenüber der Polizeiverwaltung*, 20 May 1912, Stadtarchiv Wuppertal O I 49.

21. *Täglicher Anzeiger* (27 April 1912), clipping in Stadtarchiv Wuppertal O I 49.

22. *Essener Arbeiterzeitung* (27 May 1910), clipping in Staatsarchiv Düsseldorf, Regierung Düsseldorf 30327; *Freie Presse* (9 and 24 April 1912); *Täglicher Anzeiger* (27 April 1912); clippings in Stadtarchiv Wuppertal O I 49.

23. *Essener Arbeiterzeitung* (7 January 1908), clipping in Staatsarchiv Düsseldorf, Regierung Düsseldorf, Präs. Büro 748; *Essener Arbeiterzeitung* (28 May 1910), clipping in Stadtarchiv Essen XIII/8.

24. Conference, Essen, 20 March 1907, Anlage 1, Staatsarchiv Koblenz 403/13500.

25. Regierungspräsident, Düsseldorf, to Minister des Innern, 9 August 1910, Staatsarchiv Koblenz 403/13500; Niederschrift über die Besprechung am 1. Juni 1912 im Königlichen Landratsamt in Essen über die beim letzten Bergarbeiterstreik gemachten Erfahrungen, Staatsarchiv Koblenz 403/13534.

26. Albrecht Funk, *Polizei und Rechtsstaat: Die Entwicklung des staatlichen Gewaltmonopols in Preussen, 1848–1918* (Frankfurt am Main, 1986), p. 237; *Statistisches Jahrbuch Deutscher Städte* 18 (1912): 24.

27. Oberbürgermeister, Essen, to Regierungspräsident, Düsseldorf, 2 November 1905; Regierungspräsident, Düsseldorf, to Oberpräsident, Rheinprovinz, 10 December 1905; both in Staatsarchiv Koblenz 403/13500.

28. Bericht über die Besprechung im Kreishause zu Dortmund, 22 May 1906, Staatsarchiv Koblenz 403/13500.

29. Oberbürgermeister, Essen, to Regierungspräsident, Düsseldorf, 15 January 1907, Staatsarchiv Düsseldorf, Regierung Düsseldorf, Präs. Büro 748; Regierungspräsident, Düsseldorf, to Minister des Innern, 9 February 1907, Staatsarchiv Koblenz 403/13500.

30. *Kölnische Volkszeitung* (11 February 1909); *Kölnische Zeitung* (25 June 1909); both clippings in Stadtarchiv Essen XIII/22; Ralph Jessen, *Polizei im Industrierevier: Modernisierung und Herrschaftspraxis im westfälischen Ruhrgebiet, 1848–1914* (Göttingen, 1991), pp. 98–99.

31. Regierungspräsident, Düsseldorf, to Oberbürgermeister, Essen, 23 December 1907, Stadtarchiv Essen XIII/21; Polizeipräsident, Essen, to Regierungspräsident, Düsseldorf, 16 April 1910, Staatsarchiv Düsseldorf, Regierung Düsseldorf 30327.

32. Zusammenstellung der durch Erlass des Herrn Minister des Innern vom 6. Januar 1909 von der Übernahme in dem Staatsdienst zurückgestellten Polizeibeamten, Staatsarchiv Düsseldorf, Regierung Düsseldorf 30324.

33. Regierungspräsident, Düsseldorf, to Oberbürgermeister, Essen, 16 January 1909, Stadtarchiv Essen XIII/55; Nachweisung, 1909, Staatsarchiv Düsseldorf, Regierung Düsseldorf 30268.

34. Register of Essen policemen prepared to enter state service, Stadtarchiv Essen XIII/21; Oberbürgermeister, Essen, to Regierungspräsident, Düsseldorf, 9 February 1909, Staatsarchiv Düsseldorf, Regierung Düsseldorf 30324.

35. *Essener Arbeiterzeitung* (14 January 1908), clipping in Staatsarchiv Düsseldorf, Regierung Düsseldorf, Präs. Büro 748.

36. Raymond B. Fosdick, *European Police Systems* (Montclair, N.J., 1969, reprint of 1915 edition), pp. 71–72.

37. *Rheinisch-Westfälischer Anzeiger* (30 July and 23 August 1908); Polizeiverwaltung, Essen, to Minister des Innern, 27 August 1908; Telegram,

Regierungspräsident, Düsseldorf, to Oberbürgermeister, Essen, 2 September 1908; all in Stadtarchiv Essen XIII/21.

38. *Statistisches Jahrbuch Deutscher Städte* 20 (1914): 284.

39. Bekanntmachung, Regierungspräsident, Düsseldorf, 27 May 1909, Stadtarchiv Essen XIII/22.

40. Nachweisung eingestellter Hilfsschutzmänner, Essen, 16 November 1909, Staatsarchiv Düsseldorf, Regierung Düsseldorf 30326.

41. Polizeipräsident, Essen, to Regierungspräsident, Düsseldorf, 27 October 1910, Staatsarchiv Düsseldorf, Regierung Düsseldorf 30328.

42. Polizeipräsident, Düsseldorf, to Regierungspräsident, Düsseldorf, 28 January 1910, Staatsarchiv Düsseldorf, Regierung Düsseldorf 30326.

43. Nachweisung eingestellter Schutzleute und Hilfsschutzleute, Essen, 1 July 1910 to 1 January 1911, Staatsarchiv Düsseldorf, Regierung Düsseldorf 30328.

44. Niederschrift über die Besprechung am 1. Juni 1912 im Königlichen Landratsamt in Essen über die beim letzten Bergarbeiterstreik gemachten Erfahrungen, Staatsarchiv Koblenz 403/13534.

45. See, for example, Oberpräsident, Rheinprovinz, to Regierungspräsident, 23 December 1913, Stadtarchiv Wuppertal O I 79.

46. Minister des Innern to Oberpräsident, Rheinprovinz, 11 September 1914, Staatsarchiv Koblenz 403/6594.

47. Polizeiverwaltung, Düsseldorf, to Regierungspräsident, Düsseldorf, 5 August 1914, Staatsarchiv Düsseldorf, Regierung Düsseldorf 30272.

48. Polizeiverwaltung, Barmen, to Regierungspräsident, Düsseldorf, Staatsarchiv Düsseldorf, Regierung Düsseldorf 30272.

49. Minister des Innern to Regierungspräsidenten, 7 August 1914, Staatsarchiv Düsseldorf, Regierung Düsseldorf 30272.

50. Peter Hüttenberger, *Die Industrie- und Verwaltungsstaat (20. Jahrhundert)*, vol. 3 of Hugo Weidenhaupt, ed., *Düsseldorf: Geschichte von den Ursprüngen bis ins 20. Jahrhundert* (Düsseldorf, 1989), p. 250.

51. Polizeiverwaltung, Düsseldorf, to Regierungspräsident, Düsseldorf, 12 October and 29 December 1914, both in Staatsarchiv Düsseldorf, Regierung Düsseldorf 30272.

52. Knopp, *Die Preussische Verwaltung des Regierungsbezirks Düsseldorf*, p. 309. Herbert Reinke's forthcoming article " '. . . hat sich ein politischer und wirtschaftlicher Polizeistaat entwickelt': Polizei und Großstadt im Rheinland vom Vorabend des Ersten Weltkrieges bis zum Beginn der 20er Jahre," in Alf Lüdtke, ed., *"Sicherheit und Wohlfahrt": Polizei-Praxis im 19. und 20. Jahrhundert* discusses war-induced changes in the police and policing of Rhenish cities.

53. *Bericht über den Stand und die Verwaltung der Gemeinde-Angelegenheiten der Stadt Düsseldorf* (Düsseldorf, 1918), p. 38.

54. Ibid., pp. 37–39. See also Hüttenberger, *Die Industrie- und Verwaltungsstaat*, pp. 246–49.

55. Derek S. Linton, *"Who Has the Youth, Has the Future": The Campaign to Save Young Workers in Imperial Germany* (Cambridge, 1991), pp. 205–9.

56. Mary Nolan, *Social Democracy and Society: Working-Class Radicalism in Düsseldorf, 1890–1920* (Cambridge, 1981), p. 273; Johannes Buder, *Die Reorganisation der preussischen Polizei, 1918–1923* (Frankfurt am Main, 1986), pp. 121–30, 233–34; Hüttenberger, *Die Industrie- und Verwaltungsstaat*, pp. 277–94.

57. Carl Severing, *Mein Lebensweg*, vol. 1 (Cologne, 1950), pp. 312–17; Dietrich Orlow, *Weimar Prussia, 1918–1925: The Unlikely Rock of Democracy* (Pittsburgh, 1986), pp. 147–50.

58. Herbert Jacob, *German Administration since Bismarck: Central Authority versus Local Autonomy* (New Haven, 1963), pp. 87–89; Eric Kohler, "The Crisis of the Prussian Schutzpolizei, 1930–1932," in George L. Mosse, ed., *Police Forces in History* (London, 1975), pp. 131–50; Buder, *Die Reorganisation*, pp. 90–111, 443–60.

59. Hsi-huey Liang, *The Berlin Police Force in the Weimar Republic* (Berkeley, 1970), p. 5.

60. Buder, *Die Reorganisation*, pp. 116, 309, 467, 469.

61. Kohler, "The Crisis of the Prussian Schutzpolizei," p. 132; Buder, *Die Reorganisation*, pp. 59, 314, 554–63.

62. Liang, *The Berlin Police Force*, pp. 64–73; Orlow, *Weimar Prussia*, p. 150.

63. Buder, *Die Reorganisation*, p. 447.

64. Horst Romeyk, *Verwaltungs- und Behördengeschichte der Rheinprovinz, 1914–1945* (Düsseldorf, 1985), pp. 247–48.

65. Jacob, *German Administration since Bismarck*, p. 89.

CONCLUSION

1. Raymond B. Fosdick, *European Police Systems* (Montclair, N.J., 1969, reprint of 1915 edition).

2. Ibid., pp. 319, 371–79.

3. Ibid., pp. 25, 231–32.

4. Ibid., pp. 9, 21, 24–25, 35, 68–69, 231.

5. Ibid., p. 72.

6. See, for example, Otto Held, *Die bestehende Organisation und die erforderliche Reorganisation der preussischen Polizei-Verwaltung mit Rücksicht auf die wünschenswerthe Erweiterung derselben zur Deutschen Reichspolizei* (Berlin, 1886), pp. 2–3.

7. See, for instance, *Mainzer Journal* (26 January 1885), clipping in Stadtarchiv Wuppertal O I 46. To be sure, English policemen in their own country were at times viewed in much less favorable terms. See the discussion in Robert Storch, "The Plague of Blue Locusts: Police Reform and Popular Resistance in Northern England, 1840–1857," *International Review of Social History* 20 (1975): 61–90.

8. *Stenographische Berichte über die Verhandlungen des Preussischen Hauses der Abgeordneten*, 7 February 1852, p. 337; Frank Thomason, "The Prussian Police State in Berlin, 1848–1871" (Ph.D. diss., Johns Hopkins, 1978), pp. 160, 204.

9. See especially the annual debates on the budget of the Prussian ministry of the interior in *Stenographische Berichte über die Verhandlungen des Preussischen Hauses der Abgeordneten*.

10. *Stenographische Berichte über die Verhandlungen des Preussischen Hauses der Abgeordneten*, 11 January 1873, p. 489.

11. For one notable defense of this policy, even granting the unpopularity of policemen who carried military brusqueness into civilian life, see Otto Hintze, "Der Beamtenstand" (1911), in Otto Hintze, *Soziologie und Geschichte: Gesammelte Abhandlungen zur Soziologie, Politik, und Theorie der Geschichte*, edited by Gerhard Oestreich, 2d ed. (Göttingen, 1964), pp. 103–5. Hintze argued that Prussia could not emulate the recruitment practices of the more popular English police because Prussia had a much larger military establishment whose superannuated personnel needed employment.

12. On the exploitation of police scandals by the social democratic press, see Alex Hall, *Scandal, Sensation, and Social Democracy: The SPD Press and Wilhelmine Germany, 1890–1914* (Cambridge, 1977).

13. David Arnold, *Police Power and Colonial Rule: Madras, 1859–1947* (Delhi, 1986), p. 68.

14. Sidney L. Harring, *Policing a Class Society: The Experience of American Cities, 1865–1915* (New Brunswick, N.J., 1983), p. 122.

15. Ralph Jessen, in his study of the police in the Westphalian half of the Ruhr, emphasizes the significance of the recruitment during the last prewar years of more and more communal patrolmen from mines and factories rather than from army barracks. He sees such selections as contributing to a substantial demilitarization of municipal police departments. As long, however, as former noncommissioned officers with long years of military service remained concentrated in the police ranks of Wachtmeister and above, the barriers to infusing police practice with a more civilian spirit continued to be formidable. Ralph Jessen, *Polizei im Industrierevier: Modernisierung und Herrschaftspraxis im westfälischen Ruhrgebiet, 1848–1914* (Gottingen, 1991), pp. 157–70.

16. See, for example, Albrecht Funk, *Polizei und Rechtsstaat: Die Entwicklung der staatlichen Gewaltmonopols in Preussen, 1848–1918* (Frankfurt am Main, 1986), pp. 100–5, 129–30.

17. Heinz-Gerhard Haupt, "Staatliche Bürokratie und Arbeiterbewegung: Zum Einfluss der Polizei auf die Konstituierung von Arbeiterbewegung und Arbeiterklasse in Deutschland und Frankreich," in Jürgen Kocka, ed., *Arbeiter und Bürger im 19. Jahrhundert: Varianten ihres Verhältnisses im europäischen Vergleich* (Munich, 1986), p. 246; Joan W. Scott, "Mayors versus Police Chiefs: Socialist Municipalities Confront the French State," in John M. Merriman, ed., *French Cities in the Nineteenth Century* (New York, 1981), pp. 230–45. For a description of the interaction of the French state and a socialist municipal administration, see John M. Merriman, *The Red City: Limoges and the French Nineteenth Century* (New York, 1985), pp. 184–240.

18. Jane Morgan, *Conflict and Order: The Police and Labour Disputes in England and Wales, 1900–1936* (Oxford, 1987), pp. 30–74.

19. Robert Liebman and Michael Polen, "Perspectives on Policing in Nineteenth-Century America," *Social Science History* 2 (1978): 346–60.

BIBLIOGRAPHY

UNPUBLISHED SOURCES

Bergbau Archiv, Bochum
Krupp Bergbau
20/312
Historisches Archiv der Gutehoffnungshütte, Oberhausen
30103/0; 301054; 300 143/0
Landeshauptarchiv Koblenz (cited as Staatsarchiv Koblenz in the notes)
Oberpräsidium der Rheinprovinz:
403/ 97; 118; 163; 177; 2197; 2275; 2435; 2550; 2612; 2616; 6587; 6590–
6595; 6606–6609; 6760; 6801; 6807; 6825; 6830; 7028; 7029; 7061–7063;
9047; 13432; 13434; 13491; 13498; 13500; 13534; 13537; 15995; 17962
Nordrhein-Westfälisches Hauptstaatsarchiv, Düsseldorf, Schloss Kalkum (cited
as Staatsarchiv Düsseldorf in the notes)
Regierung Düsseldorf:
86; 99; 149; 175; 177; 178; 201; 204; 206; 213; 215; 217a; 217b; 220; 813; 3027;
8611; 8612; 8614; 8618; 8620; 8626; 8645; 8688; 8695–8698; 8702–8708; 8710;
8728; 8729; 8736; 8738; 8800; 8801; 8805; 8806; 8813; 8816a; 8904; 8905; 8935;
8939; 8956; 8984; 8998; 8999; 9061; 15915; 15919; 15927; 15928; 15944; 15953;
15964; 15989; 15991; 15993; 15995; 16038; 16039; 30210; 30218; 30267; 30268;
30270–30273; 30277; 30278; 30284; 30290; 30308; 30324; 30326–30328; 30341;
30356; 30389; 30393; 30410; 30411; 30417; 30421; 30422; 30428; 30458; 30463;
30466; 30469; 46069; 46070; 46073; 46075
Regierung Düsseldorf, Präsidialbüro:
740; 742; 747; 748; 751; 841; 915
Landgericht und Staatsanwaltschaft Elberfeld:
5/ 391; 462; 465; 467
Stadtarchiv Duisburg
Polizei:
306/ 11; 77; 92; 123; 126; 144; 186; 201; 332; 349; 350; 357
Stadtarchiv Düsseldorf
Polizeiverwaltung:
II/ 780; 787; 1335; 1336; 1361; 1433; 1495
III/ 4329; 4350; 4393; 4394; 4396–4399; 4493; 4537; 4636; 4521; 5518; 5521;
5752
Stadtarchiv Essen
Polizeiverwaltung:
XIII/ 1; 5; 8; 11; 21; 22; 48; 55; 68
Stadtarchiv Krefeld
Polizeiverwaltung/Meldewesen:
4/ 936; 938; 940; 948; 949; 954; 956; 958; 961; 974; 977; 989

Stadtarchiv Wuppertal
    Polizei:
    O I 46–49; 51; 68; 79; 117; 123; 137; 156

PUBLISHED SOURCES

Abrams, Lynn. "From Control to Commercialization: The Triumph of Mass
    Entertainment in Germany, 1900–1925?" *German History* 8 (1990): 278–
    93.
Adler, Jeffrey S. "Vagging the Demons and Scoundrels: Vagrancy and the
    Growth of St. Louis, 1830–1861." *Journal of Urban History* 13 (November
    1986): 3–30.
Anderson, Eugene N. *The Social and Political Conflict in Prussia, 1858–1864.*
    Lincoln, Nebr., 1954.
Anderson, Margaret Lavinia. "The Kulturkampf and the Course of German
    History." *Central European History* 19 (March 1986): 82–115.
Anderson, Margaret Lavinia, and Barkin, Kenneth. "The Myth of the Puttka-
    mer Purge and the Reality of the Kulturkampf: Some Reflections on the
    Historiography of Imperial Germany." *Journal of Modern History* 54 (De-
    cember 1982): 647–86.
Arnold, David. *Police Power and Colonial Rule: Madras, 1859–1947.* Delhi, 1986.
Bailey, Victor, ed. *Policing and Punishment in Nineteenth-Century Britain.* New
    Brunswick, N.J., 1981.
Balkenhol, Bernd. *Armut und Arbeitslosigkeit in der Industrialisierung dargestellt am
    Beispiel Düsseldorfs, 1850–1900.* Düsseldorf, 1976.
Bayley, David H. *Patterns of Policing: A Comparative International Analysis.* New
    Brunswick, N.J., 1985.
———. "Police Function, Structure, and Control in Western Europe and North
    America: Comparative and Historical Studies." *Crime and Justice: An
    Annual Review of Research* 1 (1979): 109–43.
———, ed. *Police and Society.* Beverly Hills, 1977.
Becker, Rolf. "Gründerzeit im Wuppertal—dargestellt am Verhältnis von Polizei
    und Alltag in Elberfeld und Barmen, 1806–1870." In *Gründerzeit: Versuch
    einer Grenzbestimmung im Wuppertal,* edited by Karl-Hermann Beeck and
    Rolf Becker. Cologne, 1984. Pp. 64–108.
Behrens, C. A. B. *Society, Government, and the Enlightenment: The Experience of
    Eighteenth-Century France and Prussia.* London, 1985.
Bergmann, Günther. *Das Sozialistengesetz im rechtsrheinischen Industriegebiet: Ein
    Beitrag zur Auseinandersetzung zwischen Staat und Sozialdemokratie in Wup-
    pertal und im Bergischen Land, 1878–1890.* Hanover, 1970.
*Bericht über den Stand und die Verwaltung der Gemeinde-Angelegenheiten der Stadt
    Duisburg.* Duisburg, 1863–1914.
*Bericht über den Stand und die Verwaltung der Gemeinde-Angelegenheiten der Stadt
    Düsseldorf.* Düsseldorf, 1851–1914.

Bericht über die Verwaltung und den Stand der Gemeinde-Angelegenheiten der Oberbürgermeisterei Crefeld. Krefeld, 1855–1914.

Bericht über die Verwaltung und den Stand der Gemeinde-Angelegenheiten der Stadt Elberfeld. Elberfeld, 1857–1914.

Bittner, Egon. *The Function of the Police in Modern Society: A Review of Background Factors, Current Practices, and Possible Role Models.* Washington, D.C., 1970.

Blasius, Dirk. *Bürgerliche Gesellschaft und Kriminalität: Zur Sozialgeschichte Preußens im Vormärz.* Göttingen, 1976.

———. *Geschichte der politischen Kriminalität in Deutschland, 1800–1980: Eine Studie zu Justiz und Staatsverbrechen.* Frankfurt am Main, 1983.

———. "Der Kampf um die Geschworenengerichte im Vormärz." In *Sozialgeschichte Heute,* edited by Hans-Ulrich Wehler. Göttingen, 1974. Pp. 148–61.

———. *Kriminalität und Alltag: Zur Konfliktgeschichte des Alltagslebens im 19. Jahrhundert.* Göttingen, 1978.

Brüggemeier, Franz-Josef. *Leben vor Ort: Ruhrbergleute und Ruhrbergbau, 1889–1919.* Munich, 1983.

Bry, Gerhard. *Wages in Germany, 1871–1945.* Princeton, 1960.

Buder, Johannes. *Die Reorganisation der preussischen Polizei, 1918–1923.* Frankfurt am Main, 1986.

Cohen, Stanley, and Scull, Andrew, eds. *Social Control and the State: Historical and Comparative Essays.* Oxford, 1983.

Croon, Helmuth. *Die gesellschaftlichen Auswirkungen des Gemeindewahlrechtes in den Gemeinden und Kreisen des Rheinlandes und Westfalens im 19. Jahrhundert.* Cologne, 1960.

———. "Die Stadtvertretungen in Krefeld und Bochum im 19. Jahrhundert: Ein Beitrag zur Geschichte der Selbstverwaltung der rheinischen und westfälischen Städte." In *Forschungen zu Staat und Verfassung,* edited by Richard Dietrich and Gerhard Oestreich. Berlin, 1958. Pp. 289–306.

Croon, Helmuth; Hofmann, Wolfgang; and von Unruh, Georg Christoph, eds. *Kommunale Selbstverwaltung im Zeitalter der Industrialisierung.* Stuttgart, 1971.

Cunningham, Hugh. *Leisure in the Industrial Revolution c. 1780–c. 1880.* London, 1980.

Danckert, Werner. *Unehrliche Leute: Die verfemten Berufe.* 2d ed. Bern, 1979.

Davis, John A. *Conflict and Control: Law and Order in Nineteenth-Century Italy.* Atlantic Highlands, N.J., 1988.

Devens, Landrat. *Statistik des Kreises Essen für die Jahre 1859–1861.* Essen, 1863.

Diefendorf, Jeffrey M. *Businessmen and Politics in the Rhineland, 1789–1834.* Princeton, 1980.

Dienstinstruktion für die Polizeiverwaltung der Bürgermeisterei Duisburg. Duisburg, 1873.

Donajgrodzki, A. P., ed. *Social Control in Nineteenth-Century Britain.* London, 1977.

Dreetz, Dieter. "Der Erlass des preussischen Kriegsministers vom 8. Februar 1912 über die Verwendung der Armee zur Bekämpfung innerer Unruhen." *Militärgeschichte* 14 (1975): 561–71.

Düwell, Kurt, and Köllmann, Wolfgang, eds. *Rheinland-Westfalen im Industriezeitalter.* Vol. 1, *Von der Entstehung der Provinzen bis zur Reichsgründung.* Wuppertal, 1983.

"Eduard Viedebantt." *Die Heimat: Mitteilungen der Vereine für Heimatkunde in Krefeld und Verdingen* 6 (1927): 82–83.

Emsley, Clive. *Policing and Its Context, 1750–1870.* London, 1983.

Evans, Richard J. *Proletarians and Politics: Socialism, Protest, and the Working Class in Germany before the First World War.* New York, 1990.

———. "Prostitution, State, and Society in Imperial Germany." *Past and Present* 70 (February 1976): 106–29.

———. " 'Red Wednesday' in Hamburg: Social Democrats, Police, and Lumpenproletariat in the Suffrage Disturbances of 17 January 1906." *Social History* 4 (January 1979): 1–31.

———. *Rethinking German History: Nineteenth-Century Germany and the Origins of the Third Reich.* London, 1987.

———, ed. *The German Underworld: Deviants and Outcasts in German History.* London, 1988.

———, ed. *Society and Politics in Wilhelmine Germany.* London, 1978.

Fesser, Gerd. "Von der 'Zuchthausvorlage' zum Reichsvereinsgesetz: Staatsorgane, bürgerliche Parteien, und Vereinsgesetzgebung im Deutschen Reich, 1899–1906." *Jahrbuch für Geschichte* 28 (1983): 107–32.

Fischer, Wolfram. *Herz des Reviers: 125 Jahre Wirtschaftsgeschichte des Industrie- und Handelskammerbezirks Essen-Mülheim-Oberhausen.* Essen, 1965.

Fosdick, Raymond B. *European Police Systems.* Montclair, N.J., 1969. Reprint of 1915 edition.

Fricke, Dieter. *Bismarcks Prätorianer: Die Berliner politische Polizei im Kampf gegen die deutsche Arbeiterbewegung (1871–1898).* Berlin, 1962.

Funk, Albrecht. *Polizei und Rechtsstaat: Die Entwicklung des staatlichen Gewaltmonopols in Preussen, 1848–1918.* Frankfurt am Main, 1986.

Gailus, Manfred. *Strasse und Brot: Sozialer Protest in den deutschen Staaten unter besonderer Berücksichtigung Preussens, 1847–1849.* Göttingen, 1990.

Gatrell, V. A. C. "Crime, Authority, and the Policeman-State." In *The Cambridge Social History of Britain, 1750–1950.* Vol. 3, edited by F. M. L. Thompson. Cambridge, 1990. Pp. 243–310.

Gatrell, V. A. C., and Hadden, T. B. "Criminal Statistics and Their Interpretation." In *Nineteenth-Century Society: Essays in the Use of Social Data,* edited by E. A. Wrigley. Cambridge, 1972. Pp. 336–96.

Gatrell, V. A. C.; Lenman, Bruce; and Parker, Geoffrey, eds. *Crime and the Law: The Social History of Crime in Western Europe since 1500.* London, 1980.

Gillis, John R. *The Prussian Bureaucracy in Crisis, 1840–1860: Origins of an Administrative Ethos.* Stanford, 1971.

Goebel, Klaus, and Wichelhaus, Manfred, eds. *Aufstand der Bürger: Revolution 1849 im westdeutschen Industriezentrum*. Wuppertal, 1974.

Graff, Helmut. *Die deutsche Kriminalstatistik: Geschichte und Gegenwart*. Stuttgart, 1975.

Gurr, Ted Robert; Grabosky, Peter N.; and Hula, Richard C. *The Politics of Crime and Conflict: A Comparative History of Four Cities*. Beverly Hills, 1977.

Hall, Alex. *Scandal, Sensation, and Social Democracy: The SPD Press and Wilhelmine Germany, 1890–1914*. Cambridge, 1977.

Hansen, Joseph, ed. *Rheinische Briefe und Akten zur Geschichte der politische Bewegung, 1830–1850*. Vol. 1, Osnabrück, 1967, reprint of 1919 edition; vol. 2, pt. 1, Bonn, 1942; vol. 2, pt. 2, Cologne, 1976.

Harring, Sidney L. *Policing a Class Society: The Experience of American Cities, 1865–1915*. New Brunswick, N.J., 1983.

Hattenbauer, Hans. *Geschichte des Beamtentums*. Cologne, 1980.

Hehemann, Rainer. *Die "Bekämpfung des Zigeunerunwesens" im Wilhelminischen Deutschland und in der Weimarer Republik, 1871–1933*. Frankfurt am Main, 1987.

Held, Otto. *Die bestehende Organisation und die erforderliche Reorganisation der preussischen Polizei-Verwaltung mit Rücksicht auf die wünschenswerthe Erweiterung derselben zur Deutschen Reichspolizei*. Berlin, 1886.

Henning, Friedrich-Wilhelm. *Düsseldorf und seine Wirtschaft: Zur Geschichte einer Region*. 2 vols. Düsseldorf, 1981.

Henning, Hansjoachim. *Die deutsche Beamtenschaften im 19. Jahrhundert*. Stuttgart, 1984.

————. *Das Westdeutsche Bürgertum in der Epoche der Hochindustrialisierung, 1860–1914: Soziales Verhalten und Soziale Strukturen*. Pt. 1, *Das Bildungsbürgertum in der Preussischen Westprovinzen*. Wiesbaden, 1972.

Henning, Wilhelm. *Geschichte der Stadtverordnetenversammlung von Essen, 1890–1914*. Essen, 1965.

Hintze, Otto. *Soziologie und Geschichte: Gesammelte Abhandlungen zur Soziologie, Politik und Theorie der Geschichte*, edited by Gerhard Oestreich. 2d ed. Göttingen, 1964.

Hochstadt, Steve. "Migration and Industrialization in Germany, 1815–1977." *Social Science History* 5 (Fall 1981): 445–68.

Hoffmann, Erich. *Dr. Francis Kruse: Königlich Preussischer Regierungspräsident: Ein Lebensbild*. Leipzig, 1937.

Holtfrerich, Carl-Ludwig. *Quantitative Wirtschaftsgeschichte des Ruhrkohlenbergbaus im 19. Jahrhundert: Eine Führungssektoranalyse*. Dortmund, 1973.

Huck, Gerhard, ed. *Sozialgeschichte der Freizeit: Untersuchungen zum Wandel der Alltagskultur in Deutschland*. Wuppertal, 1980.

Hummel, Karl-Joseph. *München in der Revolution von 1848–49*. Göttingen, 1987.

Hunley, John Dillard. "The Working Classes, Religion, and Social Democracy in the Düsseldorf Area, 1867–1878." *Societas* 4 (1974): 131–49.

Husung, Hans-Gerhard. *Protest und Repression im Vormärz: Norddeutschland zwischen Restauration und Revolution.* Göttingen, 1983.

Illner, Eberhard. *Bürgerliche Organisierung in Elberfeld, 1775–1850.* Neustadt an der Aisch, 1982.

Inciardi, James A., and Faupel, Charles E., eds. *History and Crime: Implications for Criminal Justice Policy.* Beverly Hills, 1980.

Instruktion für die Polizeiverwaltung der Oberbürgermeisterei Düsseldorf. Düsseldorf, 1860.

Jackson, James Harvey, Jr. "Migration in Duisburg, 1867–1890: Occupational and Familial Contexts." *Journal of Urban History* 8 (May 1982): 235–70.

————. "Migration and Urbanization in the Ruhr Valley, 1850–1900." Ph.D. diss., University of Minnesota, 1980.

Jacob, Herbert. *German Administration since Bismarck: Central Authority versus Local Autonomy.* New Haven, 1963.

Jessen, Ralph. *Polizei im Industrierevier: Modernisierung und Herrschaftspraxis im westfälischen Ruhrgebiet, 1848–1914.* Göttingen, 1991.

Johnson, David R. *Policing the Urban Underworld: The Impact of Crime on the Development of the American Police, 1800–1887.* Philadelphia, 1979.

Johnson, Eric A. "The Roots of Crime in Imperial Germany." *Central European History* 15 (December 1982): 351–76.

Johnson, Eric A., and McHale, Vincent. "Socioeconomic Aspects of the Delinquency Rate in Imperial Germany." *Journal of Social History* 13 (Spring 1980): 384–402.

Jones, David. *Crime, Protest, Community, and Police in Nineteenth-Century Britain.* London, 1982.

Klersch, Joseph. *Die Kölnische Fastnacht von ihren Anfängen bis zur Gegenwart.* Cologne, 1961.

Klessmann, Christoph. *Polnische Bergarbeiter im Ruhrgebiet, 1870–1945: Soziale Integration und nationale Subkultur einer Minderheit in der deutschen Industriegesellschaft.* Göttingen, 1978.

————. "Zur Sozialgeschichte der Reichsverfassungskampagne von 1849." *Historische Zeitschrift* 218 (1974): 283–337.

Knemeyer, Franz-Ludwig. "Polizei." In *Geschichtliche Grundbegriffe: Historisches Lexikon zur politisch-sozialen Sprache in Deutschland,* edited by Otto Brunner, Werner Conze, and Reinhart Kosseleck. Stuttgart, 1978. Vol. 4. Pp. 875–97.

Knopp, Giesbert. *Die Preussische Verwaltung des Regierungsbezirks Düsseldorf in den Jahren 1899–1919.* Cologne, 1974.

Kocka, Jürgen, ed. *Arbeiter und Bürger im 19. Jahrhundert: Varianten ihres Verhältnisses im europäischen Vergleich.* Munich, 1986.

Kohler, Eric. "The Crisis of the Prussian Schutzpolizei, 1930–1932." In *Police Forces in History,* edited by George L. Mosse. London, 1975. Pp. 131–50.

Köllmann, Wolfgang. *Bevölkerung in der industriellen Revolution: Studien zur Bevölkerungsgeschichte Deutschlands.* Göttingen, 1974.

————. *Sozialgeschichte der Stadt Barmen im 19. Jahrhundert.* Tübingen, 1960.

————, ed. *Der Bergarbeiterstreik von 1889 und die Gründung des "Alten Verbandes" in ausgewählten Dokumenten der Zeit.* Bochum, 1969.

————, ed. *Wuppertaler Färbergesellen-Innung und Färbergesellen-Streiks, 1848–1857: Akten zur Frühgeschichte der Arbeiterbewegung in Deutschland.* Wiesbaden, 1962.

Koselleck, Reinhart. *Preußen zwischen Reform und Revolution: Allgemeines Landrecht, Verwaltung, und soziale Bewegung von 1791 bis 1848.* Stuttgart, 1967.

Ladd, Brian. *Urban Planning and Civic Order in Germany, 1860–1914.* Cambridge, Mass., 1990.

Lademacher, Horst. "Wirtschaft, Arbeiterschaft, und Arbeiterorganisationen in der Rheinprovinz am Vorabend des Sozialistengesetzes 1878." *Archiv für Sozialgeschichte* 15 (1975): 111–43.

Lane, Roger. *Policing the City: Boston, 1822–1885.* New York, 1971.

Lange, Annemarie. *Berlin zur Zeit Bebels und Bismarcks: Zwischen Reichsgründung und Jahrhundertwende.* Berlin, 1972.

Laufer, Franz. *Die preussische Kommunalpolizei: Vorschläge zu ihrer zeitgemässigen Umgestaltung.* Schwelm, 1903.

Lees, Andrew. "Debates about the Big City in Germany, 1890–1914." *Societas* 5 (1975): 31–47.

Lemke, Polizeiinspektor. *Zusammenstellung der in der preussischen Städte über je 10000 Einwohner angestellten Polizei-Exekutivbeamten.* Osnabrück, 1901.

Lenger, Friedrich. *Zwischen Kleinbürgertum und Proletariat: Studien zur Sozialgeschichte der Düsseldorfer Handwerker, 1816–1878.* Göttingen, 1986.

Leßmann, Peter. *Die preußische Schutzpolizei in der Weimarer Republik: Streifendienst und Straßenkampf.* Düsseldorf, 1989.

Liang, Hsi-huey. *The Berlin Police Force in the Weimar Republic.* Berkeley, 1970.

Lidtke, Vernon. *The Alternative Culture: Socialist Labor in Imperial Germany.* New York, 1985.

Liebman, Robert. "Repressive Strategies and Working-Class Protest: Lyon, 1848–1852." *Social Science History* 4 (February 1980): 33–55.

Liebman, Robert, and Polen, Michael. "Perspectives on Policing in Nineteenth-Century America." *Social Science History* 2 (1978): 346–60.

Linton, Derek S. *"Who Has the Youth, Has the Future": The Campaign to Save Young Workers in Imperial Germany.* Cambridge, 1991.

Loening, Edgar. "Polizei." In *Handwörterbuch der Staatswissenschaften,* edited by J. Conrad et al. 2d ed. Jena, 1901. Vol. 4. Pp. 108–17.

Lucas, Erhard. *Zwei Formen von Radikalismus in der deutschen Arbeiterbewegung.* Frankfurt am Main, 1976.

Lüdtke, Alf. *"Gemeinwohl," Polizei, und "Festungspraxis": Staatliche Gewaltsamkeit und innere Verwaltung in Preussen, 1815–1850.* Göttingen, 1982. Translated into English as *Police and State in Prussia, 1815–1850.* Cambridge, 1989.

————. "Die 'gestärkte Hand' des Staates: Zur Entwicklung staatlicher Gewalt-samkeit—das Beispiel Preußen im 19. Jahrhundert." *Leviathan* 7 (1979): 199–226.

————. "Praxis und Funktion staatlicher Repression: Preussen, 1815–1850." *Geschichte und Gesellschaft* 3 (1978): 190–211.

McHale, Vincent, and Johnson, Eric. "Urbanization, Industrialization, and Crime in Imperial Germany." *Social Science History* 1 (Fall 1976): 45–78 and (Winter 1977): 79–100.

Marenin, Otwin. "Police Performance and State Rule: Control and Autonomy in the Exercise of Coercion." *Comparative Politics* 18 (October 1985): 101–22.

Marx, Karl, and Engels, Friedrich. *Werke.* Vol. 1. Berlin, 1964.

Merriman, John M. *The Red City: Limoges and the French Nineteenth Century.* New York, 1985.

Miller, Wilbur R. *Cops and Bobbies: Police Authority in New York and London, 1830–1870.* Chicago, 1977.

Milles, Dietrich. *". . . aber es kam kein Mensch nach den Gruben, um anzufahren": Arbeitskämpfe der Ruhrbergarbeiter, 1867–1878.* Frankfurt am Main, 1983.

Mommsen, Hans, ed. *Arbeiterbewegung und industrieller Wandel: Studien zu ge-werkschaftlichen Organisationsproblemen im Reich und an der Ruhr.* Wuppertal, 1980.

Mommsen, Hans, and Borsdorf, Ulrich, eds. *Glück auf, Kameraden! Die Bergar-beiter und ihre Organisationen in Deutschland.* Cologne, 1979.

Mommsen, Wolfgang, and Hirschfeld, Gerhard, eds. *Social Protest, Violence, and Terror in Nineteenth- and Twentieth-Century Europe.* New York, 1982.

Monkkonen, Eric. "A Disorderly People? Urban Order in the Nineteenth and Twentieth Centuries." *Journal of American History* 68 (December 1981): 539–59.

————. "Municipal Reports as an Indicator Source: The Nineteenth-Century Police." *Historical Methods* 12 (Spring 1979): 57–65.

————. "The Organized Response to Crime in Nineteenth- and Twentieth-Century America." *Journal of Interdisciplinary History* 14 (Summer 1983): 113–28.

————. *Police in Urban America, 1860–1920.* Cambridge, 1981.

Morgan, Jane. *Conflict and Order: The Police and Labour Disputes in England and Wales, 1900–1939.* Oxford, 1987.

Most, Otto. "Bedeutung, Verfassung, und Aufgaben der deutschen Stadtver-waltung." In *Die deutsche Stadt und ihre Verwaltung,* edited by Otto Most. Berlin, 1912. Vol. 1. Pp. 5–51.

Müller, Michael. "Die preussische Rheinprovinz unter dem Einfluss von Juli-revolution und Hambacher Fest, 1830–1834." *Jahrbuch für Westdeutsche Landesgeschichte* 6 (1980): 271–90.

Mülmann, Otto von. *Statistik des Regierungs-Bezirks Düsseldorf.* 3 vols. Iserlohn, 1864–1867.

Muncy, Lysbeth. "The Prussian Landräte in the Last Years of the Monarchy: A Case Study of Pomerania and the Rhineland in 1890–1918." *Central European History* 6 (December 1973): 299–338.

Nolan, Mary. *Social Democracy and Society: Working-Class Radicalism in Düsseldorf, 1890–1920.* Cambridge, 1981.

Obenaus, Walter. *Die Entwicklung der preussischen Sicherheitspolizei bis zum Ende der Reaktionszeit.* Berlin, 1940.

O'Brien, Patricia. "Urban Growth and Social Control: The Municipal Police of Paris in the First Half of the Nineteenth Century." *Proceedings of the Western Society for French History* 3 (1975): 314–22.

Olshaufen, Dr. "Die Frühpolizeistunde im Deutschen Reich." *Jahrbuch für Gesetzgebung, Verwaltung, und Volkswirtschaft im Deutschen Reich* 29 (1905): 845–82.

Orlow, Dietrich. *Weimar Prussia, 1918–1925: The Unlikely Rock of Democracy.* Pittsburgh, 1986.

Palmer, Stanley. *Police and Protest in England and Ireland, 1780–1850.* Cambridge, 1988.

Philips, David. *Crime and Authority in Victorian England: The Black Country, 1835–1860.* London, 1977.

Price, Roger. "Techniques of Repression: The Control of Popular Protest in Mid-Nineteenth-Century France." *Historical Journal* 25 (1982): 859–87.

Raeff, Marc. *The Well-ordered Police State: Social and Institutional Change through Law in the Germanies and Russia, 1600–1800.* New Haven, 1983.

Reif, Heinz, ed. *Räuber, Volk, und Obrigkeit: Studien zur Geschichte der Kriminalität in Deutschland seit dem 18. Jahrhundert.* Frankfurt am Main, 1984.

Reinke, Herbert. " 'Armed as if for a war': The State, the Military, and the Professionalization of the Prussian Police in Imperial Germany." In *Policing Western Europe, 1850–1940: Politics, Professionalization, and the Public Order,* edited by Clive Emsley and Barbara Weinberger. New York, 1991.

———. ". . . hat sich ein politischer und wirtschaftlicher Polizeistaat entwickelt": Polizei und Großstadt im Rheinland vom Vorabend des Ersten Weltkrieges bis zum Beginn der 20er Jahre." In *"Sicherheit und Wohlfahrt": Polizei-Praxis im 19. und 20. Jahrhundert,* edited by Alf Lüdtke. Frankfurt am Main, forthcoming.

———. "Die Polizei und die 'Reinhaltung der Gegend': Prostitution und Sittenpolizei im Wuppertal im 19. und im frühen 20. Jahrhundert." In *Stadt und Gesundheit: Zum Wandel von "Volksgesundheit" und kommunaler Gesundheitspolitik im 19. und frühen 20. Jahrhundert,* edited by Jürgen Reulecke and Adelheid Gräfin zu Castell Rüdenhausen. Stuttgart, 1991. Pp. 129–43.

Reulecke, Jürgen. *Geschichte der Urbanisierung in Deutschland.* Frankfurt am Main, 1985.

———, ed. *Arbeiterbewegung an Rhein und Ruhr: Beiträge zur Geschichte der Arbeiterbewegung in Rheinland-Westfalen.* Wuppertal, 1974.

Reulecke, Jürgen, and Weber, Wolfhard, eds. *Fabrik, Familie, Feierabend: Beiträge zur Sozialgeschichte des Alltags im Industriezeitalter.* Wuppertal, 1978.

Roberts, James S. *Drink, Temperance, and the Working Class in Nineteenth-Century Germany.* Boston, 1984.

Romeyk, Horst. *Verwaltungs- und Behördengeschichte der Rheinprovinz, 1914–1945.* Düsseldorf, 1985.

Rösen, Heinrich. "Der Aufstand der Krefelder 'Seidenfabrikarbeiter' 1828 und die Bildung einer 'Sicherheitswache': Eine Dokumentation." *Die Heimat: Zeitschrift für niederrheinische Heimatpflege* 36 (1965): 32–61.

Rosenberg, Donald. "The Ruhr Coal Strike and the Prussian Mining Law of 1905: A Social and Political Conflict of Working Class Aspirations and Industrial Authoritarianism." Ph.D. diss., University of California, Los Angeles, 1971.

Ross, Ronald J. "Enforcing the Kulturkampf in the Bismarckian State and the Limits of Coercion in Imperial Germany." *Journal of Modern History* 56 (September 1984): 456–82.

Saul, Klaus. *Staat, Industrie, Arbeiterbewegung im Kaiserreich: Zur Innen- und Aussenpolitik des Wilhelminischen Deutschland.* Düsseldorf, 1974.

——. "Der Staat und die 'Mächte des Umsturzes': Ein Beitrag zu den Methoden antisozialistischer Repression und Agitation vom Scheitern des Sozialistengesetzes bis zur Jahrhundertwende." *Archiv für Sozialgeschichte* 12 (1972): 293–350.

Schieder, Wolfgang. "Kirche und Revolution: Aspekte der Trierer Wallfahrt 1844." *Archiv für Sozialgeschichte* 14 (1974): 421–31.

Schlossmacher, Norbert. *Düsseldorf im Bismarckreich: Politik und Wahlen, Parteien und Vereine.* Düsseldorf, 1985.

Schmidt, Paul. *Die ersten 50 Jahre der Königlichen Schutzmannschaft zu Berlin: Eine Geschichte des Korps für dessen Angehörige und Freunde.* Berlin, 1898.

Schneider, John C. *Detroit and the Problem of Order, 1830–1880: A Geography of Crime, Riot, and Policing.* Lincoln, Nebr., 1980.

Schulte, Regina. *Sperrbezirke: Tugendhaftigkeit und Prostitution in der bürgerlichen Welt.* Frankfurt am Main, 1979.

Schulze, Berthold. "Polizeipräsident Karl von Hinckeldey." *Jahrbuch für Geschichte Mittel- und Ostdeutschlands* 4 (1955): 81–108.

Schütz, Friedrich. "Das Verhältnis der Behörden zur Mainzer Fastnacht im Vormärz (1838–1846)." *Jahrbuch für Westdeutsche Landesgeschichte* 6 (1980): 291–318.

Schütz, Rüdiger. "Zur Eingliederung der Rheinlande." In *Expansion und Integration,* edited by Peter Baumgart. Cologne, 1984. Pp. 195–226.

Scott, Joan W. "Mayors versus Police Chiefs: Socialist Municipalities Confront the French State." In *French Cities in the Nineteenth Century,* edited by John M. Merriman. New York, 1981. Pp. 230–45.

Seeber, Gustav, and Wittwer, Walter. "Friedrich Hammachers Aufzeichnungen über den Bergarbeiterstreik von 1889." *Jahrbuch für Geschichte* 16 (1977): 403–58.

Severing, Carl. *Mein Lebensweg.* 2 vols. Cologne, 1950.

Siemann, Wolfram. *"Deutschlands Ruhe, Sicherheit, und Ordnung": Die Anfänge der politischen Polizei, 1806–1866.* Tübingen, 1985.

————, ed. *Der "Polizeiverein" deutscher Staaten: Eine Dokumentation zur Überwachung der Öffentlichkeit nach der Revolution von 1848–1849.* Tübingen, 1983.

Silbergleit, Heinrich. *Preussens Städte: Denkschrift zum 100 jährigen Jubiläum der Städteordnung von 19. November 1808.* Berlin, 1908.

Silver, Allan. "The Demand for Order in Civil Society: A Review of Some Themes in the History of Urban Crime, Police, and Riot." In *The Police: Six Sociological Essays,* edited by David Bordua. New York, 1967. Pp. 1–24.

Smith, Philip Thurmond. *Policing Victorian London: Political Policing, Public Order, and the London Metropolitan Police.* Westport, Conn., 1985.

Spencer, Elaine Glovka. *Management and Labor in Imperial Germany: Ruhr Industrialists as Employers, 1896–1914.* New Brunswick, N.J., 1984.

————. "Police-Military Relations in Prussia, 1848–1914." *Journal of Social History* 19 (Winter 1985): 305–17.

————. "Policing Popular Amusements in German Cities: The Case of Prussia's Rhine Province, 1815–1914." *Journal of Urban History* 16 (August 1990): 366–85.

————. "State Power and Local Interests in Prussian Cities: Police in the Düsseldorf District, 1848–1914." *Central European History* 19 (September 1986): 293–313.

Sperber, Jonathan. *Popular Catholicism in Nineteenth-Century Germany.* Princeton, 1984.

————. *Rhineland Radicals: The Democratic Movement and the Revolution of 1848–1849.* Princeton, 1991.

Spree, Reinhard. *Wachstumstrends und Konjunkturzyklen in der deutschen Wirtschaft von 1820 bis 1913.* Göttingen, 1978.

Die Stadt Elberfeld: Festschrift zur Dreihundert Feier, 1910. Elberfeld, 1910.

Stark, Gary D. "Cinema, Society, and the State: Policing the Film Industry in Imperial Germany." In *Essays on Culture and Society in Modern Germany,* edited by Gary D. Stark and Bede Karl Lackner. College Station, Tex., 1982. Pp. 122–66.

————. "Pornography, Society, and the Law in Imperial Germany." *Central European History* 14 (September 1981): 200–229.

Statistisches Jahrbuch Deutscher Städte, edited by M. Neefe. 1890–1914.

Steedman, Carolyn. *Policing the Victorian Community: The Formation of English Provincial Police Forces, 1856–1880.* London, 1984.

Stenographische Berichte über die Verhandlungen des deutschen Reichstags. Vol. 234. Berlin, 1909.

Stenographische Berichte über die Verhandlungen des Preussischen Hauses der Abgeordneten. Berlin, 1849–1914.

Storch, Robert D. "The Plague of Blue Locusts: Police Reform and Popular Resistance in Northern England, 1840–1857." *International Review of Social History* 20 (1975): 61–90.

———. "The Policeman as Domestic Missionary: Urban Discipline and Popular Culture in Northern England, 1850–1880." *Journal of Social History* 9 (June 1976): 481–509.

Stürmer, Michael, ed. *Das kaiserliche Deutschland: Politik und Gesellschaft, 1870–1918.* Düsseldorf, 1970.

Stursberg, Pastor H. *Die Zunahme der Vergehen und Verbrechen und ihre Ursachen.* Düsseldorf, 1879.

Sybel, Heinrich von. "Karl Ludwig von Hinckeldey, 1852–1856." *Historische Zeitschrift* 189 (1959): 108–23.

Tenfelde, Klaus. "Die 'Krawalle von Herne' im Jahre 1899." *Internationale wissenschaftliche Korrespondenz zur Geschichte der deutschen Arbeiterbewegung* 15 (March 1979): 71–104.

———. *Sozialgeschichte der Bergarbeiterschaft an der Ruhr im 19. Jahrhundert.* 2d ed. Bonn, 1981.

Tenfelde, Klaus, and Volkmann, Heinrich, eds. *Streik: Zur Geschichte des Arbeitskampfes in Deutschland während der Industrialisierung.* Munich, 1981.

Thomason, Frank J. "The Prussian Police State in Berlin, 1848–1871." Ph.D. diss., Johns Hopkins, 1978.

Tilly, Charles, Tilly, Louise, and Tilly, Richard. *The Rebellious Century, 1830–1930.* London, 1975.

Tilly, Richard. "Popular Disorders in Nineteenth-Century Germany." *Journal of Social History* 4 (Fall 1970): 1–40.

Unruh, Georg-Christoph von. "Polizei, Polizeiwissenschaft, und Kameralistik." In *Deutsche Verwaltungsgeschichte,* edited by Kurt G. A. Jeserich et al. Stuttgart, 1983. Vol. 1. Pp. 388–427.

Die Verwaltung der Stadt Elberfeld in den Zeitabschnitte 1900 bis 1910. Elberfeld, 1915.

Die Verwaltung der Stadt Essen im XIX. Jahrhundert mit besonderer Berücksichtigung der letzten fünfzehn Jahre. Essen, 1902.

Verwaltungsbericht. Barmen, 1856, 1857, 1860, 1873, 1910–1913.

Vogt, Irmgard. "Einige Fragen zum Alkoholkonsum der Arbeiter: Kommentar zu J. S. Roberts." *Geschichte und Gesellschaft* 8 (1982): 134–40.

Volkmann, Heinrich, and Bergmann, Jürgen, eds. *Sozialer Protest: Studien zu traditioneller Resistenz und kollektiver Gewalt in Deutschland vom Vormärz bis zur Reichsgründung.* Opladen, 1984.

Wagner, Joachim. *Politischer Terrorismus und Strafrecht im Deutsche Kaiserreich von 1871.* Heidelberg, 1981.

Walker, Samuel. "The Police and the Community: Scranton, Pennsylvania, 1866–1884: A Test Case." *American Studies* (Spring 1978): 79–90.

Watts, Eugene J. "Police Priorities in Twentieth Century St. Louis." *Journal of Social History* 14 (Summer 1981): 649–73.

Wehler, Hans-Ulrich. "Die Polen im Ruhrgebiet bis 1918." In *Krisenherde des Kaiserreiches, 1871–1918,* edited by Hans-Ulrich Wehler. Göttingen, 1970. Pp. 219–56.

Weidenhaupt, Hugo, ed. *Düsseldorf: Geschichte von den Ursprüngen bis ins 20. Jahrhundert.* Vols. 2 and 3. Düsseldorf, 1988–89.

Weinberger, Barbara, and Reinke, Herbert. "A Diminishing Function? A Comparative Historical Account of Policing the City." *Policing and Society* 1 (1991): 213–23.

Wittwer, Walter. "Zur Taktik der herrschenden Klasse gegenüber dem Bergarbeiterstreik von 1889." In *Evolution und Revolution in der Weltgeschichte: Festschrift für Ernst Engelberg,* edited by Horst Bartel. Vol. 2. Berlin, 1976. Pp. 541–64.

Zehr, Howard. *Crime and the Development of Modern Society: Patterns of Criminality in Nineteenth-Century Germany and France.* London, 1976.

———. "The Modernization of Crime in Germany and France, 1830–1913." *Journal of Social History* (Summer 1975): 117–41.

Zimmermann, Gustav. *Die Deutsche Polizei im neunzehnten Jahrhundert.* 3 vols. Hanover, 1845–49.

———. *Wesen, Geschichte, Literatur, characteristische Tätigkeiten und Organisation der modernen Polizei: Ein Leitfaden für Polizisten und Juristen.* Hanover, 1852.

Zorn, Wolfgang. "Die wirtschaftliche Struktur der Rheinprovinz um 1820." *Vierteljahrschrift für Sozial- und Wirtschaftsgeschichte* 54 (October 1967): 289–324.

Zur Prostitutionsfrage: Aus den Verhandlungen der 56. Generalversammlung der Rheinisch-Westfälische Gefängnisgesellschaft an 9. Oktober 1884 in Düsseldorf. Düsseldorf, 1884.

INDEX

Aachen, 9–10
Adolph, Polizeiinspektor (Elberfeld), 115–16
Albedyll, General Emil von, 86
Altenessen, 143
Amusements, policing of, 119–21, 124–25
Anarchism, 80, 82
Antisocialist law, 53, 54, 75, 80–82, 87, 120
Arenberg mining company, 133
Arrests, 68
Association against Silk Theft, 48
Association law, imperial (1908), 130–32
Association law, Prussian (1850), 39–40, 74, 77, 127–28, 130
Association of German Catholics (Verein deutscher Katholiken), 77

Barmen: adding police personnel, 55; antisocialist initiatives, 82; city council, 144; civic guard, 22; city's growth and development, xiv, 13–14, 89; criticism of police, 82–83; demonstrations, 128; election results, 81; hours of work for police, 101; night watch, 18–19; number of policemen, 34–36, 50, 90; pay and benefits for police, 57, 59, 101; police duties, 45, 63; police organization, 98–99; police recruitment, 93; policing popular amusements, 121, 122, 123; policing strikes, 72; proposed establishment of state police, 140; reported crime, 51; requests for garrison, 47, 83; state-appointed police director, 32, 33, 34; World War I, 151
Beggars and vagrants, surveillance of, 4, 62, 63, 118–19
Bemberg-Flamersheim, Landrat von, 147
Bergisches Land, 13, 73, 80, 81
Berlepsch, Regierungspräsident Hans Freiherr von, 83, 86
Berlin: police before 1848, 3, 4, 6; taverns in, 129
Berlin Schutzmannschaft: allocation of resources for, 29; creation of, 27–28; criticism of, 42; night patrol, 98; police school, 103; police-to-population ration, 53
Bismarck, Otto von, 87, 156
Bochum, 147
Borbeck, 143
Boston, 115
Bottrop, 122
Brun, Polizeisergeant Aloysius (Elberfeld), 105–6
Burg, 26
Bürgerwehren. See Civic guards

Cantador, Lorenz, 27
Carnival celebrations, 10–11, 212 n.70

Catholics: and organized labor, 73, 80–81; and the Prussian monarchy, 8, 22, 76–77; as policemen, 95, 96, 149–50

City councils: allocation of resources, 7, 21, 49, 51–52; and police accountability, 5, 31, 82, 157, 161; and state-appointed police directors, 33–34; arming the police, 114–15; in 1848–49, 26; election and composition, 144–45

Civic Guards: before 1848, 7, 21–23; in 1848, 26–27; World War I, 151

Clergy, 11, 41; surveillance of, 77–78

Cologne, 9–10, 11

Convicts, released, surveillance of, 42

Cost of living, 36, 56, 100

Crimes reported, 50–51, 66–67, 112, 151

Dances, 41, 120

Daum, Polizeiinspektor (Elberfeld), 81

Demonstrations, policing of, 128–29

Deutscher Kaiser mine, 136

Disorderly conduct, 65

District Polizeikommissare, 127

Drinking, regulation of, 69–70, 116, 121–22, 123

Dublin police, 7–8

Duisburg: arrests, 68; city's growth and development, xiv, 89; number of policemen, 90; ordinance violations, 117, 118; penalties imposed, 65; police budget, 91; police misbehavior and punishment, 106; police organization, 98–100; police recruitment, 92, 148; police response to criticism, 107; police scandal, 59; policing popular amusements, 71, 121, 123; political policing, 132; reported crime, 66, 112; resistance to authority, 56, 113; social services, 109–10; uses of police, 63; state police, 146, 150, 154

Düsseldorf: adding police personnel, 55; attacks on police, 112; beggar patrols, 119; city's growth and development, xiv, 13, 89; crimes reported, 67; demonstrations, 128; fulltime night patrol, 58; hours of work for police, 38; night watch, 189n.13; number of policemen, 34–35, 47, 50, 90, 136; pay and benefits for police, 16–17, 36, 56, 57, 100, 101; penalties imposed, 64; police budget, 91; police duties, 46, 47, 63; police misbehavior and punishment, 106; police organization, 92, 98–99, 126, 127; police recruitment, 92–94; police response to criticism, 107; police turnover, 58, 60, 97, 98, 99; policing popular amusements, 69, 71, 119, 122, 123–24; policing strikes, 138; political policing, 39, 80, 132; promotions for policemen, 96–97; reported crime, 112; revolution of 1848–49, 24–25, 26–27; services provided by police, 112; state-appointed police director, 32–33, 34; state police, 154; truancy, 65–66; weapons violations, 114; World War I and after, 151, 152

Düsseldorf administrative district (Regierungsbezirk): urban and industrial development, xii–xiv, 12–13, 89; policing of, 14

Elberfeld: adding police personnel, 53; allocation of resources, 36; anti-socialist initiatives, 82–83; city council, 144; city's growth and development, xiv, 13–14, 89; criticism of police, 84, 85; elections, 81; hours of work for police, 101; night watch, 18, 19; number of policemen, 15, 35–36, 49, 50, 90; pay and benefits for police, 59, 100; police budget, 91; police duties, 44, 63; police misbehavior and punishment, 106; police organization, 99–100, 127; police recruitment, 92; policing popular amusements, 69, 122; policing strikes, 72; political policing, 128, 132; reported crime, 51; requests for garrison, 47, 83; revolution of 1848–49, 24–25, 26, 30; services provided by police, 111, 112; state-appointed police director, 32, 33–34; state police, 140, 154

Elbers, Alfred, 138

Employers: and popular amusements, 119; collaboration with police, 74–75, 134, 135; expectations, 133, 136, 138; payments to police, 48

Ende, Regierungspräsident von, 74

Engels, Friedrich, 13

Essen: city council, 144; city's growth and development, xiv, 13, 89; demonstrations, 22–23, 55, 77; hours of work for police, 60; night watch, 18; numbers of policemen, 48, 51–52, 54–55, 90; pay and benefits for police, 57, 60, 100, 148; police misbehavior and punishment, 102, 106; police organization, 97, 98, 99, 127; police recruitment, 92, 94, 95, 97, 149; policing popular amusements, 70, 129; policing strikes, 74; Polish-speaking policemen, 130; political policing, 80; reported crime, 51–52, 112; socialists in, 80–81; state police, 146, 147; weapons violations, 114

Eulenberg, Interior Minister Friedrich Graf zu, 46, 53, 156

Falderen, Polizeiinspektor Franz von (Düsseldorf), 32–33, 37, 45, 49, 62

Festivals, 10, 41, 120. See also carnival celebrations; Kirmessen

Fire departments, 129

Flottwell, Interior Minister Eduard Heinrich von, 41–42

Fosdick, Raymond B., 155

France, police in, 3, 4, 28, 159, 162, 187n.71. See also Paris police

Frankfurth, Polizeiinspektor (Duisburg), 71

Gauer, Polizeikommisar (Düsseldorf), 131

Gelsenkirchen, 147

Gendarmerie, 14, 16, 36, 47; reassignment, 49, 87; size of, 6, 9, 21

General German Workers' Association, 73

Germany, police in: 155–57. See also Prussia

Gladbach, 154

Great Britain, police in, 4, 29, 48, 136, 156, 162, 221n.7. See also Dublin police; London Metropolitan Police

Gymnastic societies, 26, 39, 151

Gypsies, 63, 117–18

Hagemeister, Regierungspräsident von, 75

Hamborn, 89, 113, 143; number of taverns, 129, 136

Hamburg, 128

Hansch, District Polizeikommissar (Essen): 130, 134

Hansemann, David, 12

Hapke, Polizeiinspektor Eduard (Essen, Duisburg), 148

Harkort, Friedrich, 156

Hellwig, Polizeiinspektor (Düsseldorf), 47

Herne, 113, 114

Herrfurth, Interior Minister Ernst Ludwig, 87–88

Hinckeldey, Police President Carl Ludwig von (Berlin), 32, 72

Hirsch, Police Director Hermann (Elberfeld-Barmen), 69, 72–73

Hostesses, 121
Housing inspection, 110–11

Journeymen, surveillance of, 40
Justice ministry, 42

Kammhoff, Polizeikommissar Otto
    (Elberfeld), 80
Kattowitz, 107
Katzenmusik, 110
Kirmessen, 11, 41, 119
Kleve, 51
Koblenz, 9–10
Krefeld: city council, 17; city's growth
    and development, xiv, 13, 89;
    demonstrations, 14, 21–22; estab-
    lishment of garrison, 199n.54;
    festivals, 41; fulltime night patrol,
    58; hours of work for police, 38,
    98; night patrolmen, 92; number
    of policemen, 14–15, 49, 90; po-
    lice budget, 91; police duties, 42,
    44–45, 46, 63; police organiza-
    tion, 99; police pay and benefits,
    16, 30—31, 36, 56, 60; police re-
    cruitment, 92, 93; police-to-
    population ratio, 53; policing
    popular amusements, 71, 123; po-
    litical policing, 132; revolution of
    1848–49, 26; silk theft, 48; social
    services, 109; state-appointed po-
    lice director, 32, 33, 34; state po-
    lice, 154
Krupp, Alfred, 48, 49
Krupp steelworks, 99
Kruse, Regierungspräsident Francis,
    136–37
Kulturkampf, 76–79

Labor unions, 132–33, 139
Landräte, 143, 147
Langenberg, 37
League of Prussian Communal Police-
    men (Bund kommunaler Polizei-
    beamten Preussens), 108
Lehr, Mayor (Duisburg), 85

Liberals, attitudes toward the police,
    7–8, 12, 42, 54, 61–62, 161
London Metropolitan Police, 7–8, 28,
    156
Louis XIV, 4

Madras, India, 159
Manteuffel, Interior Minister Otto
    von, 30, 34
May Day, 78
Mayors as police administrators, 31–
    32, 83, 144, 145
Meiderich, 143
Military: allocation of resources for,
    6, 178n.31; as model for police,
    38, 103, 104, 105, 108, 152–53,
    158–59; establishment of garri-
    sons, 83, 199n.54; police interac-
    tion with, 116–17; police recruit-
    ment from, 5, 15–16, 58–59, 91–
    93, 94, 95, 100, 147, 149,
    189n.13, 201n.20, 222n.11; use
    for domestic peacekeeping, 12,
    14, 21, 23, 25, 28, 47–48, 77, 126,
    140, 150, 152; use in strikes, 73,
    74, 86, 137
Mine protection forces (Zechenweh-
    ren), 135
Moabit demonstration, 115
Motion pictures, 122
Mülheim an der Ruhr: city's growth
    and development, xiv, 13; estab-
    lishment of garrison 199n.54;
    night watch, 18

Napoleon III, 28, 159
Newspapers, 204n.66; criticism of po-
    lice, 84–85, 159; surveillance of,
    40
New York, 115
Night watches, 4, 14, 18–19, 47, 78,
    189n.13

Oberhausen, 89, 112, 154
Ordinance violations, 42, 116, 117,

118, 119, 151; penalties for, 64–65

Paris Commune, 53, 54
Paris police, 3, 4, 28–29
Perizonius, Polizeiinspektor (Barmen), 185n.42
Picketing, 135–36, 138, 161
Pius Day, 78
Police administrators, state-appointed (police presidents, police directors): 9, 29, 32–34, 141–42, 147, 152, 178n.30
Police brutality, 85, 106
Police dogs, 116
Police forces, communal: adding personnel, 53, 55; allocation of resources, 91; criticism of, 141; duties, 44, 62, 146–47, 151; new techniques, 115–16; night patrol, 58; organization of, 97–100; services provided, 109–112
Police forces, state (Schutzmannschaften): creation of, 27, 83, 140–47, 149, 150, 153–54, 158, 163; recruitment of personnel, 93, 147–48. See also Berlin Schutzmannschaft
Police law, Prussian (1850), 32, 64, 156–57
Policemen, rank-and-file (Polizeidiener, Polizeisergeanten, Polizeiwachtmeister, Schutzleute), 4, 5; accusations of brutality, 59; and employers, 133–34; associations of, 107, 108, 153; attacks on, 55, 56, 113; duties, 19, 20, 44–45, 56, 47; fulltime night patrol, 58; hours of work, 38, 60, 101; misbehavior and punishment, 84, 85, 104, 106–7, 141; numbers of, 9, 14–15; pay and benefits, 16–17, 36–37, 56–57, 59–60, 100–1, 102, 104–5, 148; plainclothes personnel, 122; Polish-speaking, 130;

promotions, 17, 95–96; recruitment, 15–16, 91–94, 95, 141, 147, 149, 153, 160, 222n.15; religion of, 22, 78, 95, 149–50; response to criticism, 107; service in World War I, 151; status, 128; training, 103–4; turnover, 58, 60, 97–98; uniforms and weapons, 105, 114–15
Police officers (Polizeiinspektoren, Polizeikommissare), 4; associations of, 107–8; attitudes of, 137–38; duties, 17, 19–20, 40, 45–46; pay and benefits, 16, 30, 37, 57, 148; recruitment, 31, 96–97, 153; religion, 96; training, 103
Police schools, 103–4
Police-to-population ratios: Berlin, 29; Düsseldorf district, 14–15, 34–35, 50, 52, 53, 89–91; Great Britain, 7–8, 29
Polish-speaking population, surveillance of, 130, 131
Political policing, 11–12, 126–27, 132, 150, 152
Postal directors, 80
Prostitution, 20, 71–72, 123–24
Prussia, police in, 3, 4, 5–6, 152–53, 157–64; allocation of resources, 29–30; New Era, 41–42; police accountability, 31; use of, 38–43. See also Berlin Schutzmannschaft; Police forces, communal; Police forces, state

Railroads: surveillance of, 40–41; transport of peacekeeping forces, 14, 73
Registration of residence, 19, 40, 41, 111, 117
Reichstag elections, 81
Remscheid, 35–36, 129
Rhine province: as part of Prussia, xiii, 8–9; 10; policing of, 9; revolution of 1848–49, 25

Ruhr coalfield, 83, 138, 143; taverns in, 129; urban and industrial development, xiv, 13, 112–13, 130; establishment of state police, 146, 150; weapons violations, 114, 115
Ruhrort, 143
Russian empire, police in, 159–60

Salvation Army, 79
Scheffler, Polizeisergeant Samuel (Elberfeld), 30
Schnapskasinos, 129–30
Sedan Day, 78
Setzermann, Polizeiinspektor (Düsseldorf), 138
Shooting societies, 26, 151
Siege law, Prussian (1851), 150
Social Democrats, 73; and the police, 107; election results, 54; in city councils, 144, 145
Solingen, 81
Spiegel, Regierungspräsident Freiherr von, 20–21
State prosecutors (Staatsanwalten), 48, 81, 82–83
Steigerverband, 134
Sterkrade, 143
Strikes: 1855 and 1857 Wuppertal dyers' strikes, 72–73; 1869–74 strike wave, 54, 73–74; 1872 Ruhr miners' strike, 55, 74; 1889 Ruhr miners' strike, 86, 87; 1899 miners' strike in Herne, 113, 114; 1900 strike at Wortmann and Elbers enamel works, 138; 1905 Ruhr miners' strike, 115, 130, 135; 1912 Ruhr miners' strike, 134, 135; 1912 Rhine ship workers' strike; police and, 132, 135–36, 137, 138, 139
Stursberg, Chaplain H. (Düsseldorf), 67
Sundays, regulations relating to, 41, 79

Taverns: curfews, 70, 82, 121, 124; licensing, 41, 69, 74, 129; numbers of, 13; surveillance of, 80
Terpe, Polizeiinspektor (Duisburg), 114
Theaters, surveillance of, 37–38
Thyssen steelworks, 133
Tingel-Tangel, 71
Travelers, surveillance of, 4, 9, 19, 40–41
Trier pilgrimage (1844), 10
Truancy, 65–66, 112, 117

United States, police in, 4, 6, 28, 115, 136, 159, 162, 163, 207n.2
Upper Silesian coalfield, 146
Urban politics and administration, 142–43, 144, 162–63

Verband Preussischer Polizeibeamten, 153
Vereinigung Preussischer Polizeioffiziere, 153
Victoria Mathias mine, 48
Viedebantt, Polizeiinspektor Eduard (Krefeld), 31
Villers, Landtag deputy Graf, 28

Walther, Polizeiinspektor Leonard (Krefeld), 17, 30–31, 62
Weapons: possession and use by public, 26, 113–14; supplied to police, 68, 114–15
Wesel, 20, 104–5
William II
Workers: perceptions of, 62–63, 64, 68; coal miners, 17, 36, 57, 74, 100–1, 113; metal workers, 26; railroad workers, 40; surveillance of daily life, 123; textile workers, 13, 14, 17
World War I, 150–52
Wortmann und Elbers enamel works, 138

Youth, surveillance of, 122–23, 131, 151–52

Zechenwehren. *See* Mine protection forces

Zeller, Polizeiinspektor (Düsseldorf), 25
Zöller, Polizeiinspektor Adolf (Duisburg), 59, 65
Zweigert, Mayor Erich (Essen), 141, 142, 149

UNIVERSITY LIBRARY
INDIANA UNIVERSITY OF PENNSYLVANIA
INDIANA, PA 15705